Beyond the Lecture

Beyond the Lecture

Interacting with Students and Shaping the Classroom Dynamic

Katie A. L. McAllister

ROWMAN & LITTLEFIELD
Lanham • Boulder • New York • London

Published by Rowman & Littlefield
A wholly owned subsidiary of The Rowman & Littlefield Publishing Group, Inc.
4501 Forbes Boulevard, Suite 200, Lanham, Maryland 20706
www.rowman.com

6 Tinworth Street, London SE11 5AL, United Kingdom

British Library Cataloguing in Publication Information Available

Library of Congress Cataloging-in-Publication Data

Names: McAllister, Katie A. L., author.
Title: Beyond the lecture : interacting with students and shaping the classroom dynamic / Katie A. L. McAllister.
Description: Lanham : Lexington Books, [2021] | Includes bibliographical references and index. | Summary: "This book is essential reading for novice instructors, for those wishing to shift from lecturing to active learning, and for experienced educators wishing to examine their teaching practice"—Provided by publisher.
Identifiers: LCCN 2020049947 (print) | LCCN 2020049948 (ebook) | ISBN 9781475858617 (cloth) | ISBN 9781475858624 (paperback) | ISBN 9781475858631 (epub)
Subjects: LCSH: Teacher effectiveness. | Active learning. | Teacher-student relationships. | Classroom environment.
Classification: LCC LB1025.3 .M345 2021 (print) | LCC LB1025.3 (ebook) | DDC 371.102—dc23
LC record available at https://lccn.loc.gov/2020049947
LC ebook record available at https://lccn.loc.gov/2020049948

Contents

Acknowledgments

This work is dedicated to my mentors: Professor Emerita Selma Wasserman, former director of Professional Programs of the Faculty of Education at Simon Fraser University, and the late Professor Eric Vatikiotis-Bateson, Canada Research Chair in Linguistics & Cognitive Science and former director of the UBC Cognitive Systems Program. Selma and Eric supported me, challenged me, and, above all, *taught* me. I am so grateful for their significant role in my life.

This book wouldn't have been possible without encouragement from friends and support from my family. From novice instructors to highly experienced educators, your passion for teaching and lively chats about our experiences in the classroom was motivating from the first words to the final chapter. I am very grateful to my parents, in particular, for their tireless support of this project.

With thanks and appreciation to my colleagues and students at the Minerva Schools at KGI. Your enthusiasm for active learning and dedication to improving higher education is inspiring.

Chapter 1

Introduction

Higher education is undergoing a reinvention. More and more instruction is moving beyond the traditional lecture to include active learning and engagement supported by technology.[1] Unfortunately, many instructors have limited experience with this pedagogy. The challenge to adapt is particularly intimidating for instructors who rely on their experience as students to inform their teaching practice.

Most colleges and universities expect novice instructors to jump into teaching without first learning to promote student engagement, foster critical thinking, or positively shape the classroom dynamic. Without training, many instructors simply continue to lecture, but those wishing to develop their pedagogy can take action and move beyond passive methods of delivering content.

Resources for interactive activities and lesson plans are increasingly available, yet advice on using these approaches, such as "ask questions" or "have a discussion," is well meaning but uninformative. To adapt successfully, the instructor must learn to interact effectively and shape the classroom dynamic.

Effective *interaction* encompasses the verbal and nonverbal interpersonal communication that takes place between an instructor and students. Skilled interaction promotes critical thinking, fosters psychological safety, increases engagement, and conveys instructor immediacy.[2]

The classroom *dynamic* encompasses the classroom climate[3] as well as the distribution of talk-time, style of engagement, and degree of instructor control.

This book addresses the development of more effective instruction across a variety of contexts, with a focus on skills that promote critical thinking and deep engagement on the part of students. As graduate students or sessional lecturers may not have access to professional development, each chapter includes activities for self-evaluation and concrete suggestions of things to try in the classroom.

The focus across topics rests on effective interactions and the overall classroom dynamic, grounded in psychology, the science of learning, and perspectives on critical thinking. Sources and quotes provide an extensive starting point for instructors wishing to explore academic research in these areas. This foundation empowers instructors to examine and justify their approach to teaching.

While the primary audience is the college or university instructor, the key concepts and suggestions in this book are also appropriate for pre-college classrooms as well as for developing effective interpersonal interactions in general.

HOW TO USE THIS BOOK

What is it like to be a student in your classroom?

How does your behavior as an instructor create that experience?

Understanding how to approach interactions with students is incredibly challenging, particularly for sessional lecturers or novice instructors at colleges or universities where the norm is to simply "jump into it." This book focuses on putting interactive teaching into practice. While every classroom is unique, the common themes and examples provide a basis for understanding what shapes the dynamic in a given context.

Experienced instructors may be familiar with active learning pedagogy, yet also benefit from taking the time to reflect on how they are shaping their classroom dynamic in particular ways—even unintentionally. With deliberate reflection, many instructors realize their assumptions may not wholly reflect the *actual* distribution of talk-time, depth of student engagement, or degree of instructor control.

For those in supervisory or coaching roles wanting to propose actionable "things to try" for struggling faculty, this book includes suggestions and discussion of what to consider when advising specific instructors.

The basics of effective communication explore interpersonal interactions and communicative dynamics through the lenses of *what we say* and *how we say it*. Online instructors receive specific attention, given the increasing frequency of such classes and the strengths and challenges associated with this particular format. From there, four foundational concepts that shape engagement with students, such as psychological safety and emotional intelligence, are reviewed in the context of the classroom.

Building on this understanding of the nature of interactions, key topics related to promoting students' engagement and critical thinking are explored, with examples, self-evaluations, and suggested "things to try" for instructors wishing to experiment with their teaching practice. The final chapter addresses specific challenges that often arise in the classroom, including conformity, instructional dissent, anxiety, and supporting second-language speakers.

This book is a resource for instructors who wish to move beyond simple lecturing in their teaching practice. Initially, one can scan the table of contents and take a closer look at areas that seem of particular interest. A follow-up read of the complete text positions an instructor to identify a focus for development and try the steps suggested for promoting growth in that area. Which areas to address and how far to proceed with professional development are a matter of personal choice.

When treating this book as a practical guide of things to try, an instructor must take the suggested statements and *adapt them to their own voice and context*. When reading sections on *things to try*, pause to consider, "How would *I* say that?" In some cases, the wording may feel appropriate; in others, you may wish to keep the *idea* but adapt it to your style. In doing so, always consider two questions:

- How would it sound in *your* voice?
- What would resonate with *your* students?

NOTES

1. Such as "clickers" to indicate simple responses to multiple-choice questions, even in very large classes.

2. Immediacy is described as the sensation of "closeness": the perceived physical or psychological distance between individuals (Anderson, 1979). Instructor immediacy facilitates participation as well as affective and cognitive learning, among other positive outcomes (McCroskey & Richmond, 1992; McCroskey et al., 1996; Rocca, 2009, 2010; LeFebvre & Allen, 2014).

3. The classroom "climate" is traditionally defined as the general quality of the atmosphere or environment, whether hospitable or chilly (Hall & Sandler, 1982).

Chapter 2

Beyond the Lecture

Year after year, I had written on the blackboard that pressure is defined as force per unit area—a definition that is printed in the book and in my lecture notes. Year after year the students copied it from the blackboard into their notebooks. What a waste of time, both for the students and the teacher! What inefficiency! And the students and I believed this lecturing constituted "teaching." What a fallacy! Mazur (1997, p. 981)

WHY MOVE BEYOND THE LECTURE?

The evidence is overwhelming. Student learning outcomes are higher in *active* versus *passive* learning environments (Deslauriers et al., 2019; Freeman et al., 2014; Rocca, 2010).[1] Active engagement gives students a proactive role in their learning. It is an opportunity to test their understanding, develop novel hypotheses, synthesize across disciplines or personal interests, and engage in critical thinking and cognitive scaffolding that promotes learning and memory. In turn, students are more able to apply and transfer knowledge to new contexts and unique challenges (Kosslyn & Nelson, 2017).

Active learning is described very broadly as anything that "involves students *doing things* and *thinking about the things that they are doing*," with a particular focus on higher-order cognitive tasks involving analysis, synthesis, and evaluation (Bonwell & Eisen, 1991, p. 19). A wealth of suggested classroom activities grounded in active learning exists in the literature. Examples of common methods include the following:[2]

- Think-Pair-Share
- ConcepTests

- Interactive presentations
- Discussions
- Fishbowl (discussion + observation)
- Socratic dialogue
- Case studies
- Role-plays
- Engagement tasks (voting, polling, generating examples, concept-mapping, etc.)

The above techniques improve comprehension, retention, and transfer of knowledge, as well as increase persistence and diminish attrition from higher education (Braxton et al., 2008). Active learning is not even an all-or-nothing choice—while "fully active" may be ideal, even a short period of discussion or brief activity inserted in a more traditional lecture makes a significant difference.

Given such positive outcomes, why don't institutions and instructors stop lecturing? It would be naïve to assert this is due to a fundamental lack of interest or willingness to change. One primary driver is simply experience: Lectures are what college and university instructors know well.

The desire to change and some sense of how to inject active learning into the classroom is a starting point. The first hurdle of understanding how to *structure* participation can be tackled with existing resources. The next challenge of how to effectively *facilitate* participation requires new skills and deliberate practice. The purpose of this book is to give instructors tools to develop their approach to interacting with students and achieve improved outcomes.

Additional challenges and barriers exist beyond skill development. While not insurmountable, an instructor wishing to include more active engagement in their classroom should consider how they wish to tackle common impediments *proactively*.

OVERCOMING CHALLENGES AND BARRIERS

Institutional Norms

The main reason we are still using this method is habit: we tend to teach the way we were taught (Mazur, 1997, p. 982).

Carl Wieman, a Nobel laureate in physics, takes this inertia further—describing a fundamental lack of incentive to change perpetuating teaching by information transmission to passive recipients. Indeed, Wieman asserts there is *zero incentive* to use active learning rather than traditional lectures grounded in "pedagogical superstition and habit" when an institution cares more about its research funding than teaching methods (2014).

In the absence of institutional pressure to change, the increasingly mature body of evidence demonstrating improved student outcomes provides instructors with a rationale to justify experimentation with active learning approaches. In a lecture-based tradition, it is helpful to recognize that active learning is not an all-or-nothing choice. As a starting point, small modifications to a lecture-based model can result in increased engagement. Even if a given course cannot make a significant change, an instructor should consider how to interact with students to promote psychological safety, agency, and critical thinking.

What about when the incentive *is* present: when an instructor has the freedom to change, the support of colleagues, and an encouraging institution? Logistics are the primary reason students do not participate in class. Instructors note the group is too large for comfort, the room's seating arrangement inappropriate, the students exhausted in a night course or late in the semester, or course policies do not foster participation (Rocca, 2010). Technology can mitigate some of these issues. Others require creative partitioning of a room, intentional design of course policy, or change in pedagogy.

The common concern that some classes are simply "too large" should be approached with skepticism (Bonwell & Eisen, 1991). Activities such as think-pair-share work with partners. With thoughtful task design, an instructor can effectively facilitate multiple breakout groups simultaneously. The question of psychological safety, often linked to students' unwillingness to speak in large classes, can be significantly mitigated by group norms and instructor behavior described in this book.

Indeed, some would argue that active learning methods are *more* critical in large classes, given the instructor's limited bandwidth for each student. In a class of fifteen, an instructor is able to observe indicators of comprehension or common confusion by reading the familiar faces in the room. In a larger class, the instructor may need to find a way to *ask* how things are going. Rather than shy away from active learning due to class size, instructors should attempt to embrace it.

As an experienced practitioner of active learning in a STEM classroom notes, "The only real difference between a class of 20 and a class of 200 is that the latter class is noisier during activities" (Felder & Brent, 1999, p. 278).

Evaluative practices for instructors that base tenure and promotion almost entirely on student course evaluations raise a unique challenge. Students in a classroom with active learning can rate their perceived learning lower than peers in a passive (lecture-based) class, despite a generally positive perception of the active learning environment (Deslauriers et al., 2019).

Quantitative analysis does not support this student perception of poor learning. In a direct comparison at the University of British Columbia, students with a highly rated traditional lecturer scored 19 percent *lower* on a physics concept survey test[3] than an equivalent cohort taught with active learning techniques (Deslauriers et al., 2019). In an effort to reconcile student perceptions with the quantitative evidence, Deslauriers et al. suggest that students may *interpret* the increased cognitive effort demanded by active pedagogy as a sign of inferior learning.

Is this a problem? Student reviews on RateMyProfessors.com[4] demonstrate a preference for course "easiness,"[5] as evidenced by correlation with the "quality" measure (Felton et al., 2008; Silva et al., 2008). While "easiness" is an inherently problematic dimension to calibrate (i.e., is a course easy due to a lack of rigor or effective instruction), it likely relates to *perceived learning*. Another dimension, "helpfulness," that typically correlates with positive scores from students and measures of learning (Otto et al., 2008), also becomes confounded depending on the students' understanding of active learning pedagogy.

For example, from a student's perspective, is it most "helpful" for a professor to answer a question directly, or use it to spark a discussion incorporating multiple students? How does a student perceive being asked a question in response, particularly when the instructor intends to promote critical thinking or further reflection? For example,

- Student: "I think culture influences this behavior. Is that right?"
- Instructor: "Let's explore that as a cause—tell me more about how that could be the case," or "Culture shapes this behavior—how might you find evidence to support your hypothesis?"

Course evaluations from first-year students in an active learning environment show varying understanding of non-lecture methods. For example, embedded within a highly positive evaluation of an instructor was the statement: "One thing that I don't like in [the instructor's] approach is redirecting most of the questions that were directed to him to other students. Sometimes it feels like wtf, I asked you, professor, why [do] you ask other students to answer?"[6]

If students are unaccustomed to an interactive dynamic that is not a straightforward progression of instructor-question:student-response:instruct or-evaluation (IRE), such negative feedback can result. However, these students were not wholly resistant to engagement. The same set of course evaluations also included as strengths that this instructor "evenly distributes how much people contribute," "really tries to engage every student in the conversation," and "facilitates discussion so well, asks follow-up questions which really challenge me and overall I learn a lot."

While students appear to value the instructor's overall approach, the slightly mixed feedback may reflect differences in their understanding and acceptance of active learning.

Positive reviews of lecture-based classes on RateMyProfessors.com often suggest many students value straightforward information transmission coupled with charisma. An expanded review of nearly 13.7 million ratings again demonstrated a statistically significant correlation between clarity, helpfulness, overall quality, and easiness scores (Rosen, 2018). If students perceive active learning as more effortful and less effective at building factual knowledge, sound pedagogical approaches could be subject to criticism. This negative critique can occur, even though students typically feel that the overall classroom dynamic is positive.

While a review of course and instructor evaluation methodology is beyond the scope of this book, an instructor employing active learning should take the time to examine the specific questions posed in student surveys. Is the presence of active learning queried directly? Do questions probe the process by which students are learning in the class, or rely on student perceptions of outcomes? What student preconceptions regarding the nature of effective teaching and learning could shape the results?

Felder (2011) makes several suggestions for instructors confronted with negative course evaluations after switching to a classroom dynamic that incorporates active learning:

- First, address complaints that are *not* linked to active learning methodology.
- Expect that active learning takes considerable time to master. Review student feedback with appreciation that the instructor's current skill level is somewhere on a learning curve.
- Consult the literature related to specific methods or in-class activities. A *procedural* mistake interfering with best practices can negatively shape the students' experience.
- Solicit candid feedback with a mid-course evaluation that invites students to characterize their experience of active learning. If negative feedback is driven by a vocal minority who believe they are representative of the class, sharing the generally positive results can defuse resistance.

Given these considerations, proactive engagement with both administrators and students is a worthwhile endeavor. When starting a course, an instructor should explain how they intend to facilitate student engagement or active learning activities and the associated expectations of students. This shared understanding can provide a more valid interpretation of student course evaluations and also explains "what is happening in the classroom" for colleagues and students.

A final institutional concern centers around the logistics of incorporating active learning into existing syllabi. Some characterize active learning as taking too long to prepare and too much time in class, given the need to move quickly through course material (Felder & Brent, 2009). The authors note that preparing lesson plans is a significant task, whether active learning is present or not. Some forms of active learning or engagement do not require additional effort to integrate. For those that may take more initial planning, the benefits are worth the time investment.

When incorporating active learning into existing lessons, common confusions or key ideas highlighted in past lecture notes suggest topics for straightforward activities. Indeed, some high-impact activities take only a few minutes of class time—pose a question, have students confer with the person in the next seat, invite a pair to explain their thinking to the group, and use this as a springboard into the topic. Structuring questions, inviting student contributions, and the instructor's response repertoire are discussed in subsequent chapters.

Getting the Students on Board

"My favorite student evaluation came from someone who wrote 'Felder really makes us think!' It was on his list of the three things he disliked most about the course" (Felder, 2011).

Why students might resist a shift from passive information transmission to active learning:

- They prefer lecturing because it is familiar. They understand how to be successful by taking notes, and in some cases lecturers are entertaining.
- Active learning takes more effort and can involve uncertainty, which can be misconstrued as "poorer" learning.
- They may be afraid to speak in class or be new to psychologically safe environments and not trust the instructor to avoid ridicule or responses that cause social discomfort.
- They may be used to immediate and direct judgment in a straightforward "instructor initiation(question):student response:instructor evaluation" (IRE) dynamic and equate that with clarity and effective instruction.

Unfortunately, such predispositions drive "resistance behaviors" in students (Finelli et al., 2018; Seidel & Tanner, 2013; Weimer, 2013). Four student resistance behaviors are common:

- nonparticipation in an in-class activity, even when asked to engage;
- distracting other students;
- performing a task with minimal effort; and
- giving poor course evaluations.

Instructors with significant experience in active learning occasionally experience outright criticism or skepticism beyond nonparticipation. This is the student who, when asked to share their ideas, instead explains *why the activity is flawed* or even undermines or disrupts the instructor's introduction of a task. While such behaviors are typically rare, an instructor may want to have some form of response ready in their repertoire (instructional dissent is also discussed further in chapter 10).

Confronted by such resistance, an instructor's heart tends to sink. It is a struggle to avoid personalizing the remark or experiencing it as a direct critique of their worth as an individual and educator. More importantly: How should an instructor respond? Is entertaining such a remark going to increase the likelihood of disruptive resistance in the future? If other students agree, is the learning goal of the day essentially a write-off?

One approach is to decide quickly whether there is a valid point for the whole class to discuss (briefly), or whether it is best parked as dissent to address after class. In all cases, instructors should nonetheless attempt to maintain openness, even if they feel the complaint is ungrounded or even mean-spirited. It is fair to engage with dissent, but essential to set the norm that activities will continue and some "concerns" will be discussed after class rather than pressing pause for everyone else.

Imagine that a student responds to a discussion prompt with a comment such as, "You asked us to explain this behavior using Maslow's hierarchy of needs, but that's pointless without considering how culture shapes behavior." How might the instructor reply? Should they agree the prompt is no good and abandon it? Should they refuse to engage with the dissent, and inform the student that the prompt is the prompt? Alternatively, might they try something else:

- "I appreciate your concern that this question is an oversimplification, but for the purposes of the course we'll start with simple cases to build our understanding. I'd be happy to chat after class about how you're finding the relative level of difficulty."
- "I appreciate your concern that we are ignoring cultural factors. It's more than we could weave in here, but let's aim to take a few minutes to discuss as a group after the activity. If you're particularly interested in cultural factors, come to my office hours and we'll chat about how to capture that concept throughout the course."
- "I appreciate feedback and suggestions for the future, please come to my office hours and we can chat further. For the purposes of today, we're going to do the activity as described."

These examples attempt to balance psychological safety for students with varying degrees of receptiveness to changing the activity on-the-fly. In all cases, however, an emphasis is placed on the student feeling their ideas are valued (even if the most appropriate place for the specific conversation is not the classroom itself).

Finelli et al. (2018) surveyed over one thousand undergraduate students in introductory engineering courses to investigate student perceptions and responses to active learning, with a focus on understanding how to mitigate resistance.

Across the eighteen classes included in their survey, resistance behavior was low, albeit not nonexistent. Overall, students appreciated the active learning techniques employed by their instructors. When asked to consider specific instructor strategies to reduce resistance, students responded positively to approaches grounded in both explanation and facilitation, but perceived facilitation as having a stronger relationship with reduced resistance.

The dimensions of explanation and facilitation used by Finelli et al. encompassed eight instructor behaviors often suggested in the active learning literature. The first three are explanation; the following five are facilitation (2018, p. 81 & 83):

- Clearly explaining the purpose of activities.
- Discussing how activities relate to students' learning.
- Explaining expectations (process and deliverables).
- Using demeanor and nonverbal cues to encourage students to engage with the activities.
- Inviting students to ask questions about the activities.
- Moving around the room to assist students with the activity, if needed.
- Confronting or redirecting nonparticipatory students.
- Soliciting feedback from students about the activities.

Two additional instructor behaviors diminish student resistance: setting the stage on the first day of class and building up active learning over time.

Setting the stage on the first day is a strategy that many instructors employ. It is particularly relevant when instructors suspect engagement in their class is going to feel different or have different demands than students have experienced in the past.

There are many versions of this "first-day talk," whether a mini-lecture or more of a discussion, but the key ideas to convey are often reasonably consistent:

- "I'd like to explain how this class is going to be different and why I value this."
- "Why are we doing this? Your learning and ability to apply these concepts will be improved—real evidence supports this." Note: One can include

other rationales as appropriate, such as learning to interact effectively with others or becoming more comfortable speaking in groups.

- "This will feel different—we can work together to make sure everyone is comfortable."
- "This will feel demanding—being engaged requires more cognitive effort."
- "Here are the expectations I have for the group." [Such as preparation, paying attention, or willingness to contribute. This may be particularly important for a flipped model where students must prepare in advance.]
- "Here are some norms we're going to want to agree to." [Such as listening, respecting ideas, or sharing talk-time. Students likely have ideas of relevant norms and expectations. It is very fruitful to solicit student priorities and incorporate them instead of merely listing your own.]
- "Here are the expectations you can have of me." [Such as listening carefully to students' ideas, making it "safe" to speak up in class, clearly explaining activities and expectations, helping if someone gets stuck, or making sure confusions are ultimately clarified.]
- "Please talk to me if you have any questions at any time."
- "I value your feedback."

If that is the start of the first day of class, what should an instructor do next? How can they make everyone more comfortable with the transition from passive to active learning? Building-up can take different forms: in terms of either the structure or the expectations for participation.

One might start with very short activities or discussion prompts in pairs before increasing the duration, group size, and complexity of tasks. This helps students learn to navigate the interpersonal dynamic of working together and develop their ability to maintain focus without direct instructor intervention. Such building-up is a very natural approach. One would not try to have students do an hour-long role-play or debate in a political science class without some practice with individual subcomponents such as crafting opening statements or structuring rebuttals.

Building up participatory expectations can take several forms, including student engagement in discussion, activities, and posing questions. The case of cold-calling will be discussed further in chapter 8, but beginning with more straightforward questions may give students experience making contributions where they feel confident. An instructor might take a more active role in an early discussion to model how to engage with other students' ideas, before shifting more of the talk-time over to students.

Similarly, one could slowly build up how clarifying questions are applied to push students to develop their thinking until extensions become the norm rather than an unexpected challenge.

All of these techniques help students become more adept at thinking on their feet. In either approach, an instructor needs to take time to reflect on the student experience and try to understand just how different or nerve-wracking active engagement might be.

THE ISSUE OF AUTHENTICITY

While lecturing is something of a one-size-fits-all approach, the instructor *as a person* fundamentally shapes the interactive dynamic. Many instructors, particularly the younger or less-experienced, attempt to play the *role* of the professor. This façade is a little too reserved, standoffish, or one-dimensional—many students typically experience this as disinterest or a lack of caring. In active learning, a little empathy and emotional intelligence go a long way toward diminishing resistance but require the students to see the instructor as a *human* rather than a *role*.

This humanizing does not mean instructors should feel compelled to share their life stories, use their first names, or play the role of everyone's pal. Each instructor should decide where the line is between their personal life and the classroom. While humor can be humanizing, be very thoughtful about in-jokes—if using them at all.

A way of framing the right balance is to be authentic—but be an authentic *leader*.

The leadership literature describes the closely related constructs of *authentic leaders* and *transformational leaders*: individuals who "are self-aware, showing openness and clarity regarding who they are, and consistently disclosing and acting in accordance with their personal values, beliefs, motives, and sentiments" and offer "idealized influence, inspirational motivation, intellectual stimulation, and individual consideration of followers" (Banks et al., 2016, pp. 635–636).

Furthermore, these individuals engage in "relational transparency" by openly, *but appropriately*, sharing their real thoughts and emotions, and in "balanced processing" by considering others' opinions and concerns and attempting to maintain objectivity during decision-making (Banks et al., 2016).

In the classroom, this may require minor adaptation. In some cases, instructors will deliberately refrain from disclosing their political views (and related values) so as not to exert influence or pressure to conform. On the whole, however, each facet of demonstrating authentic and transformational leadership can be employed by an instructor in the classroom.

Describing a few key terms in more detail,

- *Self-awareness* goes beyond merely engaging in self-reflection and under-standing one's strengths and weaknesses, but also in understanding how one makes meaning of the social world.
- Exerting *idealized influence* is the capacity for others to identify with an individual—typically by engaging in behavior that models one's values and presents opportunities for direct interpersonal interaction.
- *Intellectual stimulation* refers to presenting (surmountable) challenges, but also encouraging followers to take risks and become more confident in a psychologically safe environment.
- *Individual consideration* is of particular relevance for an instructor, where the leader seeks to understand and meet the unique needs of their followers.

A final means of conveying authenticity is *nonverbal immediacy*—behaviors that decrease the perceived physical or psychological distance between individuals. Immediacy can be demonstrated with a positive affect and tone of voice and diminished by behaviors experienced as condescending, dismissive, or aggressive. Nonverbal immediacy on the part of an instructor leads to increased fondness for the instructor and the subject of the class, increased learning and cognitive engagement, and positive student evaluations (Rocca, 2008).

Three Points to Remember about Moving beyond the Lecture

- A significant body of evidence supports the benefits of active learning.
- Proactive framing of active learning with students and administrators can reduce resistance behaviors, foster effective engagement, and result in more meaningful course and instructor evaluations.
- Be authentic—always adapt examples to your unique voice and context.

NOTES

1. See *Student Perceptions of Prof Talk* in chapter 9 for further discussion and sources.

2. For accessible examples of such activities, consult the following:

Girgin & Stevens (2005) original research described above includes think-pair-share; discussion roles; fishbowl, case studies; and student presentation with class discussion.

Huston (2009) outlines interactive or student-led activities of varying durations (from 2 to 60 min) with additional facilitation advice for instructors who may be teaching outside of their discipline.

The Christensen Center for Teaching and Learning at Harvard University hosts a wealth of instructional materials for the case method. Seminal publications include Christensen's *Teaching by the Case Method* (1981) and Barnes et al. (1994). Applications range from primary education (Wassermann's *Introduction to Case Method Teaching. A Guide to the Galaxy*, 1994) to college and business schools. For discussion of potential challenges and an example of a failed attempt at implementation, see Section XV of Herreid (2007) or Zurer (2002).

Crouch and Mazur (2001) describe outcomes of peer instruction in physics and calculus classes, modeled after methods described in Mazur's *Peer Instruction: A User's Manual* (1992) and *Peer Instruction: Getting Students to Think in Class* (1997).

3. The Quantum Mechanics Conceptual Survey was administered one week prior to the final exam in a second-year undergraduate modern physics course.

4. Ratemyprofessors.com is not affiliated or endorsed by an institution of higher education. The authors of this research paper note the issues with availability bias, in terms of students self-selecting to post anonymous reviews of their individual instructors online, although these reviews have been widely described by students as influencing their course registration.

5. As well as instructor "hotness," although that metric raises other concerns and confounds.

6. Minerva Schools at KGI undergraduate end-of-semester course/instructor surveys (2016–2020). Reprinted with permission.

Chapter 3

The Basics of Effective Communication

This chapter may seem *very* obvious—it is the basics after all—but it is essential to start on the same page. For every point that you feel is evident, pause, and ask yourself how often you are truly aware of *and* in control of these factors during your day-to-day interactions. While our folk understanding of these concepts is often not bad, we rarely take the time to reflect on putting our understanding into practice.

A good place to start is with how we define communication. One can refer to the actual content of our interactions, the topics of conversation and specific word choice, as *what* we say. This is discussed in detail in subsequent chapters. Yet, *how* we say it is no less important.

Any interpersonal interaction includes a breadth of simultaneous events—some fairly conscious and others essentially nonconscious. Recall the last sentence you said to someone: What were the words? How would you describe your tone of voice? Did your voice rise or fall? How would you describe your posture at the time? Did you smile? Were you expressing or suppressing an emotion? Was the topic important? Were you rushed?

You could probably recall some of those aspects more clearly than others. Reconsider your answers: How many were you *inferring* rather than remembering? For example, "Well, I was talking to my friend about the weekend, so I *must have* been smiling." To grapple with the basics, one must try to make all of this more open to introspection.

VISUAL CUES

Eye contact, facial expression, gaze direction, and responses: this is a reasonable, but by no means exhaustive, list of visual cues. As social beings, the four cues in Figure 3.1 convey significant information and will tend to be noticed by others. If you've ever had a conversation that felt, for lack of a better word, "a little off," it's likely the person you were speaking with was not conforming to your expectations in one of these dimensions.

Eye contact is one of the strongest signals you can give to another person—it conveys attention and interest in both the interaction in general and the specific topic. This "perception of being seen" is usually considered a positive social signal.[1] Individuals who make eye contact are generally judged as more pleasant, competent, and attractive than those who do not (Heitanen et al., 2020). That said, eye contact also demands significant cognitive resources to maintain (see gaze direction, below). One can learn to be thoughtful about when to maintain eye contact and when, and how, to look away.

Attempting to distill this complex topic into straightforward rules of thumb is challenging. Three suggestions offer a starting point for more effective eye contact:

- Make eye contact to convey interest and attention.
- Try to have this eye contact feel natural rather than forced.
- Understand it is okay to break eye contact when pausing to think or the conversation takes a natural break.

Too much consistent eye contact can appear intimidating, so take advantage of those natural pauses to give your gaze a break. Remember, you can gesture with your eyes as well—such as rolling your eyes, expressing surprise, or using your gaze to indicate someone or something of interest.

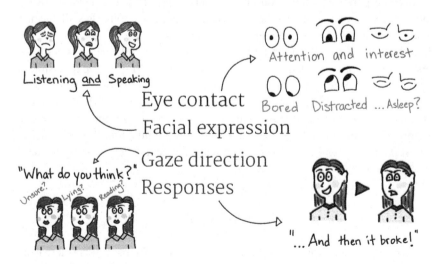

Figure 3.1 Visual Cues in the Classroom. *Source*: Copyright by the author.

As social beings, humans are good at following cues from gaze direction (Davidson & Clayton, 2016). Habitually looking in specific directions may result in students' eyes wandering around the room as well, which becomes distracting.

Closely linked to eye contact is, of course, the rest of your face. For all the jokes about "resting bitch face," there is some truth in the idea that we unintentionally convey affect (Rogers & Macbeth, 2015).

With this in mind, it is helpful to understand two things about your affect. First, what is your natural "neutral" facial expression? Second, what is your natural expression when *attentively listening* to another person? Is it the same as your neutral expression? Is it closed (negative emotional valence; skeptical) or more open and inviting? Can you feel a difference if you try ever so slightly smiling?

It's important to understand how another person could perceive your natural expression. Some instructors find they are *attending so intently* it results in a blank expression that a student might interpret as disinterest or boredom.

Conversations are not static, and faces shouldn't be either. Do not attempt to work out some sort of "ideal listening face" and then keep it plastered on in perpetuity. Genuine emotional reactions are essential for conveying attention and empathy.

In some contexts, however, it is just as important *to avoid reacting*. If you have been in such a situation before, were you successful in regulating your response? Why or why not? How does one decide what level of reaction is appropriate? This links to the concept of emotional intelligence (discussed in chapter 5).

What happens when an individual is asked a challenging question? Research has shown that if you *really* need to think about the answer, you should free up some cognitive bandwidth by breaking eye contact (Jarrett, 2016; Kajimuri & Nomura, 2016; Phelps et al., 2006). When doing this, consider two things:

- Do you just move your eyes, or do you move your whole head?
- In what direction do you direct your gaze?

Folk-literature is awash with theories of lie detection, and many include assertions that gazing up and to the right is associated with lying (it's likely not—see Wiseman et al., 2012). Similarly, gazing up rather than to the side or down can be perceived as different degrees of uncertainty.

In contexts where conveying confidence is critical, it is important to consider where to gaze when a longer pause is needed (e.g., to formulate a response to a complex, multipart question). Consider what combination of a short or long pause, gaze direction, and posture might be best suited to your context. For example, one could glance downward for a brief pause or turn one's head slightly to the side and down for more time (and mental space) to think.

POSTURE AND BODY LANGUAGE

Again, a reasonable, but not exhaustive, list—while also visual, posture is worth exploring independently of facial expressions. What we typically refer to as body language conveys, both intentionally and non-consciously, a wealth of information. Take a moment to consider two habitual behaviors:

- How do you tend to *stand* when in conversation?
- How do you tend to *sit* when in professional conversation (such as at a table with a supervisor)?

Most people have at least one (or several) default postures that will convey information to other people. Also, consider whether you tend to adapt your posture to different situations. For example, how does your conversational pose differ from how you might stand if you were giving a presentation to a small audience? What difference might this make in how other perceive you?

Postural cues alone share multiple kinds of information: from a level of authority to interest in the subject, to the degree of engagement in the dialogue, to confidence in what is said.

While specific topics like "power posing" have proved as captivating of wide audiences as they are controversial (Carney et al., 2010; Ranehill et al., 2015), being aware of your posture and a basic idea of what it conveys will facilitate more effective communication. Consider how to stand or sit in a manner that presents confidence and your undivided attention to the interaction. You may find some postures make you feel more poised and confident—try a few different options to see what feels best for you.

Are you a "hand talker"? The answer to that question can play a significant role in how you interact with others. The use of gestures in communicative interactions is widely studied and a range of purposes and best practice identified (Gunter et al., 2015; Gunter & Weinbrenner, 2017; Holler & Stevens, 2007; Kelly et al., 2012). Briefly, we use gestures for a variety of reasons:

- Gestures resolve lexical ambiguity (miming something with wings when saying "bat").
- Gestures cue the speaker (help them remember key points).
- Gestures convey intentional information (e.g., size).
- Gestures prime the audience to pay attention.

- Gestures *convey* emotion to the audience.
- Gestures are *reactive* to the emotion of the audience.

In general, speakers who use gestures effectively are considered charismatic and authoritative, with a few caveats. First, be consistent—if you repeat gestures, they should have a particular meaning. Do not overwhelm—constant hand motion is distracting; consider a limited set of gestures tailored to the content and audience. Make every motion count—use gestures to emphasize or draw attention to the most important points.

VOCAL CUES

Take a moment to consider just how much information is conveyed by your voice. This may include the following:

- Gender
- The country (or in some cases even the city) where you grew up
- Age
- Confidence
- . . .

What else should be on this list? Be aware that people may make assumptions about you from the moment they hear your voice. While you may not be able to influence these assumptions, it is important to consider how these may shape the interaction.

The first thing to consider is the tone and pitch of your voice. Most people don't deliberately attempt to modify the natural tone and pitch of their voice all the time. Yet, understanding what it "gives away" may induce you to shape how you sound at certain moments (e.g., preventing the pitch of your voice from rising too high in an emotionally charged situation).

Vocal effort is related to how you use your body to produce sound, and whether (to an observer) it appears effortful. For example, consider how actors or musicians with vocal training can project their voices *without* sounding like they are straining or yelling—producing sound recruits your whole body. Try speaking clearly and loudly (as if to someone in another room) while sitting hunched versus sitting straight. Try again while standing. Did the quality of your voice change? Did a particular posture seem to take more effort to produce the same volume?

Try speaking at different volumes (without shouting) in various postures to get a sense of how you can project more clearly without sounding strained or as if you are shouting. Understanding how to project your voice without it appearing effortful will help you appear more confident and authoritative.

It is unlikely that you speak in a total monotone, but take a moment to consider how your speaking voice sounds over time. Do the pitch and volume rise and fall? Is this related to highlighting key points, conveying emotion, or emphasizing certain ideas? Consider how you can modulate your voice to be engaging for a listener.

Uptalk—also referred to as a "high rising terminal"—is a tendency to finish a sentence with a rising intonation. This trait exhibits some regional dependency, including prevalence in parts of the United States, Canada, and Australia. It is particularly associated with the west coast of North America, from Southern California to the Pacific Northwest. While a fairly common mannerism in some regions, it is often perceived as being associated with *younger* speakers and is regarded very negatively by some audiences.

A typical objection to uptalk is that it results in declarative sentences being uttered with a rising intonation at the end—*as if they were questions* (Rhodan, 2013). Thus, the speaker may be judged as uncertain or immature. There is a significant generational difference with this perception—for younger audiences, uptalk will often pass unnoticed.

THE SUBSTANCE

Moving from *how* you speak, *what* you have to say, and how you structure that information is no less critical. Take a moment to reflect on the relative fluency of your speech (or, better yet, listen to a recording of yourself speaking). A speech dysfluency is anything that interrupts the flow of your speech—unnecessary pauses, false starts, repeated use of "like" or non-words such as "uh," "um," or "huh" are all examples.

One can also try to identify habitual words or phrases that become distracting. Habits such as consistent use of a particular adverb (e.g., "really") or a tendency to respond with "nice," or "yeah, but . . ." in a repetitive fashion are all undesirable elements in one's *response repertoire.*

It is certainly possible to train yourself out of some of these habits, but it can take significant effort (and a friend to call you out). You might also find some degree of context-dependence. Many people, with practice, stop interjecting "like" into a conversation with students but still find it peppering speech with old friends from college.

Three Points to Remember about the Basics of Effective Communication

• There is a significant interplay between *what* you say and *how* you say it.

- Most people are unaware of the significant amount of information they unintentionally convey to others.
- The deliberate use of eye contact, posture, gesture, and voice can make an individual more intelligible and judged more positively by others.

NOTE

1. While broadly true, an instructor should be sensitive to individual differences in the subjective experience of eye contact. For example, some individuals with autism spectrum disorder may experience sustained, direct eye contact as more stressful than engaging. An instructor must be prepared to read the social cues displayed by their students and adapt their behavior if necessary.

Chapter 4

Tips for the Online Instructor

Impersonal. Noninteractive. *Glitchy*. For most instructors, the thought of teaching online conjures up few positive adjectives. Instructors might recall their own student experiences with online education—just far enough in the past to be dominated by clunky user interfaces and asynchronous or at best one-way communication. In a sudden rush to go online, the tendency is to expect the least of the technology: to treat it as a platform for information transmission and nothing more. In fact, teaching online offers new opportunities for instructor-student interactions and classroom engagement.

IMMEDIACY ONLINE

Immediacy, the perceived distance between students and the instructor, is a critical driver of student engagement and a positive classroom dynamic. Nonverbal immediacy on the part of an instructor, how they convey openness, approachability, and familiarity, leads to increased positive affect for both the instructor as a person and the subject of the class (Rocca, 2008). Importantly, immediacy is present *even in an online learning environment*.

As more courses are mediated through online platforms, synchronously or asynchronously, an instructor must consider the particular skill set required to interact effectively in this context. Building on the basics, one should specifically explore,

- Visual cues: How are you going to convey attention and interest?
- Postural cues: How are you going to convey confidence and approachability?
- Vocal cues: How will you be engaging?
- The substance: How will you juggle all of the above while saying the right thing?

The considerations covered in the basics all apply to an online environment, but additional dimensions arise when engagement takes place over video.

First, lighting is critical. Insufficient light on your face means you won't be able to convey eye contact and facial expressions effectively. Additionally, it is very distracting for other users to attempt to have a conversation with a silhouette. Make sure to avoid placing a window or significant light source behind you when choosing where to teach.

Next, check your camera angles. You'll want to appear naturally present in the center of the field of view. With some laptops, this requires raising it on books to avoid being filmed from a low angle. Such angles should be avoided as they distort your face and expressions.

Some instructors use standing desks to teach in a familiar posture and recruit their whole body when making a point or conveying an idea. The field of view and freedom of movement with a standing desk facilitates breathing deeply, gesturing, shifting weight, and leaning forward.

If you don't already have a standing desk, you can create an improvised one by putting a box on top of a table or counter—this may make you feel more comfortable if you typically stand in the classroom. Standing can also prompt more normal classroom communication: being mindful of speaking too slowly or too quickly, varying your tone, and avoiding disfluencies or filler words (*um, uh, like*) that creep into speech in non-teaching contexts.

Once you have the camera properly situated, you'll want to think about how to convey attention and interest through eye contact—*even over video*. To do this, try setting up your screen so that you can easily look directly into the camera (or at least appear to; if you're a few degrees off, people often don't notice).

In a lecture environment, a student may only see their instructor from a distance. Online, you have the chance to let them see you up close and convey attention, interest, and emotion with your expression. If you make a point of looking directly into the camera, you can convey *eye contact*. Research has demonstrated that a direct gaze in bidirectional video elicits a similar psychophysiological response as in-person eye contact (Heitanen et al., 2020).

Some platforms allow a side-by-side view throughout class (such as showing both the presenter's video feed and slides). Even if that's not possible, you can consider switching between looking at slides and looking at *people* at different points in the class.

Another opportunity for instructors is the teaching location and what you wish to convey about yourself. Perceived interpersonal distance tends to diminish when we feel we know someone as a person, rather than a title. Showing your bookshelf, or a photo, or even the view out your window (being careful of backlighting) can change an instructor from a subject matter expert into a person with interests, experience, and values.

What about the student side of the camera? Many platforms offer views of all participants in an online class. Instructors who teach online frequently comment on the amount of time spent reading student's faces. Who is smiling? Nodding? Confused? Engaged or disengaged? If you're used to some physical distance from your students, consider using the wealth of information that is present when you can see a significant number of faces close-up. This may require you to clearly set the expectation that all cameras are turned on during class.

Even if you decide to spend the class time in screen sharing or presentation mode, at least consider starting your class with a view of everyone's faces (yourself included). With everyone using profiles, you have a chance to greet students by name as they arrive. Some initial "eye contact" can also go a long way to breaking down the interpersonal distance and promoting immediacy before you launch into your lesson.

Filling the screen with the video or your slides is a natural instinct, but often results in looking somewhere in the middle of the display. Unfortunately, this directs your gaze away from the camera, and won't appear like eye contact to students. If you have a very large monitor, try using a smaller window closer to the camera lens. This should allow you to look into the camera as you speak while still observing the students' reactions. You can also place notes near the camera to avoid obviously looking elsewhere. If you look at notes low on the screen or on your desk, you may appear to have your eyes shut!

On the topic of notes—while it is important to prepare, there is such a thing as overpreparation. The temptation to do this in an online class is stronger than in-person, given that the students can't see what you might have propped up off-camera or in another browser tab. Some instructors even create the teaching environment in Figure 4.1.

If you have so many notes that you are either

- noticeably looking around to find the right point in response to a question; or
- distracting yourself by thinking more about your notes than listening to the actual questions.

Then you need to pare it back.

USING THE TECHNOLOGY

The platform itself may include features such as chat and breakout groups that promote engagement. Chat is a double-edged sword for instructors. Helpful in some ways, but also extra cognitive "load" to keep an eye on (particularly if

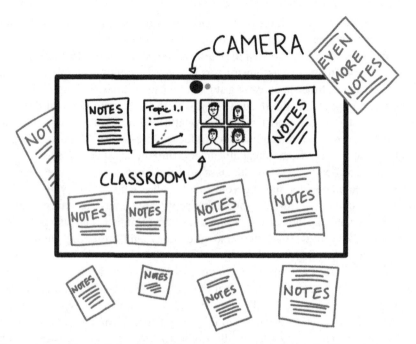

Figure 4.1   A Cluttered Teaching Environment. *Source:* Copyright by the author.

students can @instructor messages in a way that triggers a notification sound). Chat is also potentially distracting if side conversations start to take place between students. Some instructors set ground rules for chat as a means of managing these challenges, while others leave it to the students to establish norms.

Some instructors use chat as a channel for deliberate engagement during class:

- Asking students to submit questions as a means of identifying common confusions.
- Pausing class and asking everyone to write a short reflection or answer a question in chat. An instructor can ask the students to skim the responses and share out one they find particularly interesting or insightful.
- Saving the last five minutes of class for deliberate reflection and consolidation in chat. An instructor can ask students to write two or three key takeaways from the class. This will aid learning and give insight into the extent to which the students achieved learning goals.

If the class is too large for chat to be a manageable means of engagement, polls offer similar opportunities. Many online teaching platforms include at least yes/no or multiple-choice polls, and third-party websites increasingly offer polling systems for education. One caveat with yes/no polls is that some instructors find they encourage guessing and produce more limited discussion.

Frequent polling is a staple of many online classrooms and can be used throughout a class to promote ongoing engagement. These polls may take various forms:

Checking preparation or initial understanding of a concept, for example:

- Yes/No: "Were you able to complete the problem set?"
- Multiple choice: "Which of these diagrams is accurate: A, B or C?"
- Short answer: "Explain [concept] in your own words."

Gathering information that shapes the progress of the class, for example:

- Yes/No: "Should we review another example of this concept?"
- Multiple choice: "Given this algorithm, assume $g(x) = x^2$ and solve for x = 42" [incorrect options represent common pitfalls to discuss].
- Short answer: "Do you have a question for the class? If so, please share it now."

Checking current understanding of a concept, for example:

- Yes/No: "Is this a Nash equilibrium?"
- Multiple choice: "Which of the following are valid chemical structures? A, B, C, or D?"
- Short answer: "Briefly describe the process of DNA replication without looking at your notes."

Taking the "temperature" in the room or identifying the breadth of opinions present, for example:

- Yes/No: "Do you agree with [this claim / this answer]?"
- Multiple choice: "Which factor do you think has the greatest potential to drive economic development in this country? A, B, C, or Other?"
- Short answer: "What is the strongest argument you can craft *against* this position?"

Facilitating reflection and engagement related to the science of learning, for example:

- Yes/No: "Recall Kahneman's concept of 'loss aversion' from earlier. Is this 'risk aversion' the same thing?"
- Multiple choice: "What is another example of this concept: A, B, C, or D?"

- Short answer: "We'll pause for four minutes. Please make a diagram of [this concept] and share a link to your drawing here" or "Restate this concept in your own words" or "How does this relate to [the previous concept]?"

Some platforms also allow for small-group breakouts—if you usually teach your class in a room configuration that is not conducive to discussion groups, this feature may be a pleasant surprise. Breakouts can range from a think-pair-share approach in small groups, where students consider and discuss a question before reconvening, to a breakout task where students collaborate in a shared document to solve a problem, engage in peer instruction, or create a deliverable.

If your platform lacks such features, there are still some engagement tricks to try. You can solicit quick yes/no responses by asking students to hold thumbs up or thumbs down or using their arms to signal X as a means of informally polling the class. A shared notes document also allows productive engagement during class, particularly if seeded with a skeleton of topics or learning goals of the day.

Institutions shifting to a "flipped classroom" model with significant student preparation prior to the class session often ask instructors to provide video content. A common pitfall when preparing these materials is not keeping the audience or an interactive approach in mind. All of the previous considerations should be at the forefront of content creation: How will your videos display confidence, be engaging, and so on.

To mitigate the temptation to simply write the perfect monologue and deliver it verbatim, consider both the *delivery* and the *content*. First, focus on how you communicate:

- Eye contact: Approach this as if there is a real student on the other side of your camera. Use eye contact to emphasize key points and demonstrate your engagement with the topic. Consider how to use gaze as naturally as possible—don't just stare directly into the camera for the entire duration!
- Posture: How much of your body is going to be in view? Sitting or standing is a deliberate choice, as is the amount of focus on your face. Some instructors deliberately stand when preparing a video lecture so they can more effectively gesture.
- Gestures: Your camera setup will also constrain gestures. As you prepare your notes or script in advance, consider annotating where you might wish to provide specific emphasis with a gesture. Be sure to test out that your gestures are well captured by the camera, rather than curtailed or mostly off-screen. You may need to develop a specific repertoire of gestures to use in this particular context.

Moving to the content of the lecture, incorporating elements that would be present in live interactions make this more engaging. While tempting to simply write a script that is a monologue version of a textbook chapter or research paper, consider alternatives.

- Include thinking time: Allow pauses for students to process what they have heard. When there isn't a live audience, it is easy to forget that a real person is going to be engaging with the video at some point. A pause to think or even a pause to, well, *pause* the video and note key points can be very helpful.
- Ask questions: Prompt students to reflect or critically engage with what they are hearing. You may even wish to give them specific engagement tasks to complete as they take notes. Such tasks can include identifying a specific number of arguments, attempting an example problem, making a diagram or mind-map, or identifying the most or least-compelling piece of evidence.
- Offer asides: Convey your own authentic interest in the topic.

Teaching online is going to feel different, but if you resist the temptation to jump into simply presenting slides, you'll find new opportunities to connect with your students, share who you are, and engage in active learning.

SELF-EVALUATION AND NEXT STEPS

Teaching online places unique cognitive demands on an instructor. In addition to managing slides, notes, lesson plans, and student engagement, controlling the online classroom itself requires attention. The location of the camera constrains how an instructor can convey eye contact, and the camera, classroom interface, lesson plan, and notes compete for space on the screen and catch the instructor's gaze.

While eye contact builds immediacy and conveys interest, at times, the instructor will need to look away to control the interface, check notes, or free up some cognitive bandwidth to think about a challenging question. An online instructor should intentionally plan their use of gaze direction at critical moments. Looking into the camera is particularly important when,

- the instructor is emphasizing an important point or conveying a key idea; or
- a student is presenting or making a complex point.

Sometimes, this requires looking directly into the camera for a sustained period of time. In other instances, the instructor might keep their gaze *close enough* to the camera to convey attention but use peripheral vision to control the classroom or check notes. Alternatively, the instructor might glance into the camera at a specific moment, then elsewhere, as needed.

With practice, some instructors can maintain their gaze in the direction of the camera, while also attending to student videos or other elements of the online classroom.

Things to Try

A Five-Minute Gaze Direction Experiment

What is the "tolerance" of your camera for conveying eye contact with the students? You may be unintentionally losing eye contact or conveying disengagement without realizing it. As most cameras mount on the top of screens, some instructors find their eyes can appear fully closed when they glance at lower areas of the online classroom.

This tolerance varies given camera location, lighting, angles, and glasses, but it is worth investigating. Enter your online classroom, and either record yourself or record your screen (if you are visible in the classroom) as you look at specific locations:

- Look into the camera.
- Look into the camera and check what you can see using peripheral vision.
- Consult your notes or lesson plan.
- If relevant, scan the area where student videos would appear.
- If relevant, read from a slide.
- If relevant, look at the various controls and settings you may use during class.
- Test other places you frequently look, whether on- or off-screen.
- If you use a tablet and stylus, draw something (you may find you're giving students a great view of the top of your head).

Review the video and examine your gaze and posture as you look at each location. Briefly note answers to the following questions:

- How close to the camera does your gaze need to be to convey attention and interest? What can you see while staying within this radius?
- What are the top three to five places you are likely to look during a class? What happens to your gaze and posture when you look there? Would you intentionally try to manage the timing of when you look at these places?
- Are there "no go" areas to avoid looking at (given your eyes may appear to close)?
- Given this knowledge, how will you manage your gaze in class?

A Five-Minute Working Memory Experiment

Controlling an online classroom typically demands cognitive engagement *beyond* what is required in-person. Once comfortable with how the classroom controls work, an instructor can try to be deliberate in directing attention to the camera, the controls, notes, or other elements in the classroom (e.g., slides or student videos).

This deliberate engagement and switching takes working memory, executive function, and *practice* to manage effectively. Initially, new instructors often focus on the controls and their notes, pausing as they change from one to the other. Over time, start experimenting with how you can switch between tasks to spend more time looking at the camera or student videos. Make a point of testing yourself to see how seamless the classroom experience can become.

- Can you start delivering a slide by reading it, but shift your gaze back to the camera and finish paraphrasing the concept from memory?
- Can you glance at your notes or lesson plan to check multiple points, but look at the camera and finish more than one without glancing back to your notes?
- Can you use classroom controls while speaking?
- Can you use classroom controls without looking away from the camera?
- If you're uncomfortable trying to do multiple things at once, deliberately make time for eye contact. Speak while consulting your notes, glance at the camera for emphasis and confirmation, then press a relevant classroom control.

Three Points to Remember about Teaching Online

- An online classroom presents unique opportunities to foster instructor immediacy and to use active learning.
- Online classrooms are cognitively demanding. Instructors should practice maintaining a posture and gaze that conveys attention and interest, even while checking notes, controlling the classroom, and engaging with students' videos.
- A final word of wisdom from instructors experienced with synchronous online classes: "When possible, ignore the tech problems." Students may not be aware something isn't quite going as planned. When possible, try to continue without drawing attention to it.

Chapter 5

Four Key Concepts and the Classroom Dynamic

With the basics of communication covered, one can go further into understanding classroom interactions. As we become more adept at interpersonal interactions, *what* we say and *how* we say it interact to shape higher-order dynamics. As a starting point, four topics begin to weave together the *what* and *how* of our interactions:

- Psychological Safety: How do you promote an environment where individuals are comfortable engaging in discussion or dialogue and empowered to contribute?
- Emotional Intelligence: How can emotion facilitate more effective interpersonal interactions?
- Questioning: How does one ensure a discussion doesn't remain superficial? How can one engage in productive versus unproductive lines of questioning?
- Entrainment: How do individuals coordinate their actions, speech, emotions, and even ideas as they interact over time?

PSYCHOLOGICAL SAFETY

Paradoxically, the most important thing a teacher can do to encourage classroom conflict is to make the classroom a hospitable space. Only under these conditions are students likely to do the hard things on which consensus-making depends—exposing one's ignorance, challenging another's facts or interpretations, claiming one's own truth publicly and making it vulnerable to the scrutiny of others. When the classroom is a hostile place, students either withdraw into

35

privatism for safety or engage in public posturing to score points. (Palmer, 1990, p. 16)

The concept of psychological safety emerged in the context of organizational psychology. Researchers in the 1960s wished to understand how teams and businesses effectively manage significant changes to their operational or organizational dynamics (Schein & Bennis, 1965). More broadly, early investigators also tied psychological safety to a developing understanding of how to foster creativity and creative problem solving (Rogers, 1954).

Generally speaking, psychological safety refers to the perceived consequences of interpersonal risk-taking in a given context (Edmonson & Lei, 2014). In a psychologically safe environment, individuals

- feel accepted and respected for who they are;
- believe their contributions are valued;
- feel free to express themselves, contribute, or share their beliefs without fear of negative consequences.

From an early focus on change management, research on psychological safety identified broader impacts across individual employee well-being, creative problem solving by teams, and the ability of an organization to learn from successes and failures (Edmonson & Lei, 2014). Aside from the business context, it is clear that a psychologically safe environment will promote in-depth student engagement and critical thinking. In the context of interpersonal interactions, one can consider how to foster psychological safety in one-to-one situations as well as within groups.

As early as the 1950s, psychological freedom (agency), psychological safety, and a non-evaluative atmosphere were considered essential enablers of both creativity and productivity, even in scientific contexts (Forehand & von Haller Gilmer, 1964; Rogers, 1954).

In describing how to foster a psychologically safe classroom, Raths notes,

> Students will have to perceive that the teacher basically likes and respects them and that they will not be punished in some way, overtly or covertly, if they make a mistake in judgment, look foolish as they search for clarity, or adopt a value that contradicts one of the teacher's or school's. This does *not* mean that the teacher must be extremely permissive, although it does probably rule out an arbitrary or autocratic climate. More important than permissiveness is respect and concern. (Raths et al., 1973, p. 168)

Anxiety and Psychological Safety

Psychological safety directly relates to the level of anxiety experienced by students during a class. Anxiety is not only subjectively unpleasant—anxiety impedes a student's ability to "think on their feet," diminishes voluntary participation, and impairs synthesis of course concepts.

In a third-year undergraduate cognitive neuroscience class discussing the cognitive demands of online active learning seminars, a student volunteered,

> I think attentional control, as well as working memory, is pretty foundational to keeping up with the conversation [in class] as well as making connections with your existing knowledge and updating your existing knowledge because there's a lot going on. What I found interesting about this example is that [in class] I feel that executive function and the *function* of the executive function or the *performance* that we get out of our executive function can be different depending on how stressed or in danger from the reinforcement we feel. For example, I feel much more uncomfortable in classes where I know the professor will be cold-calling, and there's the possibility I might not be able to give an answer. At times that might be helpful, but it does make me feel less relaxed in class or open to knowledge or connections I would make on my own. So, there's an interesting relationship with executive function and emotion.[1]

The above quote reflects at least one of three particular forms of classroom anxiety. All these forms of anxiety are related in some way to the subjective experience of evaluation:

- Classroom communication apprehension, sometimes called communication anxiety, is "avoidance of participation prompted by evaluation apprehension or expectations of negative associations with participation" (Neer, 1987, p. 157). This anxiety surrounding performing inadequately in front of the instructor or peers is typically associated with verbally responding to a question (Rocca, 2010).
- Social anxiety refers to the fear of embarrassment in social interactions. While most students who exhibit social anxiety also exhibit communication anxiety, the converse is not the case. Many students who do not exhibit more general social anxiety will exhibit classroom apprehension/communication anxiety (England et al., 2019).
- Test or achievement anxiety is a fear of inadequate performance on evaluation but can be present in the context of low-stakes quizzes as well as exams (Khanna, 2015). This can also manifest as more general anxiety related to overall mastery of course concepts.

Why is anxiety a concern in the classroom? The Yerkes-Dodson curve in Figure 5.1 describes the relationship between stress and anxiety (here called arousal), task difficulty, and performance. This "inverted-U" shaped

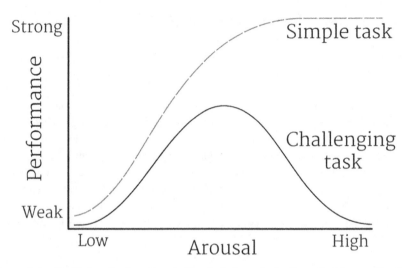

Figure 5.1   The Yerkes-Dodson Curve. Simple tasks refer to those that focus attention on a single cue, such as "flashbulb" memory, fear conditioning, or straightforward single-digit calculations. Challenging tasks require working memory or cognitive flexibility, such as multitasking, creating and adapting a strategy, or multi-digit calculations. *Source:* Adapted from figure 2 of Diamond, D. M., Campbell, A. M., Park, C. R., Halonen, J., & Zoladz, P. R. (2007). The temporal dynamics model of emotional memory processing: A synthesis on the neurobiological basis of stress-induced amnesia, flashbulb and traumatic memories, and the Yerkes-Dodson law. *Neural Plasticity*, 60803

relationship holds across a variety of contexts, including academic performance (Sarid et al., 2004; Teigen, 1994).

While the strength and nature of the relationship between anxiety and academic performance vary from study to study, a meta-analysis (Seipp, 1991) and more recent individual studies (Cooper et al., 2018) highlight the potentially negative impact. There are several key features for an instructor to recognize in this diagram:

• Some measure of arousal is needed to drive motivation and focused engagement with a task; however, when anxiety goes beyond an optimal level, performance is impaired.
• Performance on very simple or highly mundane tasks may be relatively unaffected by anxiety.
• Different tasks will have differently shaped curves—more difficult or novel tasks require less arousal for students to be motivated and focused.
• For highly difficult tasks, even moderate stress or anxiety may be sufficient to impair performance.

- Significant individual differences exist—a given classroom dynamic or task may be experienced as highly stressful by one student but less stressful for another.
- Active learning can be associated with greater classroom apprehension and anxiety, particularly for more generally anxious students (England et al., 2017).

Early estimates of the prevalence of communication apprehension suggested that 10–20 percent of Americans experience severe communication apprehension and up to 20 percent more experience moderately high communication apprehension (McCroskey, 1976). A study of 20,000 U.S. college students in the 1970s described 15–20 percent as experiencing debilitating communication apprehension (McCroskey, 1977).

Bowers and members of the 36C.099 research group surveyed 402 undergraduate students at the University of Iowa to better understand the nature and impact of communication apprehension in the college classroom. The survey began by presenting a scenario and asking, "Does this ever happen to you?"

You're attending a class here at the University. It's a class in which students sometimes make comments or ask questions, and you consider yourself prepared for the class. During the class, a question or comment occurs to you, and you think that your question or comment would be useful to you and useful to the class generally. Yet, because of some kind of inhibition or apprehension, you do not make the comment or ask the question. (Bowers, 1986, p. 372)

In this study 70 percent of students responded "yes"; this type of scenario does happen to them. Moreover, approximately 40 percent of these positive responses reported that they experience this kind of communication apprehension at least weekly. On a scale describing the severity from 1 ("very mild") to 7 ("very severe"), 12.5 percent (or 8.5% of the total sample) reported their classroom communication apprehension at a level 5 or above. Physical symptoms, reported by 27 percent of the total sample, most commonly included accelerated heart rate, general discomfort, and flushing (Bowers, 1986).

The survey continued to probe situations and causal factors that do and do not contribute to classroom communication apprehension (CCA):

Now I'm going to ask you to think of two situations. First, a class you're taking now or you've taken recently where you were *least* likely to have this feeling of inhibition or apprehension. Later, a class where you were *most* likely to have that feeling. First, the most comfortable class. Do you have it in mind? Okay. (Bowers, 1986, p. 373)

Bowers found class size was significantly related to CCA, with classes of 25 students or fewer more likely to be rated comfortable than uncomfortable, and classes of 35+ students more likely to be uncomfortable. Interestingly, the seating *arrangement,* but not where an individual student chose to sit in class, was strongly associated with CCA, with rows more associated with CCA than other configurations.

While the rank of an instructor is often confounded by class size and arrangement, Bowers found courses where students *did not know* the rank of their instructor were more likely to be comfortable. Comfortable courses were also more likely to have female instructors and uncomfortable courses male instructors, with friendliness, interest in teaching the course, and being relatively noncritical and less task-oriented associated with instructors of comfortable classes. While students appreciated being addressed by their first names, whether an instructor went by their title (Prof. X) or given name did not affect CCA.

The prevalence of CCA appears unrelated to a student's intelligence, GPA, year of study, reasons for taking a course, type of institution, or other demographic factors. Courses in communication and fine arts appeared the most comfortable, and courses in the social science and natural science are the most likely to be uncomfortable (Bowers, 1986).

What about classrooms that deliberately include practices that could prompt CCA? Interpreting the relationship between active learning and anxiety requires care, given individual differences and subtle differences in classroom dynamics.

In a study of undergraduate biology classes employing active learning, all five practices investigated caused student anxiety, from cold-calling (most anxiety), volunteering to answer a question, in-class worksheets, working in groups, to using clickers (least anxiety). Interviews with students revealed that the least-likely practices to be linked to anxiety and classroom apprehension were "waiting for a volunteer" and "discussing a topic or problem with a group of peers." The most likely to be highlighted as anxiety-inducing were "working on in-class worksheets with peers" and "instructor calling on a student for an answer" (England et al., 2017).

Another study of anxiety and active learning in large-enrollment biology classrooms found a more nuanced relationship. Depending on implementation and the classroom dynamic, certain forms of active learning, such as clicker questions and group work, could increase *or* decrease students' anxiety (Cooper et al., 2018).

Performance-oriented approaches to active learning, emphasizing speed and accuracy, tend to be more anxiety-generating (although this can be mitigated to some extent with "error framing" to help students understand their mistakes as a normal part of learning). Conversely, with careful framing and facilitation, students reported that clicker questions and group work could also decrease anxiety, given the perceived benefits for their understanding and engagement.

In contrast, active learning facilitated with cold-call or random call—two methods for calling on students who had not volunteered—only increased anxiety (Cooper et al., 2018).

For some students in highly performative and judgmental contexts, the experience of rapid-fire cold-calling impairs their ability to think in the moment as well as forming meaningful memory of the event. Describing a high-pressure cold-call, "I can remember so clearly the tone of voice, facial expression of the instructor, time of day, color of the notebook on the table, sensation of anxiety clawing its way up my throat—but not my *response*."

This example captures critical subtleties about the nature and impact of anxiety in the classroom.

In general, stressful or emotionally charged events are well remembered. *Low* levels of stress (or anxiety) may facilitate the encoding (formation) of such memories as on the left side of the Yerkes-Dodson curve. Vogel and Schwabe describe how stress has a stronger impact facilitating memory for emotional, rather than neutral, learning material. Similarly, material directly *related* to the stressor itself is enhanced, while memory for material *unrelated* to the ongoing stressor is impaired. Stress impairs retrieval of existing memory, which may underlie the impact of test anxiety on performance (2016).

Similarly, when arousal is increased by positive emotion, a subject's memory tends to be more holistic and associated with information processing that is more flexible, relational, and guided by heuristics (Levine & Pizarro, 2004). Thus, problem-solving tasks may be accomplished with more creativity and flexibility. In contrast, negative emotions facilitate information processing that is more analytical (in terms of preventing or adjusting to a threat or failure), rigid, and focused on memory for central details (Levine & Pizarro, 2004).

Further, Vogel and Schwabe describe how stress may directly impair learning in the classroom. First, stress can impair the ability to integrate new information into existing knowledge. Second, stress changes the way students think, shifting from flexible, "cognitive" forms of learning and memory toward rather rigid, "habit-like" behavior. This shift may hinder knowledge transfer, diminish cognitive flexibility during problem-solving, and lead instructors to underestimate their students' ability. Thus, stress impacts the nature and quality of memory and the cognitive processes and strategies employed during learning (2016).

For students with higher general levels of anxiety, this emotional dimension may also lead to repeatedly recalling specific in-class events where they experienced a high degree of anxiety or embarrassment. Such iteration can, in turn, increase general classroom apprehension.

While there is a clear link between low to moderate levels of arousal and performance, instructors wishing to increase focus and motivation should be very sensitive to individual differences in their students. Vogel and Schwabe suggested "cognitive challenges without excessive demands or moderate emotional arousal that results, e.g., from hearing something that is unexpected" as examples of classroom stress that may positively impact memory (2016, p. 6).

Women, low-performing students, and some minority groups may already have higher levels of baseline anxiety in the classroom. Instead of attempting to increase arousal as a driver of motivation, one should consider developing instructor immediacy, student agency, curriculum salience, and opportunities for far-transfer of knowledge and skills.

A Note on Charisma

In the Dr. Fox Lecture, a distinguished-looking, authoritative, and charismatic actor delivered a lecture containing irrelevant, conflicting, and meaningless content followed by a half-hour discussion period of little substance. Surprisingly, subjects responded favorably to the lecture—suggesting that they were "seduced" into the illusion of having learned by Dr. Fox's authority and charisma (Naftulin et al., 1973; Ware & Williams, 1975).

Researchers recorded two versions of Dr. Fox's lecture: one with a more expressive style and one without. The more charismatic version of the same content received higher evaluations, although the original study did not fully distinguish between whether students described the lecture as an informative versus enjoyable experience (Peer & Babad, 2014). This trend has been supported with subsequent observational studies and may reflect a broader positive correlation between instructor extroversion and positive course evaluations (Riniolo et al., 2006).

Charisma is described extensively in the literature on leadership, both as an approach in its own right and as a component of transformational leadership (Banks et al., 2016; Holladay & Coombs, 1994). Critically, an instructor wishing to be charismatic must go beyond a self-confident and energetic delivery style typically associated with the charismatic Dr. Fox.

In the classroom, charisma related to positive student outcomes requires an instructor to incorporate nonverbal immediacy, humor, caring, and valuing students as individuals (Bolkan & Goodboy, 2014). The authors note that this more profound form of charismatic teaching promotes students' perceptions of their learning and intrinsic motivation.

Nonverbal immediacy, caring, and valuing students are also behaviors that promote psychological safety in the classroom.

Promoting Psychological Safety

The concept of psychological safety shapes approaches discussed in subsequent chapters. As a starting point, one can consider several aspects of *what you say* and *how you say it*. First, consider what you say:

- Is your first response *judgmental or evaluative*? For example, "Nope, that's wrong" or "Great!" Even if generally positive, this can introduce interpersonal risk if students believe there will be an immediate judgment of their contribution.
- Are you able to effectively paraphrase what you have heard? Do you take care to attribute ideas to the students who may have offered them earlier in the conversation? This demonstrates that you have been listening and want to understand. It also provides an opportunity for the speaker to revise or extend their initial idea.
- Do you invite or solicit a variety of perspectives?
- Do you directly express that you value the other individual's opinion or contribution? For example, "Thank you for sharing."
- Could your response be interpreted as punishment or ridicule? For example, "How can you think that!" Even if lighthearted or intended as a joke, this can diminish psychological safety. Sarcasm should be approached with great care if employed at all—and never directed at students.

Next, consider how you say it:

- When listening, are you using eye contact to convey attention to the speaker?
- Is your expression neutral or conveying interest (rather than conveying negative emotion)?
- Are you *positively* responsive to student contributions, without conveying boredom, annoyance, or dismissal?

An instructor can also intentionally structure a seminar or lecture with psychological safety in mind. First, an instructor can offer initial framing of the discussion, so everyone is agreed concerning the focus. This can help ensure that students are more confident in their contributions being on-topic. It also prevents the discussion from feeling like an interpersonal guessing game of what the instructor wants to hear. This short preamble can also be an opportunity to set out the desired learning goals or outcomes of the day.

A second approach is to propose norms for agreement by the group. For example, an ethics class requires engagement with ideas that some will find objectionable. Indeed, if students are more willing to "test out" different perspectives or propose controversial ideas for the sake of argument, the more productive the discussion will be. In this context, one might suggest norms such as,

- "We recognize that points raised for discussion in this class *may or may not* represent a personal opinion. You are welcome to flag opinions as your own if you wish, but also free to test out ideas that are inconsistent with your personal beliefs."
- "While discussing principles of morality and ethics outside of class is encouraged, you can't 'hold' fellow students to ideas raised during the discussion after class is over (i.e., It is inappropriate to approach someone after class and demand accountability, 'How can you think that—')."
- "Recognize that we are speaking as individuals (real or hypothetical) and use 'I think . . .' or 'One could argue . . .' rather than projecting normative framing on the discussion (e.g., avoid, *'Everyone* knows . . .')."

EMOTIONAL INTELLIGENCE

"Emotional intelligence is a type of social intelligence that involves the ability to monitor one's own and others' emotions, to discriminate among them, and to use the information to guide one's thinking and actions" (Mayer & Salovey, 1993).

A considerable literature surrounds the construct of emotional intelligence, from Mayer and Salovey's four-branch model to Daniel Goleman's applications to leadership (Goleman, 1995, 2004; Mayer et al., 2016). The most widely used assessment of emotional intelligence is the Mayer-Salovey-Caruso Emotional Intelligence Test (MSCEIT), which assesses four dimensions:

- Perceiving [or identifying] emotions
- Using emotions
- Understanding [the causes of] emotions
- Managing emotions

In the context of interpersonal interactions, emotional intelligence shapes visual cues, postural cues, and vocal cues, as well as the substance of the discussion.

Consider how perceiving emotions in others can offer insight into underlying motivations.

Consider how one can manage emotional displays as a means of shaping the dynamic of the discussion.

Consider how emotions can rally people to a cause or shape an approach to problem-solving. A group with a high degree of emotional intelligence among its members will also be enabled to effectively foster psychological safety.

Emotional intelligence can directly affect both what you say and how you say it. First, consider what you say:

- "I can see this is important to you . . ." or "Does this make you feel uneasy? What might be causing you to feel that way?" The initial statement relies on accurately recognizing how emotion might be shaping what another person is saying (or the visual cues they are giving). The emotional dimension is then included in the conversation in a productive way.
- "This makes me angry because . . ." Acknowledging and owning the emotional dimension can precede a shift to engaging with the underlying issues or motivations that are most relevant to the discussion. Crucially, for emotions that have a negative valence (anger, frustration, fear), this may be best done *without* showing the emotion in tone or body language, lest it adds unwanted emphasis to the analysis. Otherwise, one risks the substance of the idea being dismissed as "just" an emotional reaction or judgment.
- "No! That's wrong!" Always consider whether emotion is the primary driver of your initial responses; one can be passionate about a subject, but an overtly negative emotional reaction can diminish psychological safety.

Next, consider how you say it:

- Consider the visual cues afforded by your facial expression and responses. Are you exhibiting empathy, by mimicking a degree of the emotional valence presented by the other person? For example, if they are enthusiastic and happy, are you smiling? If they are upset or disappointed, are you conveying a degree of concern? Importantly, one can modulate the degree to which one displays an emotional response as a means of either conveying empathy, attempting to defuse the emotion, or deliberately leading to escalation.
- Consider how your posture may convey emotion, from the tension in your frame to more overt signals such as crossing your arms.
- Consider how gestures can add an emotional dimension, when appropriate, or may need controlling if they become overbearing (particularly if they could convey anger).
- Consider how your tone of voice and effort/volume can convey emotion, whether positive or negative.

A particular challenge with emotional intelligence is recognizing when emotion will be *additive*, such as demonstrating empathy or fostering shared enthusiasm, or *negative*, such as diminishing psychological safety or overwhelming the substance of your message. This distinction is a particularly fine line for female instructors, given gendered stereotypes of the degree to which emotion guides decision-making and behavior.

For example, while Tiedens demonstrated that expressions of anger generally conferred the impression that an individual is competent and more worthy of status and power (2001), it would be premature to provide "one-size fits all" advice. In a similar experiment, Brescoll and Uhlmann found that "both male and female evaluators conferred lower status on angry female professionals than on angry male professionals. This was the case regardless of the actual occupational rank of the target, such that both a female trainee and a female CEO were given lower status if they expressed anger than if they did not" (2008, p. 268).

Furthermore, female expressions of anger are subjected to a fundamental attribution error: an angry response from a woman is attributed to her *character* ("she's an angry person" or "she is out of control"). In contrast, an angry response from a man is more likely to be attributed to the *circumstances* ("the situation is frustrating") (2008, p. 269). This distinction between internal disposition versus external situation can lead people to conclude that a woman does not have the temperament to effectively engage in the workplace without making a similar judgment of a male colleague.

In a professional context, Brescoll and Uhlmann suggest that women could adopt particular strategies to mitigate such effects, such as overtly (i.e., verbally) offering framing of the external or situational factors driving expression of negative emotion (2008).

The impact of emotional expression is nuanced. A single emotional demonstration can be a double-edged sword in terms of how others perceive an individual. For example, expressions of pride impact judgments in ways that are both positive (e.g., perceived agency or task-oriented leadership) and negative (e.g., interpersonal hostility or diminished people-oriented leadership). Expressions of other emotions, such as anger, which are often subject to gendered norms around social rules, are modulated by dominance and "affiliativeness" of a person (Hess et al., 2005).

In a study conducted in Germany, researchers found an interesting relationship: The positive effects of expressing pride versus happiness were more pronounced for women overall, yet the adverse effects more detrimental for women only on a measure of perceived interpersonal hostility (Brosi et al., 2016). In this context, the authors concluded that so-called achievement-oriented women should not withhold expressions of pride in order to conform to gendered norms of emotional expression. Indeed, "for such women, self-inhibiting pride may not only be emotionally unhealthy but also strategically ill-conceived" (p. 1326).

The specificity of such a result is significant when compared to research that describes the "backlash effects" women may professionally experience when expressing "male" emotions (Rudman & Phelan, 2008). While considerable further research could explore how these effects may generalize across culture, ethnicity, or specific contexts, evidence suggests some cross-cultural stability of gender-specific emotional experience (Fischer et al., 2004) and perceptions of emotional display.

Echoing the general considerations related to emotional intelligence above, Brescoll described emotional expression as "two complex minefields" that affect female leaders. First, determining *which emotions* are appropriate to display in a given context. Second, determining the appropriate *degree* to display a given emotion. In professional settings, women can be penalized for minor or moderate displays of emotion, particularly anger or pride. Yet, women are also expected to be emotionally expressive and sanctioned for appearing frigid or unemotional (2016).

There is no universal way to approach this challenge: culture, age, and sources of power in the classroom will all interact to shape how emotional displays are perceived. In general, instructors, particularly female instructors, should consider

- the extent to which they display stereotypically more masculine or more feminine emotions;
- how students have responded to specific displays of emotion in the past;
- the extent to which express emotion in the classroom;
- how to model emotional intelligence in the classroom;
- whether it is essential to mitigate the fundamental attribution error by highlighting relevant situational factors when displaying emotion.

Importantly, emotional display rules that work for one instructor may not be effective for another. Some measure of experimentation or feedback (from students or peers) may be necessary to fit one's behavior to a given context.

Psychological Safety, Emotional Intelligence, and Values

Psychological safety and emotional intelligence impact students expression of values. Values are fundamental; they are chosen, prized, shape action, and are modifiable upon reflection (Raths, 1959). An instructor must be aware that student contributions to class discussions may reflect their individual *values*. When students' values are involved, it is particularly important for an instructor to use teaching practices that foster psychological safety and focus on *individual agency and critical thinking* rather than *information transmission*.

Building on John Dewey's educational theories, Raths developed Values Clarification[2] as a means of outlining a theory of values as well as a process to support students identifying and developing their values (Raths et al., 1973). While a postsecondary instructor is unlikely to engage in moral education directly, the behaviors described by Raths nonetheless create a positive dynamic when class discussion is shaped by students' values. Here, instructors must

- be accepting and encouraging;
- encourage diversity, not assuming absolute right or wrong answers [for value-related ideas];
- respect the student's right to participate or not;
- respect the student's response;
- encourage each student to answer honestly;
- listen carefully to student responses;
- raise clarifying questions to promote engagement and development of ideas;
- avoid questions that may limit or threaten thinking; and
- raise questions of both personal and social concern.

Within this approach, one can identify behaviors promoting psychological safety, acting with emotional intelligence, and fostering critical thinking. Even constructive critics of Values Clarification note the student-centered and humanistic perspective accompanying this pedagogy, as well as the respect for student freedom, autonomy, and choice (Griffin, 1976).

That is not to say that *every possible value* must be accepted. While an instructor should be accepting of a breadth of perspectives, even ones they do not personally agree with, lines may be needed. Some institutions have clear policies related to hate speech or what is or is not permissible behavior in the classroom. In other cases, an instructor may need to use their judgment.

A crossed line is best dealt with clearly, firmly, and without an emotional reaction—particularly if the student may not have intended to cause a problem. For example, "I need to pause the class for a moment. This is not acceptable [Explanation of the issue and expectations for the future]." This approach may also be effective if student-student interactions become problematic, such as being dismissive of others or "friendly joking" becomes bullying.

AN INTRODUCTION TO QUESTIONING

What kinds of questions do instructors pose in the classroom? Wassermann differentiates between "unproductive," "less-than productive," and "productive" questioning, which in turn relates to both the substance and the style of posing questions (Wassermann, 1992, 2017). Consider where you have encountered examples of each kind of question.

Unproductive Questions

- "Stupid" questions
- Too complex questions
- Teacher-answered questions
- Trick questions
- Questions that humiliate

The above types of questions diminish psychological safety. They are often posed to further the narrative or position (or ego) of the person asking the question, rather than as a genuine overture for input.

Less-than Productive Questions

- Trivial questions
- Abstract questions
- Ambiguous questions
- Hit-and-run questions

While none of these types of questions *deliberately* belittle others, they will nonetheless diminish psychological safety because students are not enabled to make thoughtful or meaningful contributions to the conversation. Being put in the position of only making superficial contributions diminishes the extent to which the student feels valued by the instructor and the group as a whole.

The hit-and-run style of rapid and typically somewhat trivial questioning in Figure 5.2 is a common strategy used by individuals wanting to feel they are engaging the other party.

While it can appear engaging given the frequency of student contributions (as opposed to a lecture), this engagement is at best superficial and can diminish psychological safety. The questioner wholly controls the topic and rapid flow of questions (typically with a desired end-point already in mind). The person responding may recognize they are not shaping the discussion in a meaningful way, and even wonder whether they are being listened to at all. This dynamic will diminish their sense of agency in the conversation, foster mistrust that their ideas are considered of value, and can lead to more general disengagement over time.

Productive Questions

- Respectful of the individual
- Focus on "big ideas"
- Can be grounded in values

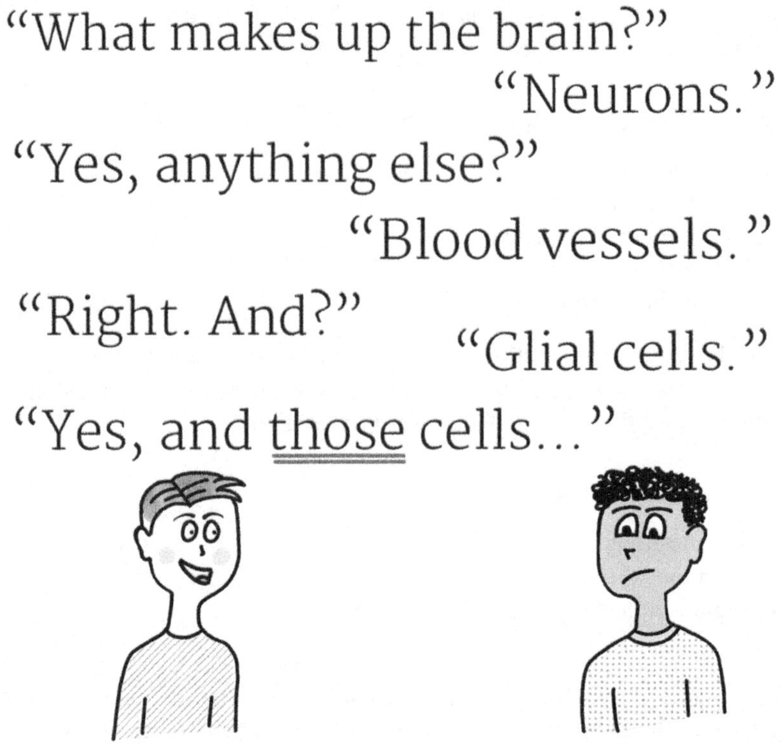

"What makes up the brain?"

"Neurons."

"Yes, anything else?"

"Blood vessels."

"Right. And?"

"Glial cells."

"Yes, and those cells..."

Figure 5.2   Hit-and-Run Questioning. While this example is particularly trivial, the student's ability to shape the discussion would remain superficial even if the questions appear more involved. Here, the questioning is rapid as the instructor steers the student toward a specific idea. *Source*: Copyright by the author.

Productive questions promote psychological safety by making space for individuals to engage deeply with a given topic and share their thinking. They can also be questions that allow individuals to clarify or share their values or personal opinions, which promotes psychological safety. Responses to these kinds of questions will typically go beyond surface-level considerations and require analysis, synthesis, or evaluation. See the chapters on (Non)evaluative Responses and Complex Questioning for further elaboration on psychological safety and promoting depth of engagement. For further elaboration and examples of these question types, consult Wassermann 1992 or 2017.

ENTRAINMENT

Picture two individuals engaged in a productive conversation. Does one person dominate? Do they use a shared vocabulary? How do they take turns? Do they appear to be "on the same page," and, if so, how can one tell?

Entrainment is the process of synchronization of two people's behavior. It is particularly present in productive conversation. Two forms relate to *what you say* and *how you say it* in the classroom: lexical entrainment and postural/vocal entrainment.

Lexical entrainment refers to the process by which two individuals in conversation use a shared set of specific words or examples. When individuals talk about particular concepts, "while there is a great deal of variability *across* conversations, there is little *within*" (Brennan, 1996; Brennan & Clark, 1996).

This entrainment can be considered a form of cooperation between the participants: removing ambiguity and fostering agreement. While this will take place naturally, one can consider how to deliberately shape the working terminology for a given conversation. When relevant, one can consider how deliberately using previous words in future context-specific conversations will facilitate understanding.

Postural and vocal entrainment refers to the process by which individuals synchronize their movements and engage in turn-taking during a conversation.

This widespread phenomenon reflects the cooperative nature of communication and builds a shared sense of rapport, familiarity, and group identity. Research has shown quantifiable differences between the postural and vocal entrainment found when friends or like-minded individuals converse, versus when strangers converse. Such entrainment is also suggested as one factor contributing to more successful clinician-patient interactions in therapeutic settings (Latif et al., 2014; Oberg et al., 2011; Richardson & Dale, 2005; Richardson et al., 2008).

In dubbing this the "chameleon effect," Chartrand and Bargh note that this mimicry of postures, mannerisms, facial expressions (and more) is typically unintentional and without conscious awareness, yet significantly contributes to perceptions of likability and friendship. They further note that individuals considered "dispositionally empathic" exhibit this entrainment to a greater degree (1999).

While the basis for this behavior may be largely nonconscious, one can nonetheless reflect on the extent to which you might engage in this behavior. Specific habits, such as whether an individual typically sits or somewhat stiffly stands, may also facilitate or hinder this type of entrainment. Being deliberately receptive to this form of coordination may positively impact the communicative dynamic.

Mirror neurons are a topic that has received a lot of attention in the pop-psychology literature of the past two decades. Investigation of mirror neurons began with an intriguing discovery. When an individual observed another individual perform an action, neurons would fire in areas of the *observer's brain* as if they were also making the gesture or motion (Rizzolatti et al.,

1996; Rizzolatti & Craighero, 2004). The discovery seemed to relate to something we intuitively understand as humans. Don't we wince when another person stubs their toe? Don't we look at someone reaching toward an object and *understand* what is happening? When you interact with someone who is angry or sad, isn't there a tendency to understand their emotion and perhaps even feel that way yourself?

Mirror neurons were initially proposed as the neurobiological basis of this "action understanding," then extended to be described as the basis of learning from observation and even the foundation of human empathy and our social reality (Ramachandran, 2009; Lehrer, 2008). While this compelling claim made for many popular articles, other neuroscientists favor a much more conservative interpretation of the evidence (Hickok, 2009; Gruber, 2016).

While the jury is still out on the specific role of mirror neurons, it is worth recognizing that your facial expressions, gestures, and body language may have a significant and direct effect on the other party in a conversation. Consider how your gestures and displays of emotion may be consciously and unconsciously shaping the dynamic of your interactions.

NOTES

1. Minerva Schools at KGI undergraduate course in-class discussion (2019–2020). Reprinted with permission.

2. In short, the process of Values Clarification described by Raths et al. (1973) of choosing, prizing, and acting is described as:

Choosing: freely, from alternatives, after thoughtful consideration of the consequences of the alternatives.

Prizing: cherishing, being happy with the choice, and being willing to publicly affirm the choice (value).

Acting: doing something aligned-with or shaped-by the chosen value; acting repeatedly and consistently in accordance with the value.

Values Clarification exploded into teaching pedagogy in the late 1960s and 1970s, with Raths et al.'s *Values and Teaching* selling over half a million copies (1966, 1978). Individuals with clear values, according to the authors, are enabled to be positive, purposeful, enthusiastic, and proud. A practical follow-up, *Values Clarification: A Handbook of Practical Strategies* (1972), outsold its predecessor and cemented the position of Values Clarification as a significant approach in education and counseling of the time (Kirschenbaum, 2000). While this trend continued through the early 1980s, with over 200 dissertations and 60 academic articles from 1978 to 1985, overall interest and application waned as pedagogy shifted and critiques mounted (Kinnier, 1995).

While generally positive, early empirical studies were often far from conclusive, hindered by small sample sizes and often insufficient control (Kirschenbaum,

1975). Across a second wave of studies in the late 1970s, dependent variables ranged from "Self-esteem, self-concept, and personal adjustment," "attitudes and abilities in science and ecology," "classroom behavior" (as evidenced by a substantial increase in active participation and decreases in inappropriate behavior during values clarification activities), to simply "values."

In a detailed analysis of the individual studies, Lockwood concluded that claims related to a positive impact on classroom behavior appeared warranted, including an increase in observable participation. However, the degree of generalization across age groups was as-yet unclear. Other claims remained inherently more challenging to assess, and instructor experience or competency emerged as a significant covariant (1978). A recent study supports the efficacy of this interaction style: instructors reported a classroom dynamic described as more "enjoyable and motivating," and student feedback was overwhelmingly positive (Lisievici & Andronie, 2016).

Chapter 6

Quality, Not Quantity

Defining Effective Engagement When Promoting Active Learning

"How can I explain the wild variety of teachers who have incited me to learn—from one whose lectures were tropical downpours that drowned out most other comments, to one who created an arid silence by walking into class and asking, 'Any questions?' " (Palmer, 1990, p. 11)

What is engagement? The definition may seem self-evident, but as one moves beyond the traditional lecture, something straightforward like "participation" is an insufficient construct. Consider the "hit-and-run" style of questioning introduced previously. This type of interaction includes an abundance of participation but is not a desirable style of student engagement.

Similarly, Ben Stein's "Anyone? Anyone?" teacher in *Ferris Bueller's Day Off* would not become a model instructor by merely adding a few cold-calls. Defining engagement in terms of quality, rather than simply relying on quantity, is a necessary first step in moving toward a more effective model of interactive instruction.

Recall the last time you heard someone essentially ask, "Aren't we all having fun?" That tired refrain, frequently a statement masquerading as a question, often comes from an individual in charge. Indeed, instructors engaging in hit-and-run questioning tend to find it a rewarding, invigorating experience. At the center of the classroom, secure in their role as the smartest person in the room, they solicit a stream of affirmation of their narrative and offer a stream of affirmation in return. What fun!

The above teaching style is an inherently *performative* approach. The instructor has a script and weaves in student engagement to fit their desired outcome. Students often perceive such instructors as charismatic and highly intelligent—indeed, they seem able to make any student contribution "fit" almost effortlessly.

The problematic element, through the lens of effective engagement, is the degree to which the performative instructor is controlling the room. There is no room for new ideas, no novel synthesis, no emergent understanding that makes use of the disparate perspectives and backgrounds of the students. Everything is fit to a predetermined narrative.

Such an interaction style, as discussed previously, does not promote psychological safety or convey respect for students' ideas or values. Beyond the lecture, instructors have to define engagement in a way that takes into account both of these critical factors. The most important first step is recognizing the role of the instructor's ego in shaping the dynamic of the classroom. Consider the following:

- To what extent is the instructor invested in *specific topics* being the focus of the discussion?
- To what extent is the instructor invested in *specific examples* becoming *the exemplars* for the discussion?
- To what extent is the instructor invested in *specific "Ah-ha!" moments* occurring during the discussion?
- Does the instructor *believe* that they are an engaging speaker, with valuable things to say?
- Is the instructor *concerned* with losing credibility if not perceived as "the expert" in the room?

This list might appear to be the very definition of an instructor; however, some elements can undermine the desire to have deep and active engagement on the part of students.

At its heart, instructor ego maintains control in the classroom: control the content, the narrative, and the outcome. The instructor's ego can drive some of the unhelpful behaviors, such as lecturing, hit-and-run questioning, or shutting down student comments, that should be avoided. A further tension lies in the fact that while an instructor may have learning goals for the day, they also have an idea of *how* to achieve these goals. In some cases, these can be particularly specific, such as when certain examples are considered seminal in the field or specific "Ah-ha!" moments have occurred before.

Student engagement is fundamentally risky for an instructor's ego as it can shape the discussion in unexpected ways. Indeed, any move from superficial to deep engagement carries the risk of altering the direction of the class. While a good motto may have to be simply "expect the unexpected," doing this requires one to approach a topic with student-directed engagement in mind. First, identify specific learning goals associated with the topic of the day and articulate them clearly. Next, identify avenues to achieve these goals, such as analyzing particular examples, exploring a case study, or other activities.

A well-designed case study or activity can address most problems of quality versus quantity of engagement. Still, any section of instructor-led debrief can slip back into an overly controlled dynamic. For matters of tradition or class size, one may need to conform to the expectation of a *lecture-style* delivery. Nonetheless, one can incorporate active engagement into these types of contexts, provided the instructor is ready to cede a measure of control.

LEVELS OF STUDENT ENGAGEMENT

One can define three levels of engagement in the classroom: superficial, deep engagement with limited student control, and deep engagement with extended student control.

Superficial engagement is the classic model of soliciting frequent-yet-shallow contributions from students. The most common example of this is the hit-and-run style of questioning described by Wassermann (2017). In this questioning style, the instructor punctuates their narrative by asking students to fill in the gaps but wholly controls the result. While students do contribute and may appear highly engaged, there are specific, desirable answers to each question.

A similar approach is one where the instructor engages students beyond a narrative flow, but the questions are straightforward and related to clarification, demonstrating fundamental knowledge, or simple synthesis. All of these questions have "right or wrong" answers. An instructor can turn these types of questions over to the students while retaining control of anything that could shape the direction of the discussion more broadly.

For example, the instructor may ask questions such as,

- "Who discovered the structure of DNA?"
- "In your own words, how can you describe Bayes' Theorem?"
- "Consider the examples—what was the common theme?" or
- "Given the discussion today, what is one key idea to take away?"

If the latter questions feel different from the former, consider this: While they do allow the student to express a more detailed point of their own making, the summative nature means the student's idea will not shape what comes next. If another student is asked to comment, they are unlikely to build on such a summative point (and more likely to express some novel idea of their own). At best, the student might get a name check by the instructor as they wrap up, "That's a great point [Student X]. I think. . ." In this dynamic, the instructor always gets the last word.

This kind of engagement in a *single interaction* can feel rewarding given the frequent acknowledgment of students coupled with a verbal reward for providing the correct answer (often praise). Such questions can have a place in the classroom: In some contexts, recollection of factual knowledge or straightforward problems may be a necessary *first step* in learning a skill or concept. Over time, however, students are likely to realize that they are not shaping the discussion. As this lack of agency is eventually discouraging, using this kind of engagement as the primary mode of student contribution is to be dissuaded.

Deep engagement with limited student control is where the students play a significant role in shaping the discussion, but the instructor controls the process in a manner that tightly constrains the outcome or output. A familiar instance of this is where students generate an example or identify a context for further analysis, but the instructor wholly constrains the approach, and a specific "right answer" is the end objective. While the students have chosen a topic of interest, the final output and insight will appear the same regardless of which example or context is selected.

Consider a biological statistics class concerned with understanding sampling and basic statistical analysis. In the example below the instructor begins by determining both the specific analysis and the context in which it is applied. They don't use reflective restatements or other techniques that would encourage students to develop their initial ideas. Engagement moves quickly from one student to another.

- Instructor: "Today, we're going to learn about the chi-squared test. Let's do this by performing an analysis of whether two species associate in a given environment. If we take the San Francisco bay area, what two species might we be interested in?"
- Student W: "How about seals and sea lions."
- Instructor: "What factors suggest we might we expect them to associate?"
- Student W: "Well, they live in the ocean and eat the same things."
- Instructor: "What other factors might there be?"
- Student X: "They are adapted to the same climate."
- Instructor: "Diet and climate, could there be more?"
- Student Y: "Geographically, it makes sense: both are found in North America."
- Instructor: "Are these sufficient for our hypothesis that they do associate to be plausible? What do you think, Student Z?"
- Student Z: "Yeah, these seem like the big ones. I can't think of a good reason why not."
- Instructor: "It sounds like we're on board with this being a plausible hypothesis, so let's try a chi-squared test. Here's some sampling data: we'll call the first set seals and the second set sea lions. . ."

Here, the instructor was ready to entertain a short debate about the plausibility of the association between the two suggested organisms and could have pushed for more synthesis of relevant factors to consider. They might have solicited two different species if the first didn't pass muster with the class.

While that let students feel they had some agency in shaping the topic of discussion, the sampling data was already in the instructor's presentation. The students' ideas of why there might be a relationship were immaterial to the analysis and the outcome. There was no deep engagement with the particular exemplars, no in-depth investigation of a student-suggested hypothesis, and no context-specific factors became the subject of scrutiny.

Consider another example where there is a measure of deeper engagement, but the instructor doesn't quite cede control of the narrative to explore a student-generated hypothesis. Here, the instructor does probe and offer reflective restatement, but the takeaway fits the instructor's narrative rather than directly incorporating the students' ideas.

- Instructor: "We've learned about intrinsic and extrinsic motivation, and organismic integration theory posits that these are not mutually exclusive. Can you think of an example where we might see a blend of these types of motivation?"
- Student X: "University—I'm interested in what I study, but I also want to get a degree."
- Instructor: "Tell me more about what is intrinsic and extrinsic here."
- Student X: "Well, the interest and enjoyment in learning about psychology are intrinsic, but the degree itself is extrinsic because I'll use it to get a job and make money."
- Instructor: "Is this consistent with how others think of being at university?"
- Student Y: "Yeah, I also please my family by being here. That's kind of intrinsic and extrinsic, I guess."
- Instructor: "So some factors may themselves be both?"
- Student Z: "Yeah, but in individualistic cultures it would be more about pleasing yourself. My culture is more collectivist, so we think about it differently."
- Instructor: "Interesting. It sounds like there can be some individual differences, but the key idea that intrinsic and extrinsic motivation is a spectrum seems to hold."

If invited to elaborate from their own perspective, Student Z could probably have made a nuanced point about the relative importance and overall framing of specific factors across cultures. Instead, the instructor quickly shifted to their own takeaway of motivation as a spectrum.

Deep engagement with extended student control is where the students become significantly more in charge of the topic and direction of the discussion. While the instructor would approach the session with learning goals, relevant examples, and questions to spark discussion, student contributions could shift the focus of the conversation or propose a hypothesis to investigate further. In many cases, students could define the analytical approach to a problem and may reach different conclusions (or output) as a result. Adapting and continuing the previous example:

- . . . Student Y: "Yeah, I also please my family by being here. That's kind of intrinsic and extrinsic, I guess."
- Instructor: "Some factors may themselves be both." [Reflective restatement]
- Student Z: "Yeah, but in individualistic cultures it would be more about pleasing yourself. My culture is more collectivist, so we think about it differently."
- Instructor: "Tell me more."
- Student Z: "There are powerful expectations around pleasing your family, which is reinforced socially—I guess kind of like an extrinsic reward, but we've also internalized that this is important, so because I value it, it feels intrinsic to me as well."
- Instructor: "Do others experience this similarly or differently?"

[Several students voluntarily share their experiences]

- Instructor: "What do we hear across these examples?"
- Student Y: "Culture plays a role in both the degree of intrinsic/extrinsic motivation associated with a given factor, but also which factor carries the most weight in shaping behavior overall."
- Instructor: "How do we feel about this? Was this captured in our readings, or are we looking at things differently?"
- Student W: "The readings didn't mention it, but isn't it just extrinsic in these cases? If they tell you to be a doctor, is there any intrinsic motivation?"
- Student Z: "I still think so. . ."

[Students debate—eventually the instructor helps call time on the discussion]

These two model discussions had the same learning goal (understanding intrinsic and extrinsic motivation as a spectrum). However, in the second the discussion shifted to focus on a point particularly important to the students (cultural factors), and the ultimate takeaway would include student-generated insight about how culture shapes motivation.

Similarly, the instructor could use a more flexible process in the seals and sea lions example. *How should we investigate associations?* As a potential starting point, it could lead to a debate about different species or the applicability of *t*-tests versus chi-squared analysis. Still, it would achieve the end learning goal of understanding how to test for a relationship between two variables.

Discipline-specific differences do exist, yet the perception that extended student control is well suited only to discussions in the arts, the humanities, and social sciences is misguided. The following questions all address specific, fundamental concepts in undergraduate math and physics, yet the answer will depend on the assumptions and approach suggested by the students.[1]

- Why does toast tend to land jam-side down when sliding off a table (or does it)?
- Imagine a boat that could transport the entire class from Port Alberni to the Bamfield Marine Sciences Centre. What is the horsepower of the engine?
- Susie the spider slips off a branch, reaches terminal velocity, then lands in her web. How many times does Susie bounce in her web before coming to rest?
- What is the probability of an electron in a truck's tire tunneling through a speed bump rather than going over it?

While the above questions are not as well defined as a standard "given x, solve for y" type of problem, they nonetheless follow that format. Yet, real problems in science and engineering are not so straightforward. As Felder highlights,

> Most engineering course time is spent teaching students to solve well-defined problems that have (so we believe) one correct answer. However, most real nontrivial problems don't fit this description: the questions are vaguely defined, and the "correct" answer usually begins with "It depends." Moreover, all of our courses are based on well-defined compartmentalized bodies of knowledge: we teach thermodynamics in the thermodynamics course, fluid mechanics in the fluid mechanics course, and rarely do the twain meet in the minds of the students who take these courses. Show me a professor who has not been greeted by blank looks and mumbled denials when he has asked about material from other courses, and I will show you a professor in his first week of teaching. (1985, p. 176)

Given the opportunity to generate their own examination questions, Felder's chemical engineering students generated a wide variety of open-ended questions that required creativity, synthesis, and divergent thinking. In engineering courses more broadly, creativity encompasses both *convergent* and *divergent* thinking, including analysis and evaluation to dig deeper into ideas. A fruitful avenue of pedagogical development would foster openness to "exploring, rather than solving, problems" and "encourage students to embrace ambiguity, avoid premature closure, and increase reflection" (Daly et al., 2014, p. 437).

Mathematical creativity and divergent thinking are also deliberately fostered using problems where a typical approach would lead students astray. Describing such a problem in analytical geometry, an instructor notes, "Creativity is expressed in the search for different solutions, from different mathematical areas . . . when the immediate solution doesn't work, and you attempt to look at the problem differently . . . looking at the same given data from a different angle" (Levenson, 2013, p. 283).

Instructors can cede control even when students' understanding is at an early stage of building basic knowledge of a concept. Mazur describes the effectiveness of peer instruction in introductory physics courses and notes, "Instead of teaching by telling, I am teaching by questioning" (Mazur, 2009, p. 51). Similarly, elaborative interrogation is a particularly effective learning technique (Dunlosky et al., 2013) used in quantitative and qualitative disciplines. Weinstein et al. describe this method with an example of using "how" and "why" questions to explore the physics of flight (2018).

Inductive, rather than deductive, approaches also promote students' agency in their learning. Here, an instructor may share observations, examples, or data and let students take the lead in inferring principles, developing theories, and creating models. The basic, fundamental concepts are presented once this context of realistic and complex problems is already established (Felder & Brent, 2004; Prince & Felder, 2006).

An introductory undergraduate statistics class, for example, can conduct a dice rolling experiment, practice calculating simple probabilities, then explore questions that do not have a single, straightforward answer. In this context, such questions might include, "What [outcome] would it take to surprise you?" or "What is the probability of your prediction being off by more than x?" or "What are some likely explanations for [this disparity in the outcomes]?" (Ernst, 2011).

THE CRITICAL FIRST QUESTION

The most important tool for an instructor is a well-thought-through first question, statement, prompt, or example. Begin by identifying the purpose of the session and *specific* learning goals associated with the topic of the day. Articulate these clearly. Use this to develop an overarching "first" question—this may sometimes take the form of a statement or an example but must be structured in a way that welcomes engagement. This first question is not to be posed *and* concluded at the outset, rather, it provides direction for everything that takes place in the class session.

Next, identify avenues to achieve the learning goals of the day, such as analyzing particular examples, exploring a case study, or other activities. Use this to create a rough scaffolding of sub-questions, prompts, or activities that underlie the first question.

Critically, this may be less of a firm plan and more of an opportunity for the instructor to *think it through* in advance. It may be necessary to add questions, drop questions, or extend in an unexpected direction given students' contributions, interest, and confusions. Throughout these on-the-fly changes, the first question continues to guide the instructor and the class as a whole.

DEEP ENGAGEMENT AND ACTIVE LISTENING

In this style of deep engagement, psychological safety is essential for creating an environment where students feel empowered to contribute and make *speculative* suggestions. This safety grows as students make contributions reflective of themselves and their values, which shape the narrative and direction of the discussion.

When students are in a mode of deep engagement, the instructor has to actively listen in order to determine how to facilitate the discussion. *Active listening* is a demanding task that requires one to listen carefully as well as infer what is implied by student contributions. In doing so, an instructor should consider the following questions:

- How might this relate to the learning goals of the day?
- Does the student's contribution reflect a desire to shape the discussion in a particular way? If so, why is this important to them? To what extent should this be encouraged at this specific point in class?
- Does this student tend to dominate class? Would the group be interested in pursuing their example or digression at this time?
- [If contribution is in response to an instructor's question] Does this address the question that I believe I asked? If so, how? If not, why not?
- If we don't discuss this now, can I propose a concrete follow-up of some sort (chat after class, office hours, recommend a reading, etc.)?

The above can all be taken into account to shape how the instructor engages with student contributions. While it initially feels like a lot to monitor at once, an experienced instructor might distill it down to both:

- thinking flexibly about what could promote learning related to the goals of the day; and
- keeping an eye out for ideas that are particularly important to a given student.

Promoting student agency is the critical construct underlying this approach to facilitation. Recent literature incorporates agency in frameworks of active learning (Jamaludin & Osman, 2014; Reeve & Tseng, 2011), self-determination theory (Hospel & Galand, 2016), and student motivation (Goldman et al., 2017).

Historically, agency and autonomy are present in pedagogical best practice (Chickering & Gamson, 1987; Wassermann & Eggert, 1976), instructor roles (Brown & Krager, 1985), approaches to engagement and the classroom dynamic (Davies, 1990; Nystrand & Gamoran, 1990; Thomas, 1980), and approaches to specific subjects (Packer, 1970).

SELF-EVALUATION AND NEXT STEPS

Complete a self-assessment to gather data on what is happening in your classroom right now. Take one class or seminar that you facilitated recently under consideration. Reflect on the student engagement and roughly classify the interactions as:

- Superficial engagement_____
- Deep engagement with limited student control_____
- Deep engagement with extended student control_____

Consider how much of the total student engagement felt like each type and assign a rough percentage to each one. Be as critical as you can as to whether the students truly had control in shaping the outcome of the interaction. Note instances where you feel students may have experienced agency in shaping the discussion, but secretly you would have been ready to redirect almost immediately.

Complete a self-evaluation to explore why the above is taking place. Given your understanding of the balance of engagement taking place in your classroom, consider what concern might be preventing you from giving students more agency and control

- _____ I need to make sure particular topics are the focus of the discussion
- _____ I need to use (or enjoy) particular specific examples
- _____ I want to see particular "Ah-ha!" moments occurring during the discussion. The students enjoy them, and they drive home the key points.

- _____ It will become unproductive and disengaging if certain students monopolize the floor and ramble.
- _____ I don't like the students going "off-piste" by bringing in other topics, examples, or synthesis beyond the syllabus. I risk losing credibility when they get into topics I don't know well.
- _____ Other (specify)

See if you can put a rough red/amber/green rating against each of the above. Red highlights a particularly significant barrier; green signifies things that you don't feel are shaping your behavior (amber would be somewhere in between). Be honest! It's not uncommon for one to be more concerned with credibility than one might realize.

The above assessment and evaluation combine to create a more holistic picture of how you control the classroom. Consider identifying ways in which to experiment with how you utilize interactions.

Things to Try

First, consider *how* you could approach giving up more control while interacting in a manner that conveys confidence and fosters psychological safety:

- Project maximum confidence, even in the face of uncertainty. If you feel put on the spot, trust yourself to use visual and postural cues to signal that you are actively thinking about the student's idea. Build a response repertoire that will give you immediate ideas of things to say, so you're not afraid of being tongue-tied.
- Model that "wait time" is okay. It is absolutely acceptable to take several seconds (or more) to decide whether a tangent should be encouraged or to develop a response to a particularly unexpected contribution. If you want students to think before they speak, don't be afraid to model this behavior for them. You can even label these in your head as a "tangent pause" or a "synthesis pause" and attempt to practice deliberately taking 3 to 5 seconds of thinking time when a tangent or unexpected synthesis takes place. Some instructors might even play this back to their students, for example, "I'm taking a moment to consider if this can link back to our key idea today [pause]. I think . . ."
- Do not over-engineer—shift your preparation from anchoring on "what must happen in class" to "what learning to achieve in class." While it may be comforting to have everything planned out very clearly, this creates stress if you're unprepared to manage deviations. Do prepare a skeleton of how to approach the topic, with key examples and questions in mind, but make sure you have a thoroughly developed understanding of the desired

learning outcomes. This will allow you to redirect to the learning outcomes in a more flexible way, rather than attempting to steer toward an overly specific idea of what should be happening.

- While observing students having an "Ah-ha!" moment is one of the great delights of teaching, you may have to step back from planning them directly (e.g., this point, at this specific time in the class, will result in a lightbulb moment). Trust that a focus on desired learning goals and seeding of examples or ideas will let students get there on their own. Forcing "Ah-ha!" moments that may have occurred organically in previous classes is disengaging for students if they recognize an attempt at engineering a purportedly profound moment of insight (even worse is recounting past moments to current students).
- Recognize that it is okay to decline to answer a student's question that goes beyond the topic of the day, but follow-through on the promise of follow-up. A perfectly acceptable response is, "I'd like to look into that for/with you—why don't you remind me via email, and we can chat more in office hours."

To make this more concrete, Table 6.1 describes suggestions for approaching these particular concerns, while Table 6.2 provides examples of phrases you could have ready in response.

What if you feel you are offering students extended control yet they are not taking it? First, consider your response repertoire and how it might be either shaping psychological safety or a sense that students don't need to contribute because the instructor will just give the "right answer" anyway. This will be discussed further in the next chapter.

Three Points to Remember about Effective Engagement

- Student engagement must be defined more broadly than the frequency of participation.
- The instructor's perception of their need to maintain control can inhibit their willingness to promote deep engagement.
- One can turn over control, and give students more opportunity for deep engagement, without compromising learning objectives or credibility.

Table 6.1   How to Address Concerns Related to Ceding Control

Concern	Seminar (~3–30 students)	Small or Large Lecture (30–100, 100+)
Topic	As you introduce the topic of the day, explicitly solicit agreement from the students in terms of what they aim to understand by the end of the session. Use this as a basis for arbitrating when the discussion might be getting off course and redirecting without diminishing student agency. With students agreed to objectives, you can also invite *them* to evaluate whether the group needs to refocus. They may even begin to proactively weigh-in to course-correct if they sense the discussion getting off-track.	As you introduce the topic of the day, clearly frame the desired learning outcomes, explain why they are important, and say something about how they can expect to engage with the topic(s) over the course of the class. This will provide context for why you might need to move the discussion along at some point, even if some students wish to engage further.
Examples	Many fields have "canonical" examples associated with them. If you feel particularly invested in them ("I can't teach consequentialism without the trolley problem!"), then do use them as a starting point, but carefully plan how you will give space for students to apply their own analysis. Alternatively, share the canonical example and then solicit analogous examples or counterexamples from students to compare and contrast further.	In a small lecture, one could have students in groups of 5–10. After introducing the "desired" examples, students could generate more within their group. A subset of these, self-identified as particularly compelling, could be shared. Alternatively, a small or large lecture could ask students to generate and compare their own examples in pairs. If there are canonical examples to use, consider how students can make more open-ended contributions related to evaluation or analysis.
"Ah-ha!"	Redefine "Ah-ha!" in terms of the learning outcome more generally rather than tightly constrained with a specific example and timepoint in the discussion. Or, consider what new moments of insight you might find if the students have more control.	
Credibility	Gently put the onus on the student to explain further the idea they wish to introduce. It's fair to caveat outright that something is "outside of your wheelhouse" and offer your reaction "on behalf of" how your field would approach the question, but without feeling accountable for explaining the student's point for them or providing a "correct" answer.	

Table 6.2 Example Phrases When Sharing Control with Students

Concern	Seminar (~3–30 students)	Small or Large Lecture (30–100, 100+)
Topic	"This is interesting, but I need to move us back to . . ." "Are we getting away from [topic/learning goal]?" "Are we interested in taking 10 minutes to explore this further? We might have to [describe trade-off in topics covered]."	"For time, we'll have to move on now. I'm happy to chat about this after class."
Examples	"There's an example that's considered important in this field—I'd like to put it on the table for you to consider . . ."	
Credibility	Student: "How does [computer science principle] apply to [philosophy]?" *Potential responses from a philosophy instructor:* "Please explain [computer science principle] for us. I don't think we're all familiar." "Tell me more about what led you to consider this link." "What might be a hypothesis?" Invite other students to evaluate the hypothesis. "While we're not all familiar with the specifics, [to other students] does the *overall logic* seem to hold?" "This is going beyond the scope of the discussion for today, let's park it for now, and we can chat more in my office hours." "This is getting more technical and is beyond the scope of the course. Let's stop here, but you might want to talk to [another instructor in computer science]."	

NOTE

1. The first three questions are based on the author's recollections of problem sets completed as a student in the Science One program at the University of British Columbia. Such questions were almost always followed by the guidance, "You will need to make some assumptions."

Chapter 7

(Non)Evaluative Responses

Promoting Critical Thinking and Psychological Safety

With a working definition of engagement, one can now consider how to create a dynamic that promotes both *voluntary* and *proactive* engagement on the part of students.

Voluntary engagement is exemplified by students offering to contribute when the opportunity presents itself, often in response to a specific question from the instructor. In many classrooms this is the typical "hand raise," although other norms related to speaking out can also arise.

Proactive engagement is exemplified by students identifying and acting on opportunities to extend the conversation, question assumptions, or move the discussion in new directions. Here, the students are moving beyond simply responding by taking an active role in shaping the discussion.

EVALUATION AND THE RESPONSE REPERTOIRE

The response repertoire of the instructor comes into play when promoting student engagement. While there can be considerable variability in an individual's responses *within* a given interaction, most instructors tend to rely on a subset of common ways of responding to students during a seminar or lecture. This primary response repertoire fundamentally shapes the classroom dynamic.

Judgmental or evaluative responses such as "Great answer!" "Exactly!" "Yes, very well done" or their counterparts, "Poor" "That's wrong" and "You've missed the point" are a common staple of many instructors' response repertoire. A distinction exists between judgmental responses that capture a *value judgment* and evaluative responses that *engage with the substance* of a

69

student's contribution. Judgmental responses rate, praise, or criticize without providing actionable information about what has occurred.

There are three critical reasons why instructors should not rely on responses that can be perceived as judgmental:

- Judgmental responses *stop thinking.*
- Judgmental responses *create risk and diminish psychological safety.*
- Judgmental responses *frame the discussion in terms of correct and incorrect responses.*

First, the instructor needs to recognize that a judgmental response can be the strongest possible signal that students can *stop thinking* about the topic in question. When a student receives "great answer" as feedback, what more thinking is there to do on the subject? The student can now disengage because they got it "right." The other students in the room will see no need to attempt to extend or offer an alternate perspective. The instructor has given a highly normative signal about what responses are ideal. Further contributions could be discouraged or, worse, deemed a "bad answer."

A positive judgmental response can also be a strong signal that no direct follow-up is coming. Consider how frequently instructors might immediately shift to the next topic of conversation after identifying a "great answer." Such a pattern of behavior is readily identifiable and will promote a dynamic where students do not seek to probe or build on previous contributions.

If there are "great" answers, then it stands to reason that there are also "terrible" answers. For many students, judgmental responses *create risk and diminish psychological safety.* Immediate and public judgment of a contribution, particularly when framed in terms of binaries such as "great" and "bad," can be a source of significant anxiety and decrease risk-taking (Black & William, 1998; Kluger & DeNisi, 1996). Attempting to address this by emphasizing positive reinforcement and diminishing direct negative criticism or critique is often insufficient.

Even a culture focused on the positive aspects of contributions can be anxiety-inducing, with every contribution dogged by the nagging questions, "Is this one going to be good? Am I going to get a '*great answer*'?" It also creates a dynamic where students become hyperaware of who is getting frequent "great answers!" This can lead to students identifying themselves or their peers as "smart" or "dumb," as instructor favorites or unfavored. A culture of one-upmanship may result, as students compete to gain tokens of positive reinforcement throughout the class.

Interpersonal risk aside, judgmental responses frame the discussion in terms of *correct and incorrect responses* by signaling that there is a specific "right answer" to the question at hand.

Some questions do have specific right answers and checking this straight-forward knowledge can be an important starting point in learning about a topic. One may need to begin a class by soliciting definitions of concepts or answers to a problem set. In this context the instructor can provide a "yes" or "no" or "correct/incorrect" without a direct *value judgment* of the student or their work. Including judgmental language such as *"Clever!* Yes, that's the right answer" does not serve a useful function.

Such interactions focused on straightforward evaluation do have a place in most classrooms. Yet, in a learning environment focused on complex questioning and critical thinking (see chapter 8), this is not how one would wish to engage students for the majority of a class.

A right answer often relies on a "right process" and a specific interpretive lens, which significantly constrains creative problem solving. If an instructor's repertoire includes an abundance of short judgmental responses, it suggests that their approach to questioning is inappropriate for promoting critical thinking.

Instructors should also consider the extent to which a brief judgmental response is formative and constructive. Does it help the student understand what they are doing well or what they might wish to do differently? Does it help them understand the *process* they used to reach their output? Consider the kinds of evaluative feedback that could substitute for "great answer." For example,

- "Creating that analogy made for a particularly insightful reframing of the author's idea."
- "That is a novel and informative connection to make between these two fields."
- "Your analysis does not appear to have a logical fault or weakness in the premises, which means it is sound and valid."
- "I can see that others found your integration of economic and social considerations compelling."

Similarly, when one says, "that's weak," "not quite," or "I don't think so," it obscures more meaningful feedback. Such judgmental remarks do not address the issue:

- "Some [specific] part of your statement is factually incorrect."
- "That does not seem to be a fair representation of the author's views."
- "That is incomplete or superficial."
- "Those premises do not support your conclusion."
- "Your hypothesis may be implausible or challenging to test."
- "I saw some skeptical faces in the room when you shared your third premise."

- "We'll need you to explain that some more in order to understand."

An uncomfortable question for many instructors is whether short judgmental responses are simply *lazy feedback*. Given the above more accurately reflect student contributions, why not provide that meaningful elaboration? Yes, it may be more time-consuming; however, there are short versions of every statement above. See chapter 10 for further discussion of meaningful feedback.

A further question is whether the instructor needs to weigh in evaluatively after a given point. Instead, other students could be invited to engage with the contribution as a means of assisting with evaluation or extension, with facilitation by the instructor. Consider how this can look in practice:

- Student A: "I don't think the author's argument is compelling. She is making a case for everyone needing to massively reduce our carbon footprint, and doing so urgently, but just last week flew to give a TED talk in New York and then London. Clearly, it's not that important if she doesn't practice what she preaches."
- Instructor: "[Student B], is your thinking similar, or would you say something different?"
- Student B: "Well, I'm also skeptical, but more because of the data."
- Instructor: "The data is more compelling for you. What is compelling about the distinction you're making?"
- Student B: "Well it's unfair to say her argument must be wrong because of something about the person, that's a fallacy, but when I look at the data I don't think the focus should be so much on individuals. She's not showing the relative impact of individuals versus corporations. . ."

Many instructors would be tempted to jump in immediately and "call out" the ad hominem fallacy as soon as it is voiced. Above, the instructor relied on another student to recognize the nature of the argument. What if they had not? As discussed earlier, giving up control means being ready to expect the unexpected. In a case like the above, it could have resulted in several students jumping on the bandwagon of the ad hominem fallacy.

For most instructors seeing multiple students latch onto a fallacy would cause them to intervene, but one can still consider how the evaluative component is framed. "Student A actually started us off with a fallacy . . ." is very different from, "As I listen, I can't help but wonder if we're addressing the logical argument of the author or focusing on her personally." Both would guide toward the "necessary" insight, but the latter would likely be experienced very differently by the first student.

Instructors must grapple with the question of when and how frequently to weigh in. Certain common confusions might be best addressed before they become entrenched, but one can consider how often such action is necessary. Does the confusion truly detract from the learning goals of the day, or could it be part of coming to grips with the topic? The process of learning and developing higher-order analytical skills frequently requires students to engage with uncertainty and resolve confusions.

If letting students run with something "incorrect" is anxiety-inducing, the instructor should remember it as an important avenue for promoting critical thinking on the part of the group as a whole. A sophisticated response repertoire can include strategies to bring such issues to light at summative moments.

WHY JUDGMENTAL RESPONSES PERSIST

Short judgmental responses are deeply ingrained in many response repertoires. Common objections to avoiding their use include the following:

- "Students need to know when they get it right."
- "Students need to know when someone has given a wrong answer."
- "Students won't like it! They're used to being told when they have great answers."

First, consider the issue of "knowing when they get it right." A class focused on exploring an open-ended case study, crafting a critique, or developing a policy proposal would not have a specific right answer. Even "great answer" would be an inappropriate attempt to capture the nuanced nature of students' contributions or conclusions. Meaningful feedback in these contexts could focus on the process and decision-making that took place, rather than the "correctness" or brilliance of the outcome.

Instructors who are not engaging in a *performative* dynamic should be less invested in the articulation of very specific "right answers." If one engages students in shared evaluation, facilitates reflection, or offers substantive feedback, the relative strengths or weaknesses of a given response will be evident.

While some questions do have straightforward correct or incorrect answers, an instructor's response can vary from more formative and evaluative to more personally judgmental. Examine the differences between the following responses:

- "Thank you. Yes, $t=0.42$ using those steps" or "Perfect! $t=0.42$. That's a smart way of doing it."
- "I see. Yes, your suggested t-test is appropriate here" or "Clever! Yes, a t-test is a great idea."

- "We'd expect the conditional probability to be 1/13. Let's try calculating the prior probability together" or "You're way off base—it should be 1/13. It looks like the prior is wrong."

If students are at a point in their understanding where a set of straightforward facts are needed, one can still consider how to phrase affirmation. For example,

- Instructor: "What are Marr's three levels of analysis?"
- Student: "Computational, what it's doing and why; algorithmic, how it's doing it; and implementation, the actual physical structure: the brain or the computer."
- Instructor 1: "Great answer! Yes . . ." or "Smart! Yes . . ." (judgmental)
- Instructor 2: "That's a very clear articulation . . ." (evaluative affirmation)
- Instructor 3: "Thank you . . ." (nonevaluative, although it can signal appropriate response)

Similarly, if instructors are concerned that students need to be told when they are correct, they are typically *even more* concerned that students need to know when they are incorrect.

Negative judgmental responses shape the classroom climate. When students perceive an instructor as being overly critical or liable to put them down, they will participate less. While clearly the case with overt verbal aggression or negative nonverbal behavior (e.g., sarcasm, put-downs, or frowning), this may extend to judgmental remarks. Verbally *challenging* a student can increase their anxiety, cause the student to become defensive, or perceive the instructor as looking down on them (Rocca, 2009).

Here, "challenging" is not intended to encompass *all* interactions that prompt students to extend or justify their contributions. Instead, it refers to a specific type of response and interaction style that reflects an instructor's argumentative tendencies or engagement in contentious or precise communication behaviors (Myers & Rocca, 2000, 2001). Such challenging remarks are often counterproductive and not necessary to extend student thinking, push for clarity, or foster engagement with students who experience classroom communication apprehension.

They are also not necessary to promote in-depth participation more broadly. "Those who "are good listeners and do not judge their students can encourage participation . . . [those who] are supportive of and patient with their students also can promote participation" (Rocca, 2009, p. 23).

When considering the use of judgment and evaluation, one should first assess whether a dynamic focused on correct/incorrect responses is appropriate. Then consider how the group might work together to identify and evaluate strengths and weaknesses without direct instructor judgment. Finally, decide whether an alternative response affords more meaningful, formative feedback.

This does not mean an instructor should avoid engaging with student misconceptions. Straightforward corrective feedback on a task with a right or wrong answer can enhance learning of a new skill; however, the context, type of task, and learner's proficiency mediate effectiveness and impact (Wisniewski et al., 2020).

Hattie also describes the powerful role of *disconfirming* feedback, where an instructor might start with, "Let's assume [what you said is correct] . . ." and work through an example or implication that sheds light on the error (2012). This approach leads to a greater depth of understanding than simply providing a factual correction.

Consider several different responses to a student initiating a group analysis:

- Instructor: "Suppose we are interested in understanding in-group and out-group dynamics. What levels of analysis could we use as a basis of our analytical approach?"
- Student A: "We should look at individuals, the groups they form, and society as a whole." [Note: these are a relevant set of levels of analysis]
- Instructor Response 1: "Great answer! Those will definitely work. Okay, what are the relevant factors at those levels?" . . . This response offers praise and affirmation but lacks specific feedback as to why the contribution is effective before moving to the next question. Students may have some insight that the *specific* response was deemed appropriate for the *specific* question. However, an opportunity to promote more critical thinking about levels of analysis is arguably missed.
- Instructor Response 2: "You suggest three interacting levels of analysis—let's build on this. What are the relevant factors at each level?" . . . This response does not offer overt praise but does affirm the contribution as an effective starting point. It also signals something more general about the concept, which can be used as formative feedback (i.e., that interactions between levels are significant to consider). While there is a form of evaluation taking place, it is more *descriptive* than *judgmental*.
- Instructor Response 3: "A clear starting point. Tell me more about why those levels are appropriate for the context?" . . . This response is more neutral from a judgmental perspective but does affirm the idea as sound. It invites the initial student to extend their thinking while engaging in an evaluative process. Presumably, students listening may also reflect on the rationale offered.
- Instructor Response 4: "Student B, would you propose a similar or different approach to the analysis?" . . . This response is also initially neutral

but brings in a peer to offer an evaluative perspective. Consider the difference between psychological safety elicited by this statement versus a more narrow and evaluative framing of the question, "Student B, why are these levels effective for our analysis?"

- Instructor Response 5: "Okay. There can be different ways to approach this. Hands-up if you would structure your analysis using these levels." . . . Here the instructor is pivoting to the group as a whole to offer evaluation. This has to be done with care, as a student could feel picked-on unless there are *genuinely* different ways to approach this problem. If everyone were to vote against the suggestion, the instructor might need to be ready to offer an alternate perspective or explain the rationale for voting.

A key difference above was the source of the evaluation—whether from the instructor, a peer, or by inviting extension or reflection by the initial student. The first response also used overt praise to reinforce the student's contribution. Praise risks becoming the focus of the response rather than anything the instructor could say that might be more formative. It is more likely to stop other students from considering alternatives (or their own evaluation) and in this example can dangle the carrot of "great answer" over any subsequent contribution. While evaluation was present in the later responses, it was not a short judgment of "great" or "poor."

Another approach is to withhold the immediate evaluative response but offer more summative feedback after additional student responses or discussion has taken place. One approach is paraphrasing key points covering several student contributions, then identifying a shared yet specific strength or weakness and suggestion for the future. Summative feedback avoids singling out any one contribution as the focus of praise or negative evaluation.

Alternatively, summative feedback can be more general. For example, "I hear us identifying levels with links to root causes. Starting with causes helps mitigate the tendency to focus on common-but-irrelevant levels. Let's keep an eye on this in the future."

The issue of how students, particularly those used to immediate judgmental evaluation, tend to respond when an instructor changes their response repertoire is complex.

Students' perceptions, particularly their *initial* perceptions, of a less judgmental dynamic are often mixed. While many students can recognize the benefit of an environment that promotes psychological safety and student–student interactions, most are accustomed to being praised or having contributions judged immediately as correct or incorrect. For particularly strong students used to a stream of affirmation, the sudden lack of praise can be jarring. This can lead to resistance behaviors from strong students, including confusion, hostility, and even anger. However, with care, these can be mitigated over time.

Perceptions of effective teaching are strongly dependent on what students' value as educational outcomes. It is not uncommon to see instructor reviews on sites such as ratemyprofessors.com that essentially say something along the lines of "Great instructor! Download the slides, memorize all the bolded points, and get an A. Very clear what we need to know."

Some students expect to be rewarded for diligence and accuracy without critical thinking. When an instructor replies to a question with, "What do you think?" or "Tell me more [about what led you to ask that]," it will feel different to the student than a direct judgment such as "Yes" or "No, you should think of it this way instead."

Without a shared understanding between instructor and student, unfamiliar active learning techniques can be met by confusion and resistance: "One thing that I don't like in [the instructor's] approach is redirecting most of the questions that were directed to him to other students. Sometimes it feels like wtf, I asked you, professor, why [do] you ask other students to answer?"[1]

Depending on the age and past experience of students, one can offer a rationale or ground rules for this different kind of engagement. These will vary by instructor and context, but could include the following:

- "I'm going to take on the role of the moderator. Everyone should be attending and ready to engage with the ideas that are offered because we are going to create and test solutions together."
- "I'm going to try not to be heavy-handed or interject frequently—it's important for your learning that you try out different ideas—but I will make sure we don't leave with misconceptions."
- "Once we move beyond the basics, there may not be straightforward correct or incorrect answers. My role will be to push for as much depth as possible and help make sure we are comfortable with what we achieve."
- "I may not call on people in the order that hands were raised. It's no reflection of what I think of your contributions—part of my role is to balance talk-time across students."

PRAISE AND PUNISHMENT

"These concerns about praise are not the same as claiming that students do not like to be praised; they do" (Hattie & Timperley, 2007, p. 97).

A further challenge in a judgmental dynamic is that students become accustomed to the little rush of positive emotion that comes when praised.

This understanding of praise as positive reinforcement is well grounded in behaviorism, but its impact on student motivation, learning, and the classroom dynamic is of concern.

Since early research first suggested that *extrinsic* rewards can undermine *intrinsic* motivation to engage in behavior or complete a task (Deci, 1971), the use of incentives or rewards in the classroom has been the subject of significant debate. Described as the "undermining effect," cognitive evaluation theory (CET) (Deci & Ryan 1980; Ryan et al., 1983) and the more overarching self-determination theory (SDT) suggest that offering external rewards can be counterproductive to fostering student motivation and engagement (Deci & Ryan, 2012).

Competing meta-analyses in the late 1990s brought different opinions to the forefront. One group claimed rewards are effective in fostering student engagement and do not diminish intrinsic interest in activities (Cameron & Pierce, 1994, 1996; Eisenberger et al., 1999).

The other argued that rewards in the classroom would drive the undermining effect—where motivation depends on extrinsic factors and intrinsically motivated engagement is diminished (Deci et al., 1999a,b, 2001).

There is an interplay between the nature of a reward and the specific context. For example, one study found verbal rewards have a *positive* impact on motivation to perform a simple task, but a *negative* impact (undermining effect) on more complex tasks (Hewett & Conway, 2016). Children and college students differ in the magnitude of the impact of verbal or tangible rewards, with specifics of task interest, reward type, expectancy, specificity, and contingency shaping positive or negative effects (Cameron, 2001).

While the behavioral impact of tangible rewards was mostly negative, different contingencies resulted in different effects (Cameron, 2001).

Where verbal rewards have been associated with college students demonstrating increased motivation for low- *and* high-interest tasks (Cameron, 2001; Cameron et al., 2005), "verbal reward" encompasses a wide range of instructor behaviors in these studies. Thus, an instructor should consider the potential impact of different verbal rewards, such as affirming a student's competence at a task, praising the individual, and offering written feedback related to performance standards or goals.

Interestingly, not all instructor feedback improves performance. In fact, a third of feedback interventions in one study *decreased* student performance (Kluger & DeNisi, 1996). Feedback generally becomes less effective when focused more on the *self* (the characteristics of the person) than the task or process. Compared with other feedback interventions, praise, rewards, and punishment were least effective (Kluger & DeNisi, 1996; Wisniewski et al., 2020). Beyond affecting motivation and risk-taking, praise is rarely effective as *feedback* as it fails to inform the student about task goals, progress, or actions to take (Hattie & Timperley, 2007).

Where instructors believe praise is highly effective, it is likely they are accompanying it with information about the process or performance, for example, "You're really great because you have diligently completed this task by applying this concept" (Hattie & Timperley, 2007, p. 96). Unfortunately, when a student receives a combined message like "Great! But you should have spent more time explaining each step," they may attend to the praise at the expense of engaging with the feedback (Hattie, 2012). Indeed, students are so attuned to judgment they may hear it even in comments purely intended as descriptive (Brookhart, 2008).

Regardless of one's personal beliefs about the interplay between intrinsic and extrinsic motivation, a cautionary note regarding the use of praise is that "the more rewards are used, the more they seem to be needed" (Kohn, 1999, p. 17).

In the short term, praise can make students sit up and take notice, but over time it is not an effective strategy for shaping the classroom dynamic. As praise becomes habitual and normalized, it has a diminished impact on student behavior. The instructor's praise becomes background noise, most notable in its absence and an increasing interpersonal risk for those not praised *as much as expected*.

Praise often accompanies a strongly instructor-driven dynamic, where students are praised for conforming to the instructor's expectations. In many cases, praise becomes a form of *control* in the classroom.

This matter of control can also shape the extent to which students are willing to take risks in the classroom—whether by choosing more challenging tasks or by engaging more creatively. Where praise becomes a reward for conforming to expectations, studies have suggested such risk-taking is diminished (Kelsey, 2010).

Instructors who promote the autonomy of their students engage in a significantly different pattern of behaviors than those who favor a more controlling dynamic. This is particularly relevant when praise is used as a contingent reward in the place of more qualitative informational feedback (Reeve & Jang, 2006). Here, praise with informational feedback could be a statement such as "Good work thinking that through—you've found a key issue." While there is still an element of praise ("good work") there is an informational component beyond the reward itself.

Even praise intended as purely qualitative feedback can go awry given subtle nuances of phrasing. The word *should* or other *embedded expectations* provide two examples of how comments intended as feedback can become more controlling:

- "Excellent, you *should* keep up the good work" includes pressure to continue performing at a certain standard. This pressure might be absent if the instructor were to simply share that the student is considerably above average (Deci et al., 1999a).

- "I haven't been able to use most of the data I have gotten so far, but you are doing really well, and *if you keep it up* I'll be able to use yours" versus "Compared with most of my subjects, you are doing really well," where the former is experienced as controlling pressure but the latter is not (Pittman et al., 1980).

An important issue is how an instructor can express enthusiasm and encouragement without using praise that becomes a contingent reward or overly controlling. *What you say* and *how you say it* become equally important in this context.

Returning to the issue of lazy feedback, one can swap a contingent reward for formative feedback. Compare the difference between the following:

- "Great job—keep it up!" [Contingent]
- "Bringing together three factors gives significant depth of analysis." [Formative]

When some form of positive reinforcement is desirable, *hints* (Reeve & Jang, 2006) and *questions* (Kohn, 2001) may offer an effective alternative.

When carefully framed, hints are linked to autonomy-supporting instructional behaviors and an internal locus of learning (Reeve & Jang, 2006). Again, one can contrast a hint that functions as a contingent reward with one phrased as formative feedback, by swapping,

- "Great job! You're on the right track now!" with
- "Ah-ha! It appears you're making more progress with [your revised algorithm]."

Questions can also be a form of positive reinforcement in their own right—when carefully framed, Kohn highlights how they help students reflect on their accomplishments and share enthusiasm for the task or content (2001). In order to be effective, questions should be specific and promote thinking about something concrete. For example,

- What was the most challenging aspect of applying Marr's levels that you overcame?
- How did you work out which analogy was the most appropriate?
- When did you realize this approach to the algorithm was going to be effective?

When responding to an ineffective or incorrect student contribution, consider phrasing the response so that it does not increase classroom anxiety by diminishing psychological safety. While some answers to specific questions are incorrect or inappropriate and need to be addressed as such, an instructor can still aim to ensure their response does not:

- have a negative affective component;
- humiliate the student; or
- imply that the student does not have the capability to improve.

The capability to improve relates to the concept of students having a primarily *fixed mindset* versus more of a *growth mindset*. Rather than frame a student's ability as fixed ("That's okay, maybe math is not one of your strengths"), one can acknowledge the challenges inherent in learning and frame it as a case of one's skills or understanding being a work in progress (Dweck, 2015). This framing of "not yet" rather than fundamentally "not able," coupled with a genuine acknowledgment of the effort inherent in learning, creates a mindset where students embrace challenges and are resilient in the face of setbacks (Dweck, 2010).

In contrast, in a fixed mindset intellectual ability is viewed as a trait—one either has it or one does not. Dweck found this fragile belief in one's own capability leads students to engage in a confirmation bias of sorts, by seeking tasks that will "prove" their intelligence and avoiding challenges where they might struggle. Rather than motivating students, praising a student's intelligence supports this fixed mindset view of the world, with all the anxiety and vulnerability associated with it (2007).

Similarly, the *brilliance belief* is a fundamental way of relating to certain subjects, namely, those in which the general perception is that raw, innate talent enables success. Philosophy, math, physics, and music composition are all subjects with a high degree of emphasis on brilliance—and all subjects where fewer than a third of U.S. PhDs are female (Leslie et al., 2015). The researchers observed a similar trend, underrepresentation in subjects linked to brilliance, in African American PhDs.

To explain this data, Leslie et al. put forward the *field-specific ability beliefs hypothesis*. Women and minorities are stereotyped as "lacking innate intellectual talent," which in turn negatively influences the participation rate by these groups in fields where brilliance is considered a necessary requisite for success (2015). Diversification, they suggest, could be increased by academics downplaying the role of genius or innate intellectual talent in their fields.

The implication is clear for instructors: praising intelligence, even in a well-meaning attempt to encourage or motivate a student, should be avoided. A not-uncommon statement of praise, "You're so smart!" risks reinforcing both a fixed mindset and the brilliance belief.

While the above discusses *what* can be said; *how* it is conveyed is no less important. Bursts of extremely positive affect[2] risk becoming contingent rewards—we are social beings after all—but an overly flat affect can be disconcerting or discouraging for students. Instructors should act with emotional intelligence to allow their natural warmth and interest to be present in the interactions, while being sensitive to issues of reward and punishment.

An instructor should use emotional intelligence to avoid fluctuations in affect perceived as favoritism or instances of reward. Being aware of the frequency and intensity of one's positive responses can also help an instructor ensure they are not inadvertently parceling out emotional responses in a way that could drive competition for affirmation.

If one is genuinely excited by the class, stifling that emotion can make an instructor appear inauthentic. Rather than hide their enthusiasm and appreciation, instructors can attempt to ensure it is experienced as a genuine response independent of direct judgment.

CULTURE AND EVALUATION

Cultural differences play a significant role in shaping expectations surrounding evaluative responses and the use of praise and punishment in the classroom.

The use of relatively indiscriminate praise might be a notably Anglo-American phenomenon (Hufton et al., 2003). In a cross-cultural study, the authors noted that while Russian, English, and American instructors all felt that praise could motivate their teenage students, the form and frequency of praise varied significantly. While Russian instructors self-reported using praise, "to an English observer, they seemed to be making little more than a bare acknowledgment of acceptable response" (Hufton et al., 2003, p. 377).

Moreover, the frequency of praise varied significantly between these classrooms, appearing sparingly in Russia and so frequently in American primary classrooms that teachers "sometimes ended up devaluing the evaluation to the point where its function was merely phatic" (Alexander, 2000 p. 369).

Students accustomed to rote-learning may expect immediate and direct judgment of responses as correct or incorrect. Uncertainty can be unsettling and proactive framing from the instructor (as described above) becomes particularly important.

Other teaching styles in different cultural contexts may rely on deliberately using judgmental responses as contingent rewards or punishments. Strongly negative critique, even bordering on deliberate humiliation, are regarded as providing motivation. These become particularly problematic when they diminish psychological safety in general, as well as the individual student's sense of competence and their ability to learn.

- "That's way off. How could you think that?"
- "No—if you don't even understand this, I can't teach you more."
- "Everybody knows that's not the case."
- "You must be the only one stuck on this."

These kinds of comments make students afraid to contribute due to the potential for strong social sanctions. They also convey that the student is not *capable* of learning. Students accustomed to this type of dynamic may need significant framing, observation of their peers, and deliberate practice to become more comfortable engaging in class.

OTHER PERSPECTIVES ON EVALUATIVE RESPONSES

In some educational pedagogies, even the above response repertoire is still too evaluative or judgmental. According to proponents, the greatest level of psychological safety and student-guided exploration, creativity, and analysis can take place only in the absence of *anything* that could be construed as judgmental. In contrast with instructors who believe evaluative encouragement stimulates further participation, such responses are seen to attenuate discussion. Even the common response of "That's interesting" should be avoided as being another form of "Good answer" (Wassermann, 1992).

Overt enthusiasm in response to student contributions, such as "Wow!" or gestures of being impressed or excited, are also of concern as they are likely to be unevenly applied and experienced as a form of contingent reward.

Interest in the discussion and contributions from students is best conveyed through intentional eye contact, a warm affect, paraphrasing or "playing back" key ideas to students, valuing contributions, and asking questions indicative of active listening. Summative responses may be used to express appreciation for engagement or contributions *in general*. As Wassermann notes, "Letting go of evaluative responses does not mean being unappreciative of students' ideas. But there is a considerable difference in impact between 'Good idea, Fiona,' and 'Thanks for sharing your thinking on that issue, Fiona' " (1992, p. 28).

The response repertoire supporting this is deliberately narrow, where a direct response beyond paraphrasing, reflective restatement, or posing a question is accompanied by at most:

- "I see."
- "Tell me more."
- "Thank you [for sharing]."

SELF-EVALUATION AND NEXT STEPS

Begin by using the below as a general questionnaire to explore your approach to facilitation:

- Have you provided your students with framing (explanation) of how you facilitate discussions? If so, what did you explain? If not, what is essential to convey?
- How would you describe the general tone of your response repertoire? In what way is it contingent, rewarding, or aversive? In what way is it neutral? In what ways does it provide formative feedback?
- How do you engage with a student's idea or express enthusiasm for the topic? Could this be interpreted as a contingent reward?
- What sources of power are most present in your classroom? To what extent might you rely on the power of evaluation, reward and punishment, or charisma? How does that shape evaluation and formative feedback in your classroom?

Next, assess your behavior in-class while focused on "what you say." Use a recording, a peer observer, or take a tally sheet to class and document the number of responses to student contributions according to each general type. Consider the relative balance of response types and how it may affect psychological safety, motivation, and students' ability to obtain formative feedback.

Using a recording, a peer observer, or a tally sheet in class, document the frequency with which you offer evaluation *immediately* versus *summatively*.

The following is an example of immediate evaluation:

- Instructor: "What levels of analysis should we use to explore this behavior?"
- Student A: "Single-cell recording and individual behavior."
- Instructor: "Single-cell is too granular. Can we think of something at a higher level?" [Immediate evaluation]

The following is an example of summative evaluation:

- Instructor: "What levels of analysis should we use to explore this behavior?"
- Student A: "Single-cell recording and individual behavior."
- Instructor: "Student B, would you agree or propose something else?"
- Student B: "I think neural circuits would be more effective. Or regions of the brain."
- Instructor: "Single-cells, circuits, regions, and individual behavior are on the table. Student C, what do you think?"

Table 7.1 Examples of Different Types of Instructor Response

Instructor Response Type	Examples
Nonevaluative/ Nonjudgmental	"I see" "Tell me more" "Thank you"
Judgmentally positive/praise/ contingent reward	"Great answer!" "Excellent!" "Clever, keep it up!" "That's really smart!"
Judgmentally negative/ contingent punishment	"Nope!" "Poor effort" "You don't get it" "You're missing the point" "You entirely failed to answer the question" "This is not your strength"
Evaluative responses with formative or informational feedback, including *hints* and *questions* described above (whether students are correct or incorrect)	"That's correct/incorrect [because . . .]" "A concise summary of the author's point" "That's more precise than most definitions" "This evidence appears unconnected to your thesis" "That sounds plausible. Is it also testable?" "You seem to be making more progress since you changed your approach" "What was the most challenging part of this analysis?"

Note: These are intended to demonstrate each type, rather than provide examples of best practice.

- Student C: "I think we can focus on circuits and behavior because we're talking about how people respond to rewards. That's considered a pathway in the brain."
- Instructor: "In this case, circuits and behavior will reflect the majority of the research in the field. The level of description that you have heard before is indeed a clue." [Summative evaluation]

While there isn't a specific target ratio of immediate versus summative evaluation, a more immediately evaluative dynamic may impede critical thinking and reduce student engagement. In short, immediately judging a contribution as "right" tells students to stop thinking and conveys there are *specific* desirable contributions. Judging a contribution as simply "wrong" may discourage future attempts at engagement or creativity.

Finally, assess your behavior in-class while focused on "how you say it." If possible, record yourself in class in order to assess how your affect may convey evaluation, praise, or punishment. Positive affective cues can include:

- Smiling
- Positive tone of voice
- Open and relaxed posture, or
- Using eye contact, posture, and gestures to convey *active listening,* as described in the previous chapter.

In contrast, negative affective cues can include:

- Frowning
- Negative tone of voice (harsh, disappointed, etc.)
- Tense or closed posture, or
- Using eye contact, posture, and gestures to convey disinterest or skepticism of a student's idea.

After viewing yourself, reflect on when you were offering affective cues and how this could be experienced as supportive, evaluative, or judgmental:

- Could positive affective responses be perceived as contingent rewards? Could this become demotivating for students who do not tend to receive a positive response to their contributions?
- Could negative affective responses be perceived as contingent punishments? Could this diminish psychological safety or motivation to contribute?
- Does the balance of responses appear evenly distributed? Do some students earn the majority of the instances of positive affect? Do other students bear the brunt of the negative affect?

Things to Try

For each short judgmental remark in your response repertoire, consider how it could be reframed to offer informational or formative feedback. For example, "Great!" could be replaced with short comments that offer feedback related to the following:

- Depth, clarity, or synthesis
- Development of a novel perspective
- Consistency with factual knowledge or perspectives in the field
- Plausibility or testability of the hypothesis or suggestion, or
- Application of practical knowledge, such as the scientific method or unbiased reasoning.

Similarly, try altering your approach to instances where you respond with a remark like "Great!" without intending to provide direct feedback. Identify a natural, yet more neutral, response to use instead. This change could diminish the perception of indiscriminate praise and keep the other students thinking, without a premature signal from the instructor that the discussion has peaked or the matter is definitively resolved.

When providing feedback tied to evaluation, ensure that your comments are *formative* and forward-looking rather than merely justifying the assigned grade.

For a discussion or activity that you anticipate facilitating in the future, consider

- identifying in advance where you might use summative evaluation/feedback instead of responding to every contribution directly;
- identifying in advance where and how self or peer evaluation could be employed;
- how a *hint* could be used to provide affirmation and encouragement;
- how a *question* could be used to provide affirmation and encouragement. What, in particular, could you ask students that would help them reflect on what they have accomplished? Is there a particularly challenging element that is worth highlighting?; and
- what you might appreciate about the class' engagement with the topic. Does it require persistence? Creative problem solving? Tackling dense material or particularly challenging concepts? Developing novel hypotheses? Justifying arguments? Identify what you might wish to highlight for the group as a whole at the end of class.

When responding to an ineffective or incorrect student contribution, consider how to phrase your response so that it doesn't unduly diminish psychological safety. In cases where you wish to respond directly, examples include the following:

- "Tell me more about [how you arrived at that]." This will put the student on the spot and you will need to be ready to engage with their explanation, but it allows them to potentially self-discover where something may have gone awry.
- "That's a logical approach and [this part] is consistent with [the answer/the literature/an expected outcome], however . . . ." This affirms where there is strength in their approach while also providing clear formative feedback.
- "Given your explanation, I can see why you approached it this way, however . . ." or "I see where you were going, however . . . ." Both of these demonstrate understanding and compassion for the student before offering constructive feedback. If the student's approach reflects a common confusion, this may be helpful to highlight as well.

You may also consider adding specific responses to your repertoire that promote student evaluation (by self or by other students). For example,

- "Tell me more."
- "What aspect did you find most challenging?"
- "Where are you more confident? Less confident?"
- "What assumptions underlie this conclusion?"
- "What factor do you think is most important?"
- "How might this generalize to other contexts?"

- "If you were to do this again, what would you do differently?"
- "Would you approach their problem in a similar way?"
- "If I asked you to extend the previous idea with 'and' or 'but,' what would you say?"
- "You appear to agree/disagree, what are your thoughts?"
- "What is a specific strength in what you've just heard?"
- "What potential weaknesses might be in this approach? What would you do differently?"

Finally, make a point of checking your response repertoire for anything that could reinforce a fixed mindset or the brilliance belief. In particular, be on the lookout for statements like:

- "You're so smart!"
- "Genius!"
- "You're just brilliant at this!"
- "If it's not one of your strengths, just do your best."
- "Not everyone can think like a [programmer/philosopher/physicist . . .]"
- "This field just requires that special something extra. You have it or you don't."

A final caution from Carol Dweck relates to praising *effort* instead of learning—a common misconception of the growth mindset. Dweck notes that praise such as "Great effort! You tried your best!" or "Don't worry, you'll get it if you keep trying" may make a struggling student feel better in the moment, but does not address why the student is unsuccessful or give them the tools to grow and learn in the future (2015). Indeed, Dweck notes that if the student is using the wrong approach or has a fundamental misunderstanding, persistence will not lead to success and being told "you'll get it if you keep trying" can be particularly discouraging.

Instead, consider how to express appreciation for their effort, but ensure there is an actionable avenue for growth: "I appreciate your persistence here. Let's consider what to do differently next time/Let's discuss what we learned from this."

Shifting to a classroom dynamic where *everyone* is engaged in promoting learning and formative feedback often leads to a culture shock for students. Duckor notes that students in such a dynamic often initially question:

Why is the teacher asking 'why?' so much?

Why is the teacher [using tools that deliberately distribute talk-time]?

Why is the teacher waiting a bit before taking answers, instead of just calling on Mary and John, who have their hands up?

Why is the teacher putting *all* answers on the whiteboard, even the wrong ones?

Why is the teacher always answering a question with another question?

Why can't the teacher just solve the problem and write the correct answer on the board so we can move on? (2014, p. 29)

It is extremely common to encounter these sentiments. Indeed, examples of real student feedback in chapters 2 and 9 voice exactly these issues. When such questions arise, instructors, rather than changing their approach to class facilitation, should interpret it as a sign that some discussion of pedagogy is needed.

Three Points to Remember about Judgmental and Evaluative Responses

- Short judgmental responses do not provide meaningful formative feedback to students.
- Judgmental responses, praise, tangible rewards, and affective cues can function as contingent extrinsic rewards/punishments and impact student motivation and engagement.
- Praise can decrease risk-taking and reinforce fixed mindsets and the brilliance belief.

NOTES

1. Minerva Schools at KGI undergraduate end-of-semester course/instructor surveys (2016–2020). Reprinted with permission.

2. Such as a wide smile, enthusiastic nodding while smiling, giving signs of being "very impressed" with facial expressions or gestures.

Chapter 8

Complex Questioning

Framing Questions to Promote Deep Thinking, Analysis, and Creativity

The teacher has the right to question; the student the obligation to respond. As questioner, the teacher enjoys the reserved right to speak again following the response, usually exercised by putting another question and thus evoking a further response. When a student permissibly contributes unsolicited information or puts a question the teacher tends to reply with a counter-question, thus regaining control of the exchange. (Dillon, 1981a)

As discussed in chapters 6 and 7, the use of questions in the classroom is shaped by one's desire to maintain control and offer formative feedback. In the traditional dynamics described by Dillon, a question-answer relationship can foster dependency and passivity in students. The instructor heavily orchestrates the discussion, with outcomes focused around factual truth or conventional "right answers" (1981a).

While this approach is common, one can examine whether instructor-led questioning is an appropriate means of shaping the classroom dynamic. When questioning is appropriate for the learning goals of the day, carefully constructed questions can more effectively promote engagement and deep thinking.

TO QUESTION OR NOT TO QUESTION— THAT IS THE QUESTION

When might an instructor *not* ask questions? Many instructors will label a section of a class a "discussion" if there is student participation and question-answer exchanges that are both leisurely and about "loftier matters than usual" (Dillon, 1981a). A classroom dynamic of instructor-led Q&A is often called a discussion, but is that an appropriate description?

An alternate framing of the instructor's role facilitating student discussions uses a straightforward, yet challenging, maxim: "If not perplexed, do not ask a question" (Dillon, 1981a). That is, an instructor should ask a question only if they are genuinely perplexed and *need* to solicit information in order to resolve confusion.

Perplexity is appropriate for an instructor to model because it demonstrates the psychological safety to ask genuine questions. Students need to see that it is okay to say, "I don't understand" and ask for clarification. Without genuine questioning, there is little meaningful inquiry despite active participation.

Advancing this alternative framing of discussion, Dillon (1981b) suggests that instructors should not question:

...As a standard response to student contributions (Dillon, 1981b). Instructors who *consistently* respond to student contributions with a question of their own focus the interaction on the instructor rather than fostering student-student dialogue. Questions in this dynamic typically reflect the *instructor's perspective*, which maintains a strong measure of control over the topic and direction of discussion. Instructors tend to rely on questioning as a standard, habitual means to stimulate student thought. Yet, including alternatives to questioning may be more effective and afford some variety (see alternatives, below).

...When a student pauses, falters, hesitates, gets stuck, or appears to have finished speaking (Dillon, 1981b). In developing the concept of "wait time," Rowe noted that in a typical classroom a student has roughly *one second* to respond to a question before the instructor will repeat the question or call on another student. Moreover, an instructor typically allows *less than a second* between a student finishing, faltering, or pausing, and the instructor's response (Rowe, 1974). Might a student have more to say, if given the opportunity? When a student falters or hesitates, does jumping in to ask a question help them work through their uncertainty?

...To "draw out" a student who is not participating (Dillon, 1981b). The matter of *cold-calling* is discussed further below. However, Dillon (and others, for example, Rocca, 2010; England et al., 2017) suggest that directing a student to speak up diminishes psychological safety for that individual and the group as a whole. Forcing contributions also risks eliciting superficial or irrelevant responses, including "I don't know," which diminish the discussion. This questioning dynamic shifts the students' role from active listening, puzzling over the content, and evaluating when and how to contribute, to being guarded against the cold-call.

...To reveal the personal feelings or experiences of a student (Dillon, 1981b). While instructors want to connect to students on an individual level, there is a significant difference between directly asking the question, "How has this issue affected your life?" and inviting discussion of the issue by those comfortable sharing. An instructor should consider their individual students and the context to determine whether a direct query of personal involvement is appropriate. Recalling the discussion of engaging with values in chapter 5, care is needed when facilitating discussion of particularly personal topics.

...To make, or *score*, a point (Dillon, 1981b). Any question intended to make a specific point is an unproductive question and better served with a straightforward declaration of the idea or more genuine exploration. An instructor attempting to *score* a point during class has forgotten that a discussion is not a *debate*, and students should not be viewed as opponents to be defeated. While some instructors enjoy arguing with their students, negative impacts, such as increased communication apprehension and decreased immediacy, must be considered.

...To elicit an idea that has occurred to the instructor (Dillon, 1981b). Such an approach aims to elicit *the* idea rather than *an* idea. It is disingenuous in discussion and better replaced by a straightforward declaration of the instructor's idea. Such questions also limit student control (as in chapter 6).

...As the reply to a student's question. Dillon highlights that it can take control, reject the student's right to shape the topic, and fail to model how one can join another in inquiry (1981b). Importantly, not all counterquestions have these negative effects. With care, this issue can be minimized (see *Framing Questions to Promote Critical Thinking*, below).

...With a *why* question. Dillon's objection is twofold and mirrors concerns from other authors: First, he characterizes *why* as "the most imprecise interrogative word available and the most inimical to expression of thought" (1981b, p. 18). Second, he describes how the genuine intent of a *why* question, elaboration of the student's thought process or idea, can be experienced by the student as including negative judgment. "Can you explain why? (because I don't think you are correct to say X)" or even "Can you explain why? (I think you are stupid to think/feel/say X)" (Dillon, 1981b; Wassermann, 1992, 2017).

...At the beginning of a course or to start a discussion (Dillon, 1981b). The problem is not questions as discussion starters per se but fostering a *norm* where students do not expect to take initiative when engaging with a new topic. Once a heavily instructor-led dynamic becomes embedded in a course, it is difficult to shift to one where students feel responsible for proactively engaging in and maintaining the discussion. The critical "first question" described in chapter 6 may be a statement, prompt, or example.

Several types of instructor questions are considered outside of the typical question–response structure, and Dillon (1981a) notes they can be used to do the following:

- Define the issue at the outset; focus the discussion or clarify the "right problem" at the midpoint.
- Ensure understanding of the content or flow of discussion ("I'm sorry, can you repeat that?" or "Can you please elaborate so we're all clear?" or "Can you remind me who mentioned culture?").
- Regain control of the classroom dynamic or discussion if things get out of hand ("Are we following our ground rules?" "Are we getting off-topic here?").

Aside from these specific procedural examples, and the exception for when one is *genuinely perplexed*, Dillon (1981b) proposes seven alternatives to instructor questions that are aligned with both the purpose and process of a true discussion. These may be used in combination with productive questions to create a more constructive, varied dynamic.

First, offer a declarative statement. When an instructor expresses their own state of mind (confusion, certainty, etc.), thought, opinion, or reaction as an equal partner in the discussion, it contributes to the momentum of the discussion. Such declarative statements are particularly effective when they articulate an idea that could give form to a question. Declarative statements elicit responses of similar or longer duration than those elicited by questions (Dillon, 1981c).

When engaging with student responses to such a statement, the instructor must be careful with their use of judgmental or evaluative remarks.

Second, provide a reflective restatement summarizing the previous contribution. Such paraphrasing signals the importance of active listening and helps the class as a whole develop a shared understanding of specific points. It also offers implicit formative feedback by highlighting what is clear or unclear and allows the initial student to rethink and respond with a clarification or elaboration.

Third, declare a state of perplexity ("I'm confused by what you're saying"). Dillon notes that an instructor can use an indirect question if it is an *honest representation* of the state of the discussion. For example, "I'm just thinking about whether that would make a difference" or "I'm trying to remember if X is the case" or "I wonder what happens under those conditions" (1981b p. 19). Such questions should not be used with the intent of scoring points, as described above.

Fourth, invite a student to elaborate on their previous contribution. When authentic, one can offer an invitation such as "I'd like to hear more of your views on that." Dillon also notes that a softened imperative such as "Could you share an example?" solicits further depth or explanation. This style of prompting is experienced differently than the demand for justification or "Why do you think that?" A more clearly nonevaluative version of this invitation is embodied by Wassermann's "Tell me more" (1992, 2017).

Fifth, invite students to raise questions. Student-student interactions lead to more meaningful engagement and diminish restrictive instructor control over the discussion. Dillon also notes that as the instructor dominates the questioning, the dynamic shifts such that students are less inclined to pose their own questions or voluntarily engage.

Sixth, simply make room for the current speaker to formulate a question if they are confused or faltering. Jumping in quickly to pose questions to "help" a student clarify their ideas may miss the point or cause further confusion. The instructor should allow the student to articulate a question that captures their confusion. Waiting prevents the instructor from taking control of the discussion and allows the student to solicit the help they need, rather than what the instructor *infers* that they might need.

Finally, wait time (Rowe, 1974), or deliberate silence (Dillon, 1981b), coupled with an affect that conveys attention and readiness for active listening, can be the most effective technique to elicit student contributions. Moreover, such contributions will typically be longer and include more analysis, evaluation, or creativity than those elicited by an instructor's rapid questioning (Rochester, 1973; Rowe, 1974).

The above may appear weighted toward employing alternatives to questioning. However, questioning and non-questioning techniques are not mutually exclusive. Instead, these techniques offer an initial refinement of the purpose of questioning and a menu of alternatives that an instructor can use to provide more variety (Dillon, 1981a). Extending this further with complex questioning and a varied response repertoire takes the classroom dynamic beyond the standard approach of instructor-question: student-response: instructor-evaluation.

To further explore how questioning shapes the classroom dynamic of a discussion, sit in on a class (or refer to Appendix 1) and carefully examine how the instructor elicits student contributions.

- Would you consider this a "class discussion" rather than an instructor-led activity? Why or why not?
- Is the instructor using questioning and non-questioning techniques? Is this being done effectively?
- Where would you wish to modify the instructor's response(s)? Why would you suggest this modification?

FRAMING QUESTIONS TO PROMOTE CRITICAL THINKING

What characterizes a productive question? Wassermann described them as being respectful of the individual, focused on big ideas, and grounded in values (see chapter 5), but what do they look like in the classroom? A productive question aims to go beyond surface-level considerations and elicit responses that include analysis, evaluation, creativity, or synthesis. Above all, they are *authentic* questions—where the instructor is genuinely interested in the student's response. Such questions must be framed carefully in order to avoid inadvertently constraining the response.

If questioning aims to elicit critical thinking, one must first attempt to understand how that should be defined. The original taxonomy outlined by Bloom and collaborators in the 1950s ordered thinking skills in a hierarchy from lower- to higher-order: knowledge, comprehension, application, analysis, synthesis, and evaluation (Bloom, 1956). Bloom's taxonomy gained widespread use in curriculum development, teaching practice, assessment, and evaluation.

After almost forty-five years, the original framework was revisited and revised to (a) adopt a multidimensional approach that captures both knowledge and cognitive processes, and (b) reorder the hierarchical approach to place greater emphasis on *creating* than *evaluation* (Krathwohl, 2002).[1]

While these changes added granularity, they did not mitigate two fundamental critiques of the taxonomy: that its *hierarchical* nature is inherently problematic and that presenting different thinking skills as unique *natural kinds* may be a misrepresentation.

Bloom's taxonomy is often presented as a pyramid, which tends to lead to the interpretation of some form of meaningful hierarchy: that *knowledge* is basic and trumped by *evaluation* or *creation* as end-goals of learning. Instead, while knowledge is a necessary condition for deep processing or synthesis, it should not be dismissed as fundamentally "less than" other elements in the taxonomy.

Similarly, the lines between concepts such as applying, analyzing, and evaluating are not strict boundaries, nor do they exist in isolation. In practice, these skills can interleave and a given task may recruit various elements in combination.

Rather than viewing the pyramid as unidirectional, consider how instances of analysis, evaluation, or creation *reinforce* knowledge and further develop the ability to apply concepts. Similarly, while building a base of knowledge in a given discipline is important, higher-order tasks may be more effective at developing fundamental understanding than fact-based retrieval (Agarwal, 2019).

This is also evident in problem-based learning, where instructor-facilitated problem solving enables students to learn content and develop thinking skills as they tackle questions that do not have a single correct answer (Hmelo-Silver, 2004).

Adapting the original taxonomy and its revisions in Krathwohl (2002), one can instead use it as

- a framework for *characterizing* and describing different types of questions, prompts, or student contributions;
- a way of exploring the *depth of processing* involved; and
- a means of evaluating whether *understanding* is present.

Table 8.1 expands the taxonomy to include both the nature of the student contribution and examples of the language that an instructor might use in their question or prompt in order to elicit a particular type of student contribution. Appendix 2 provides examples of instructor prompts and student contributions coded using this taxonomy.

Several points of interest within this taxonomy are worth highlighting.

First, the distinction between *recall* and *understanding*. Recall is synonymous with rote learning, where the student can remember material in essentially the same form it was presented. A primary confound with this form of learning is that a student's ability to demonstrate recall is not indicative of their level of understanding.

For example, a student may be able to make a statement of recall such as "Hebb said 'neurons that fire together wire together' and we call that Hebbian learning," but that does not mean the student *understands* either the mechanism described or its significance. What does it mean to "wire together" and how does that explain a phenomenon like learning? A student may demonstrate recall but be utterly unable to respond to a follow-up question that probes their understanding.

While some consider factual recall to be a necessary first step in the learning process, one can nonetheless question whether it constitutes *meaningful* learning in its own right. Recall focuses on *retention* rather than the ability to transfer learning to new contexts. In considering overarching goals of education, the latter is clearly more important, and the distinction between no learning and rote learning is less apparent. Framed broadly, "retention focuses on the past; transfer emphasizes the future" (Mayer, 2002).

Second, consider the distinction between questions with and without a specific "correct" answer. Questions framed with specific answers tend to be associated with a more instructor-controlled dynamic. While some straightforward application or deliberate practice of a calculation or analysis may be useful, this *tends* to be more associated with recall than understanding. Essentially, the more predictable the response, the less likely the question suggests an opportunity for transfer, creativity, or synthesis.

Third, keeping to specific types of thinking is challenging, if not impossible. While the typical verbs provide some consistency of framing, analyzing can blur into evaluating, creating can require applying, and understanding can shift into recall. Mismatches can also occur when a question or prompt intended to elicit one form of response results in another. Indeed, an

Table 8.1 Classification of Student Contributions Using a Revised Version of Bloom's Taxonomy

Classification of student contribution	Typical verbs in the instructor's prompt or question that elicit this type of student contribution	Description of a student contribution of this type
Aside	None—such contribution either occur spontaneously or don't follow the instructor's prompt	A wholly off-topic interaction or an aside that is generally relevant to the *topic* of discussion but not specifically within the *flow* of the discussion
Recall *With correct answer*	Define, Recall, Identify, Attribute ["Who said . . ."], Label ["What is . . ."]	Recall of straightforward factual, conceptual, or procedural knowledge. There is a specific correct answer but providing this does not necessarily demonstrate an individual's understanding of a concept or the ability to apply it in another context—even if prompted.
Understanding *With correct answer*	Paraphrase ["In your own words . . ."], Classify, Explain [something straightforward and known], Summarize	Demonstrates an individual's understanding and/or requires them to interpret information, but the instructor aims to solicit a fairly specific correct response.
Understanding *Without a specific correct answer*	Interpret, Describe ["In your own words . . ."], Highlight, Classify, Infer, Exemplify ["What is an example . . ."]	Demonstrates an individual's understanding and/or requires them to interpret the information or concept without being led to a specific correct answer. In some cases, this can also be providing a straightforward example intended to serve as the basis for further investigation of a concept or procedure.
Applying	Solve, Calculate, Apply, Use, Implement, "Do X," "Take X and . . .," Draw, Diagram	A straightforward application of a concept in a given context or situation. This is typically either applied to a present example or as an instance of near transfer (application to a new but very similar situation or context). Some cases will have correct answers, such as completing a novel but straightforward calculation.
Analyzing	Analyze, Compare/Contrast, Relate, Restructure, Organize, Break Down, Transform	Analysis of a concept, information, or example in a manner that goes beyond the surface or holistic level to consider the relevant sub-structure or components and how they relate. A novel perspective on structuring or applying an analytical approach, especially in the context of far transfer, would be a particularly sophisticated application.

Evaluating	Justify, Defend, Evaluate, Agree or Disagree, Critique, Criticize, Check, Improve ["Identify a strength/weakness . . ." or "How could this be improved?"]	Critically engaging with a concept, information, or example in order to generate a judgment or evaluation with justification. Generating a novel basis of evaluation, especially in the context of far transfer (application to a new and very different situation or context), would constitute a particularly sophisticated application.
Creating	Create, Generate, Design, Build, Construct, Invent, Make, Provide	Using a given concept or piece of information as the basis for generating something new. In some cases, this will be a novel and detailed example specifically intended to illustrate a given concept. A particularly sophisticated application could include far transfer and/or rely on a novel perspective to shape the output.

Note: This taxonomy allows an instructor to identify words or phrases that might prompt a student to respond using a specific type of thinking skill. These "typical" verbs are not a mutually exclusive or exhaustive set, and students may not always respond with the intended thinking skill. *Asides* are included for completeness (i.e., if an instructor wishes to code all student contributions in a class session). Some suggested verbs found in this table are adapted from Krathwohl's taxonomy (2002).

instructor's desire to elicit a certain type of contribution does not guarantee a particular type of response.

Despite these confounds, reviewing a lesson plan or assignment and classifying the questions or prompts, and thus likely student contributions, is a helpful exercise. Appendix 2 provides further examples of instructor prompts and student contributions. One should note that this is an exercise in classifying *intended* learning and may not reflect the actual thinking and learning that takes place. Indeed, given the tendency for students to aim to reduce their cognitive load in the classroom (Raths, 2002), an instructor must be thoughtful in monitoring and evaluating the contributions that are taking place and prompting extension when necessary.

Proponents of the flipped-classroom model typically highlight that if students engage with knowledge recall and basic understanding *ahead of time,* they are more prepared to engage in transfer and synthesis in class discussion. This can take the form of gathering the basic facts from a reading and using study guide questions to test their understanding and attempt some straightforward applications. This kind of preparation, they argue, is best done outside of the classroom and may lead to greater learning outcomes (Mason et al., 2013; O'Flaherty & Philips, 2015; Roehl et al., 2013).

An instructor can also revise how they frame questions or prompts in order to gauge *understanding* and challenge students to extend their thinking. A particular focus is how to frame those questions based on building and checking basic factual, conceptual, or procedural knowledge. For example, consider the kinds of answers elicited by two different framings of the same question:

- "What is a model organism?"
- "In your own words, what does it mean to describe something as a model organism? What do you see as significant?"

The former question is likely to elicit a quote from a textbook—a factually correct statement without elaboration. The latter question requires *thinking.* Thinking about a way to describe the concept and reflecting on why it is meaningful. Questions that require thinking are more likely to give the instructor a clear indication of the student's level of *understanding.* Taking the time to think it through also promotes *retention* of the concept.

Questions can also build "habits of thinking" related to analyzing, evaluating, and creating (Wassermann, 1992, 2017). Habits of thinking take various forms. In this context, one could aim to build an ingrained tendency to

- identify and analyze underlying assumptions;
- reason from data and develop novel hypotheses;

- use evidence to provide justification; and
- explore multiple perspectives.

To promote such habits of thinking, instructors can consider the scope and scaffolding of their questions or prompts over the course of a class. One approach is to take time to consider how questions will promote different thinking skills and achieve learning goals. Prior to a class, aim to do the following:

- Identify the key idea or purpose of the day and the associated learning goals. Use this to determine the overarching "first" question, statement, or example that is anchored in the learning goals and sets the tone and topic for the session. This first question is not to be posed *and* concluded at the outset; rather, it provides direction for everything that takes place in the class session.
- If relevant, identify the basic knowledge or contextual understanding necessary to engage with the topic. Create focused questions or discussion prompts that will ensure everyone has a necessary level of *initial* understanding. These must promote understanding rather than simply demonstrate recall.
- Create a scaffolded set of sub-questions or prompts that follow that critical "first question." These questions should elicit contributions, tasks, or deliverables that are most relevant to the learning goals. Determine how to embed habits of thinking in these questions. For example, is the topic of the day particularly ripe for developing novel hypotheses or testing assumptions?
- If a skill requires deliberate practice, consider how to create time for application during class and the appropriate balance of near- and far transfer.

Critically, this may be less of a firm plan and more of an opportunity for the instructor to *think it through* in advance. Specific questions that appear likely to be particularly productive are worth noting, but the instructor's primary focus should be on facilitating the natural progression of the class while maintaining a link to the first question and learning goals.

A further means of challenging students to extend their ideas is shifting from the basic IRE-interaction[2] to one where a *second* wait time is deliberately used to promote deep thinking. Rather than bombarding students with rapid questions or flitting from one to another, consider how a given student's ideas develop when given an extended opportunity to think.

- Instructor: "Here's the data where the researchers took the cognitive assessment task and tested subjects from three different age groups. What do you observe? Student X?"

- First wait time typically ~1 second unless trained to wait appropriately (Rowe, 1974).
- Student X: "I see that overall performance gets worse with age, but they are also slower to start and take longer to make each move. So maybe they are just thinking more slowly overall."
- Second wait time typically ~0.9 seconds unless trained to wait appropriately (Rowe, 1974).
- Instructor: "You hypothesize that this reflects a generalized impairment in speed of processing."
- Third wait time. The student is considering the instructor's reflective restatement (the instructor could have used another prompt that solicits reflection or elaboration).
- "Yeah, I think so. It seems to be a way to explain all three graphs. If the impairment was . . ."

While all instances of wait time are important in the above interaction, the *second* and even *third* wait times are arguably more critical than the first. Here, the student is reflecting on their initial idea, re-analyzing the data, evaluating their conclusion, and drawing supporting evidence. Peers are engaged in the effortful cognition of analyzing what has been said and developing their own position. This second wait time also allows the instructor to consider their reaction, whether commenting, asking another question, or moving to a new topic.

The bulk of deep thinking may be taking place during these second and third wait times, rather than after the initial question. When sufficient wait time is a normal part of classroom interactions, it helps students learn to think *before* they speak.

The Socratic dialogue is another conventional approach to classroom interaction. In this dynamic, the instructor continually challenges students to extend their thinking and probes the underlying web of interconnected ideas and assumptions. Again, the role of the instructor is to push the dialogue beyond recall: "Feeding students endless content to remember (i.e., declarative statements or 'facts') is akin to repeatedly stepping on the brakes in a vehicle that is, unfortunately, already at rest" (Elder & Paul, 1998, p. 297).

Preparation for a Socratic dialogue is very similar to the methods described above (such as identifying the big idea and preparing a list of relevant questions). Most of the instructor behaviors described by Elder and Paul (1998) also overlap with what has been described previously

- responding to all student answers with a further question that requires the student to extend their thinking. Treating all ideas as in need of refinement and development;
- valuing all student contributions;

- probing for justification in the form of evidence or supporting knowledge;
- seeking to understand the fundamental ideas and agendas that underlie an assertion or conclusion;
- asking questions that tease apart the interconnected web of thoughts and assumptions associated with an idea;
- treating all ideas as responses to a particular question. When the question is implicit, aim to make it explicit; and
- drawing out and recognizing the particular points of view or interpretive lens that accompany ideas, assumptions, or conclusions. Challenging students to consider other points of view.

This kind of contingent questioning, where previous student contributions shape the instructor's prompt, promotes extended student talk and engagement (Boyd & Rubin, 2006). Importantly, some approaches to Socratic dialogue aim to push students to discover specific constructs or truths, while others aim to foster more open-ended investigation.

"Socratic dialogue" is sometimes used to refer to *any* class discussion that is guided by continuous instructor questioning. However, the original intent of this method was for the instructor to question in order to surface a *contradiction* with the student's initial position. This contradiction is used to identify a fallacy in the initial assumptions, which is then used to refine the original idea.

OTHER FORMS OF QUESTIONING

Other forms of questioning shape the scope or dynamic of the discussion itself. These tend to exert some measure of control on the part of the instructor.

Questions That Invite Framing or Focus

- Are we focused on the right problem in this context?
- Of the potential hypotheses suggested so far, which one should we test in detail?
- Of the available analytical methods—which approach should we apply?
- How would you articulate this as a specific hypothesis?
- What have we discovered here? How could you describe what is generalizable?
- How could we broadly describe this approach? Are there others?

Questions That Promote Reflection or Reevaluation

- You're saying [paraphrase]?
- What are we assuming/What assumptions do we need to make?

- How is this consistent with [what came before]?
- How does this build on [what came before]?
- We've been developing a [hypothesis/mental model], but what evidence suggests it is plausible? How might we test it?
- Tell me more.

Questions That Evaluate the Need for Further Discussion

- Shall we continue with this idea, or are we ready to move on?
- How have we achieved the learning goals so far?
- Let's brainstorm for five minutes and then pause to evaluate in more detail . . . What's an initial idea?
- Let's pause here. Can [someone] summarize what we've covered so far?

Questions That Bring Closure

- Given the discussion, what is [a/the] key message we should take away? [What is generalizable from this?]
- What do you need to remember in order to use this effectively in the future?
- How could we use this in the future?

THE MATTER OF COLD-CALLING

Cold-calling, soliciting a contribution from a student who has not indicated a desire to participate, is a staple of law and business classrooms and present in many other contexts. In most cases, this takes the form of an instructor calling on a student whose hand is not raised and *requiring* them to make some form of verbal contribution, typically by responding to an instructor-posed question.

There are conflicting opinions regarding the purpose, efficacy, and merits of cold-calling. Instructors who use cold-calling often highlight the technique as a straightforward method to require a high level of preparation and engagement from all students. Instructors who avoid cold-calling do so given concerns about increasing student anxiety, disrupting thinking, and maintaining an instructor-focused locus of control.

The Case for Cold-calling

Advocates of this method of eliciting student contributions typically believe a classroom dynamic with frequent cold-calling

- "draws out" quieter or less confident students;
- prevents students from disengaging or mentally "checking out" and "keeps students on their toes";
- leads to increased engagement over time;
- leads to increased student preparation; or
- fosters a positive classroom dynamic where students are empowered to contribute, and a breadth of perspectives enriches the discussion.

Two particular considerations bear on the above: first, whether cold-calling increases or diminishes student anxiety (both general anxiety and classroom communication apprehension); and second, whether it impacts student preparation for class.

In a study[3] of undergraduates enrolled in discussion-based communications courses, Souza et al. found that although factors other than cold-calling *increase* student comfort participating in class discussion, comfort may not *decrease* with cold-calling (2010). At the end of the semester, the control group self-reported a higher degree of "ease" of discussion participation than the experimental group, despite reporting significantly less ease in a pre-survey. No significant difference in "comfort" was found between the groups.[4] As other proponents of cold-calling note, "Although it is certainly possible cold-calls can be humiliating (and we do *not* encourage this), it does not necessarily follow that *all* cold-calls are" (Dallimore et al., 2006, p. 355).

This measure of "ease" was interpreted to suggest that cold-calling can make a class more challenging for students, given the need to be fully prepared and required to respond at any time. Souza et al. suggest that such difficulty is desirable, as it could indicate students being challenged both intellectually—in terms of mastery of the content—and communicatively—in their ability to construct, rebut, critique, and defend arguments (2010).

As more students in the cold-call classrooms commented on engagement in their post-surveys than those in the control classrooms, Souza et al. suggest there is greater engagement in classes that deliberately incorporate cold-calling into their pedagogy.

When considering these elements of comfort, ease, and engagement, it is important to note that all four instructors in the study represent particularly skilled educators. Souza et al. noted among their key characteristics

- being formally recognized for effective teaching;
- actively working to create a supportive classroom environment that encourages engagement;
- overtly valuing student contributions across a breadth of viewpoints and giving students the freedom to make such contributions; and
- promoting familiarity and immediacy with the instructor, peers, and course overall.

Nonvoluntary participation requires that the student is put on the spot—singled out for an individual, public contribution. As such, it is not surprising that some instructors believe it helps sustain student attention. Does it also increase preparation? An exploratory study[5] of a master of business administration (MBA) discussion course suggested that classroom cold-calling both moderated a relationship between preparation, participation, and comfort with class discussion; and marginally affected preparation (Dallimore et al., 2006).

Another study of a master's level statistics course at Harvard University found that cold-calling and mandatory web-posting had a positive effect on the amount of time students read before class but not on academic performance (Levy & Bookin, 2014).

The level of cold-calling in this Harvard experiment was described as "low to moderate," despite only a single student (out of forty) being selected for cold-calling in a given class session. The student was asked two or three related factual questions, which adequate class preparation enabled answering. Students were not able to simply defer or "pass" the question: The instructor would alternate silence and probing for approximately 2 to 3 minutes. While qualitative feedback did indicate some students felt stressed about being cold-called, others indicated that the likelihood was low (and thus, presumably, it was not a preoccupation for them) (Levy & Bookin, 2014).

While cold-calling demands nonvoluntary participation, does it also increase *voluntary* engagement over time? A further observational study of in-class behavior coupled with pre-post-survey demonstrated that classes with high cold-calling exhibited

- individual students answering more questions voluntarily (which increased over time);
- a higher overall number of students answering questions voluntarily (which increased over time); and
- self-reported comfort engaging in discussion increased over time, while comfort in low cold-calling classes remained stable (Dallimore et al., 2012).[6]

Can cold-calling be used to promote engagement by subsets of students who are typically quieter in class? Gender-based differences in student engagement are influenced by many factors, including instructor gender, responsiveness to student gender, stereotypes, and gender-balance within the classroom. When differences are observed, classes tend to exhibit diminished female participation (Opie et al., 2019; Tatum et al., 2013; Salter & Persaud, 2003).

In a managerial accounting course split into low and high cold-call conditions, women answered the same number of *voluntary* questions as men in classes with a high degree of cold-calling, yet in classes with a low degree of cold-calling women answered fewer questions than men (Dallimore et al., 2019). [7]

At a university with an instructional model focused on active learning, student responses on end-of-semester course and instructor surveys included positive comments related to cold-calling:[8]

- "Really push us to think. The art of cold-call and the style of questions."
- "[Instructor] is one of the best professors I have had. I wish [they] could cold call more! Some students need a little bit of a kick in the morning."
- "There was no cold calling so that there was no real need to do the readings."
- "How to improve—facilitating discussions—COLD-CALLING."
- "I also remember that [the instructor] tried out increasing [their] tendency to cold-call in class which keeps everyone at the edge of their seats, at least for me."

The Case against Cold-calling

While some approaches to instruction recommend cold-calling, many do not or suggest it only under very specific and limited circumstances. Instructors who deliberately avoid cold-calling tend to do so on the basis that requiring nonvoluntary participation

- diminishes psychological safety;
- disrupts thinking;
- reinforces position-based power and/or an instructor-question: student-response: instructor-evaluation (IRE) pattern of engagement;
- inappropriately prizes one form of engagement;
- does not build skills for the real world; and
- ignores other, more effective, ways to sustain interest, engagement, and motivation.

Student participation in classroom discussion hinges on *confidence*, which is diminished by the relative fear of feeling inadequate in front of others or the more general "classroom apprehension" of receiving a negative evaluation or other negative consequence as a result of participation (Rocca, 2009).

Many instructors highlight classroom psychological safety or concern that students will feel embarrassed, disrespected, or humiliated as rationales to avoid cold-calling (Rocca, 2010). Others raise the issue that students could interpret patterns of cold-calling as either special-treatment or punishment of specific individuals (Dillon, 1981b).

As previously discussed in chapter 5, cold-calling as a means of facilitating active learning causes a greater increase in anxiety than other techniques such as volunteering to speak, participating in group work, or answering clicker questions (England et al., 2017).

While other active learning techniques increase or decrease anxiety depending on the classroom dynamic and instructor facilitation, cold-call or random-call only increases anxiety (Cooper et al., 2018). Students interviewed for this study recognized cold-calling as a method of increasing participation but expressed that the resulting anxiety negatively impacted their in-class performance and overall learning.

Students instructed in their second language, those with greater anxiety, or those with medical issues resulting in more frequent absences report heightened classroom anxiety when cold-call techniques are used (Broeckelman-Post et al., 2016).

Without robust support for positive outcomes associated with cold-calling, many instructors do not recommend it due to the potential to increase anxiety (Rocca, 2010; Moguel, 2004).

How does cold-calling affect student thinking? While proponents believe the likelihood of nonvoluntary participation keeps students cognitively engaged, others believe that it is counterproductive: cold-calling *disrupts*, rather than *promotes*, thinking.

In a classroom dynamic shaped by cold-calling, they argue, students will focus on being ready with a response, rather than continuing to think deeply about the topic or problem under discussion. A student who continues to think or develop a new position risks being left with an incomplete idea at the moment of being cold-called. Essentially, students feel pressure to have a minimum viable response ready at all times. Such "guarding against the cold-call" takes precedence over deeper critical thinking (Dillon, 1981b).

These concerns suggest cold-calling comes at the expense of the depth or sophistication of overall engagement. Directing someone to respond when they are still pondering or forming their argument is far more likely to elicit a superficial response, or even "I don't know." It neglects giving students the time to think deeply and determine what (and when) they would like to contribute (Dillon, 1981b). A student caught without a minimum viable response at a given moment may feel embarrassed at being forced to present an idea-in-progress and having it subjected to evaluation by the instructor or their peers.

While voluntary responses shouldn't be considered perfectly formed ideas—indeed, students should be encouraged to raise exploratory ones—the likelihood of soliciting a contribution that is superficial or irrelevant is significantly higher when cold-calling at random. As a result, the class discussion may be buffeted by superficial or incomplete ideas.

Putting a student in a position where they have to offer an "I don't know" response is even worse. While this is mitigated in a psychologically safe, nonjudgmental environment, it is nonetheless a challenging admission for most students. It can imply they are *generally* unable to contribute rather than simply unprepared or not quite ready *at that moment.*

Focusing the spotlight on unfinished or interrupted thinking can further diminish psychological safety due to the negative experience of judgment and a student's perception that the instructor may not value giving them time to develop their ideas fully. This is compounded by cold-calling approaches where students are forced to *remain* on the spot to respond, even when they feel they have nothing to contribute.

It is important to know if students are "getting it," and proponents of cold-calling often suggest soliciting random input provides an important glimpse of the general level of understanding in a class. Similarly, proponents worry that focusing on voluntary contributions will only capture the *strongest* comments and mask confusion. This concern is mitigated by a classroom dynamic where students are active participants in their learning and have the confidence and psychological safety to raise questions and "imperfect" ideas. Here, highlighting a confusion or question is a valued and respected contribution.

From a student perspective, there is a significant difference between an environment where they feel empowered to raise their hand and say, "I don't understand" and one where they are put on the spot to report, "I don't know" while still introspecting or developing an idea.

A classroom with frequent and rapid cold-calling can *tend* toward a dynamic focused on IRE-interactions, include more "test" questions with specific answers (Moguel, 2004), and even signal that spontaneous contributions from students are unwanted (Dillon, 1981b).

Engaging in *frequent* cold-calling also prioritizes the ability to offer an immediate, in-the-moment response rather than summative reflection or other forms of contribution. While "preventing disengagement" is a commonly stated goal of cold-calling, it ignores the fact that students may be engaging in other thinking-related behavior. What some instructors take as signs of disengagement may be related to personality traits, learned behavior, or situational factors, and a tendency to engage deeply with the material in a more reflective and introspective manner (Medaille & Usinger, 2019).

As Hopper notes, "There are many students, and I am one of them, who may appear to be disengaged, even catatonic, when they are in fact silently but vigorously grappling with a concept or problem" (2003, p. 25). Broadly equating silence with disengagement may be more indicative of an instructor's preconceptions of learning than representative of what is transpiring in the classroom. Furthermore, requiring in-the-moment participation or interrupting introspection may be at odds with the individual needs of particular students.

Developing the ability to act without hand-raising is sometimes a further goal of a dynamic without cold-calling. Here, students have the opportunity to attempt to paraphrase or summarize, consider when to pose questions, or defer to other speakers. They also learn more effective turn-taking and how to integrate body language and eye contact into judgments of when to engage in the discussion (Tredway, 1995). This may also allow an instructor to effectively model the behaviors, such as listening, thinking, and interacting with others effectively, that they desire to foster in students (Dillon, 1981b, Tredway, 1995).

Learning to act without hand-raising or being "called on" is a critical skill for college students. Success in internships is often strongly linked to the ability to insert themselves into a team meeting or discussion.

Relying on cold-calling ignores other means of fostering engagement. While proponents of cold-calling often suggest that some percentage of students would *never* speak in class without it, other educators strongly disagree. Fostering engagement from students who may be more reticent or from cultural backgrounds without active learning may take significant time and patience, but it is achievable.

If silence is construed as a lack of motivation or preparation, a common suggestion is that the *threat* of a cold-call can address both behaviors (a sentiment expressed by some instructors as well as some students[9]). If the fear of being called on is the principal motivation to prepare for class and pay attention, then perhaps the instructor should reevaluate both the course content and their approach to teaching.

Certain formats, such as the case method (Christensen, 1991) or peer instruction (Mazur, 1997a,b), are particularly conducive to fostering discussion and engagement. Instructors can also have private conversations with quieter students to understand how to facilitate their participation more effectively.

In some cases, prearranged summative moments are an opportunity for a more introspective student to provide insight. Different ways of framing questions may support second-language speakers whose language skills would leave them struggling to answer rapid cold-calls. Even understanding how active participation promotes learning and hearing that the instructor values students' ideas and opinions can make a significant difference in classroom apprehension.

Students may be more inclined to volunteer with specific ground rules in place: for example, that the instructor will *offer an opportunity* rather than *demand* the student respond to follow-up questions, so they are not afraid of being "left hanging." Another approach is establishing that a student can, if they falter, turn to the instructor for help paraphrasing or recalling a technical detail. While many instructors would assume such options are available, students may not take it for granted.

From the same cohort of undergraduate students that provided the positive comments above, end-of-semester course and instructor surveys also included the following comments related to cold-calling.[10]

- "How could the instructor improve: Maybe less cold-calls."
- "Hands aren't really used, instead it's more focused on cold-calling which is unfortunate when someone has a thought they really want to share."
- "It is actually hard to assess the difficulty. People can say anything if they are cold-called (bullshitting)."
- "Cold-calling keeps us on our toes, but it can be nice to throw the question out to the class."
- "The cold calling was especially hard at first, so I think taking some direct steps to foster a more familiar atmosphere would be great, so that these early moments don't feel so colossal."
- "Ask the question before cold-call a student and give us some time to think about it. [social science] questions usually take time to think."

Inviting Contributions versus Cold-calling

There is significant common ground underlying the arguments for and against cold-calling. First, all students contributing promotes both individual learning and the quality of the class discussion.[11] Second, psychological safety is of paramount importance to the classroom dynamic. Third, becoming adept at engaging in discussion is a skill that requires practice on the part of students and likely modeling by the instructor.

"Cold-calling" elicits an almost visceral revulsion in many instructors: It's disrespectful. It's authoritative. It can humiliate. It recalls past experiences with highly judgmental hit-and-run approaches to questioning.

In promoting cold-calling as a means of fostering increased engagement and preparation, Dallimore, Hertenstein, and Platt note that one can "view cold-calling as encompassing varied instructional techniques ranging from icy cold to decidedly tepid" (p. 355). In their own (and similar) studies, the research methodology defined cold-calling as *any instance* when a student was called on without their hand raised. Such a definition neglects to highlight critical subtleties of instructor behavior when engaging with students.

First, cold-calling is rarely the sole means of soliciting contributions. While one instructor in Dallimore et al. (2012) did not use any cold-calling, all others used a *mixture* of cold-calling and voluntary responses. The mean percentage of students cold-called in the "high cold-calling" group was 61 percent (33–84%) compared with 10 percent (0–24%) in the low cold-call group (2012). While some instructors do not cold-call, it is rare to see an instructor *exclusively* cold-call (unless they are deliberately using a random-call technique and there are no student questions).

The use of pre- and post-survey feedback, as well as the characteristics of the participating instructors, highlighted that instructor ability likely plays a significant role in how many students experience a variety of cold-calling techniques. Students who noted instructor-behavior making them feel comfortable in the classroom highlighted the instructor's flexibility and ability to foster an "encouraging, supportive and respectful environment" (Souza et al., 2010).

Experienced instructors often use specific techniques to build up nonvoluntary participation. This can include pre-class work where students are aware they may be required to share, starting with straightforward or highly nonevaluative questions to ensure each student can successfully field a question, or reserving cold-calling for activities where students have had ample time to think or discuss their contributions in advance (Dallimore et al., 2004, 2012). This is sometimes called "warm-calling" when referring to instances where the students are able to prepare or confer prior to sharing and the request to speak is unsurprising.

Where researchers identified cold-calling as the fundamental difference driving positive outcomes, other elements of instructor style may have also played a role. Additionally, the proportion of cold-calling and timing of different types of questions may vary significantly in meaningful ways.

In one study, students in the "high cold-calling" classes were also answering, and presumably being asked, significantly more questions overall. This more engagement-focused dynamic could shape the observed results, regardless of the percentage of cold-calling.

The increase in voluntary responses may also be a means of guarding against cold-calling—attempting to contribute when feeling more confident in an effort to avoid the instructor calling on them when they are not. Anecdotal conversations with students and preliminary research suggests this is the case.[12] Another plausible explanation is that if cold-calling encourages students to prepare more, then the majority of students may be more comfortable voluntarily contributing (Dallimore et al., 2012).

The context of such studies may also shape student perceptions of cold-calling and self-reports of the classroom experience. Those who are young, inexperienced, and immature are less likely to participate in class (Rocca, 2009). When research is conducted in graduate seminars, or contexts where participation is expressly understood as a core competence to be developed (such as in communications, law, or business), students may be more receptive to nonvoluntary participation or believe it a standard approach to instruction.

A fully controlled study—an instructor teaching the same lesson plan with the same number of opportunities to elicit a contribution, using cold-calling in one class section and relying on volunteers in the other—has not yet been done. The *distribution* of classroom apprehension or anxiety specifically related to cold-calling is also unclear. While a class, *on average*, may become more comfortable with nonvoluntary participation, some proportion of students will experience significant anxiety as a result of such techniques. If the proportion is similar to communication apprehension, 10–20 percent of students may be significantly affected.[13]

Rather than focusing on "cold-calling" as the determining factor of engagement, particularly given the wide variety of instructor behaviors involved, one can frame the issue as how to "invite contributions" from students. While some instructors may nonetheless solicit contribution from students whose hands are not raised, the concept of inviting contributions must have the following four concrete guardrails:

- It should not include hit-and-run questioning or other trivial approaches to engagement.
- It should not diminish psychological safety and must be sensitive to classroom communication apprehension. Students must be able to *pass* on a given question without disappointment, censure, or public negative judgment from the instructor.
- It should be receptive to different learning styles.
- It should include appropriate wait time.

An instructor inviting participation must engage in active listening, model best practice in discussion, and offer meaningful opportunities for students to contribute. These opportunities can include a mixture of the questioning and non-questioning elicitation techniques described previously. Similarly, while some students may be invited to contribute without having raised their hands, it is not the primary means of soliciting contributions.

Quiet students are not simply *assumed* to be disengaged, although an instructor may wish to check that assumption with specific individuals or use engagement tasks that mitigate that concern.[14]

When students are invited to contribute by name an instructor can use questions that are not focused on one very specific right answer. This allows students to determine a level of engagement that is suited to their present level of understanding or confusion. This also removes a potential cold-calling pitfall: if an instructor attempts to avoid asking a student a question they cannot answer correctly, they create a self-fulfilling prophecy of ability (Wiliam, 2014). Other avenues offer even more flexibility:

> Rather than asking students to answer a math question, the teacher could pose two questions of differing difficulty and ask, "Which of these two questions is harder and why?" The ensuing discussion will raise all the important mathematical issues that the teacher needs to cover, but the question has been posed in an inclusive way that enables more students to contribute, thus supporting differentiated instruction. (Wiliam, 2014, p. 18)

While questions intending to solicit straightforward recall or application are often considered "softball," they may in fact carry significantly more interpersonal risk than those considered more challenging. While the former is either answered correctly, incorrectly, or with "I don't know," a supposedly more challenging question may afford different avenues of engagement. Offering a starting point, identifying an uncertainty, and even explaining why it's challenging to answer are all valued contributions. Similarly, inviting a student to react to a statement may be a more productive (and inviting) starting point than a question.

In order to foster psychological safety, instructors must convey that they value student contributions and use nonpunitive responses. If a student is invited to contribute by name, they must be able to decline without sanction. While inviting contributions from students who have not volunteered may *always* introduce some measure of increased anxiety to the classroom dynamic, the instructor can at least make a conscious effort to minimize the extent to which it may be debilitating for some students.

Allowing some predictability and preparation is one approach to building student confidence and attempting to mitigate the impact of nonvoluntary participation on psychological safety. There is a significant difference between being cold-called without warning and being invited to contribute by

- sharing materials prepared in advance, such as problem sets or pre-class work;
- elaborating on a poll response or in-class task where there has been time to think; or
- sharing ideas/answers that have been discussed with other students, such as with a think-pair-share activity or breakout task.

Providing clear feedback to students about their participation may also reinforce psychological safety—expressing appreciation, sharing observations, and providing suggestions are all helpful. This feedback can address the frequency of participation, the depth or "technical" content of contributions, how they engage with their peers' ideas, or other facets of interpersonal interaction.

If it is not possible to do this for an entire class, consider gently approaching the quieter students. If participation is mandatory or affecting a course grade, identify strategies or norms to empower them to contribute:

- Perhaps they need assurance the instructor will not "leave them on the spot." One of the most impactful norms is allowing students to *pass* on a given question without disappointment, censure, or evaluation from the instructor.
- Perhaps they would be more comfortable sharing material prepared in advance (e.g., study guide responses). Classroom apprehension is notably diminished when students can engage in advance preparation before contributing (Rocca, 2010).
- Perhaps they would be more comfortable attempting to contribute if they understand the instructor is aware of their anxiety and ready to "make it okay" with a sympathetic paraphrase if they falter or get tongue-tied.

This kind of office hours (or at least outside of class time) interaction can play a significant role in decreasing classroom apprehension. In fact, across a study of ten causal variables, Weaver & Qi (2005) found that faculty-student interaction had the most significant impact on class participation as reported by students. See chapter 10 for further strategies for anxious students.

For those students who may be naturally introspective or prefer to listen carefully, take notes, and analyze, attempt to harness this approach to learning rather than interrupt it. Create an opportunity for them to take a provide a summary or feedback and thus take a deliberate role in the discussion or activity. One can attempt to balance opportunities for in-the-moment contributions with other kinds of engagement.

In some contexts, such as business, law, and communications, participation can itself be considered a primary learning outcome. Students may have firm participatory expectations of themselves and their peers and see cold-calling as a discipline-specific norm. While an instructor need not conform to their peers, it is important to understand how norms within a discipline or school may shape students' expectations and classroom apprehension. It can also provide insight as to whether students are likely to approach class with behaviors related to "guarding against the cold-call."

Instructors wishing to employ nonvoluntary elicitation should carefully consider the implications of the *frequency* of this form of inviting contributions, the specific *questions*, *prompts*, and *points of discussion* linked to voluntary versus nonvoluntary contributions, and the *impact* on psychological safety and anxiety. With care, this can be done in a way that is experienced positively by many (and perhaps even most) students. Students with low classroom communication apprehension, in particular, may have positive perceptions of such engagement.

A student in the same cohort of first-year undergraduate social science course evaluations above, stated: "I have described this extensively before. [The instructor] is excellent with class participation, having a balance between cold calling and hand raising, and always asks deep and challenging questions. Love the beginning of class and how much [instructor] cares about students!"[15]

When possible, instructors should examine student feedback. Students may still report being impacted by the "acute stress" of a cold-call, undertaking guarding behaviors, or an impatience with what they perceive as their peers "bullshitting" when cold-called. Such concerns can be present even when instructors believe cold-calling is warmed up and normalized.

Instructors wishing to avoid nonvoluntary elicitation in their classrooms may wonder about the breadth of voluntary participation that will occur. How long does it take for everyone to be frequently participating? Days? Weeks? *Months*? Conversations with instructors who *never* cold-call highlight that voluntary participation by all students is achievable, but an instructor must be ready for it to take *time*. According to these instructors, the resulting depth of discussion and student engagement is worth the wait (and effort).

OBSERVING AND INTERJECTING

How does an instructor determine when to engage with groups of students completing an in-class task? Student feedback supports the importance of circulating the room and keeping an eye on how things are going (Finelli et al., 2018). In this regard, instructor behavior varies significantly in terms of whether this is silent and more *reactive* or vocal and more *proactive*.

Many instructors will set a question or task, let the groups get started, and when circulating the room *proactively* engage with students. This usually takes the form of approaching a group and checking-in by asking a question:

- "How is it going?"
- "Do you have any questions?"
- "Can you take me through what you have so far?"
- "Do you think you're going to get through it okay? Do you need help? More time?"

Proactively engaging with a group is a common instructor behavior and will usually be met with appreciation and a positive response from the students. Indeed, many instructors make a point of going group by group and asking such questions. Some wait for a natural pause, while others attempt to jump in and out of the active conversation.

What happens after the instructor moves on? In some cases, the moment of reflection will have refocused the group. Perhaps the instructor offered a hint that helped them move forward or resolved a procedural confusion. In other cases, however, the group will lose their momentum or train of thought. Well-intentioned instructor check-ins that take place as a *matter of course* can temporarily derail the student-driven element of the activity.

Instructors can consider how to signal their availability and interest as they circulate the room, even making eye contact with specific students or pausing within obvious "listening range," as appropriate. In doing so, the instructor should observe the groups carefully and attempt to gauge the following:

- Do they appear to make progress?
- Do they believe they have "completed" the task?
- Are any students visibly off-topic or disengaged?
- Is the talk-time balanced among students, or are one or two dominating the group?
- Is there a level of conflict that *they are not capable* of handling on their own?

If a group is stuck or struggling, then it may be appropriate to step in (particularly if the issue is procedural—understanding the task or deliverables). Considering the approaches to non-questioning and affirmation described previously, an instructor can decide whether an interjection should take the form of a question, offering an observation, or providing a hint. All allow students to reflect on their progress and ask questions that come to mind. An observation or a hint can also be a means of offering affirmation without the typically judgmental direct praise.

SELF-EVALUATION AND NEXT STEPS

Discussion

If you use "discussion" in your classroom, take a few minutes to reflect on what that means to you. Briefly write down answers to the following questions:

- How do you define a "discussion" in your classroom?
- What does it look like in practice? If possible, think of a recent concrete example.

- What is your role? How frequently do you contribute or engage in facilitation?
- How do students engage? Do you heavily mediate their contributions? Do they build on or extend each other's ideas?
- Do you use both questioning and non-questioning techniques? In what way?

Now, review your notes and take a moment to reflect on how "discussions" *tend* to take place in your classroom and consider the following:

- Would you differentiate between a "discussion" and an "instructor-led activity"? Why or why not? What is the significance of such a distinction?
- How might your role or interaction-style *facilitate or inhibit* student contributions and psychological safety?
- How and when do you exert control over the *content* or *dynamic* of the discussion?
- What is one thing you enjoy about discussions in your classroom? If you would like to have more of this, how might you bring it about?
- What is one thing (you think) students enjoy about discussions in your classroom? If possible, solicit student feedback or consult course evaluations. If you would like to increase student enjoyment, how might you bring it about?
- What is one key challenge you experience with in-class discussions? How might you approach mitigating that?

Questioning

Explore *when* and *how* you pose questions to the class. This can be in the context of discussions, tasks or activity prompts, or any Q&A opportunity, including pausing while lecturing to pose a question. Consider a typical class and write down answers to the following questions:

- When do you use questions that prompt *recall* or demonstration of basic factual, conceptual, or procedural knowledge in a straightforward manner? Roughly what percentage of your questioning is of this type?
- When do you use questions that require a straightforward *application* or *demonstrating understanding*? Roughly what percentage of your questioning is of this type?
- When do you use questions that invite *analysis, evaluation, or creation* related to a given concept or topic? Roughly what percentage of your questioning is of this type?

While each type of questioning may be appropriate in different contexts, examine the overall balance and timing. Carefully consider the following:

- Are you confident that you have a clear picture of what your students understand?
- What percentage of your questions have a specific "right answer"? Why is that?
- Does your style of questioning allow for agency on the part of students?
- Does your style of questioning allow students to exhibit *transfer*—demonstrating skills or concepts in one context that were learned in another?

Examine the above and identify one aspect of how you approach questioning that you might try changing. It could relate to *when* you ask questions or the *type(s)* of questions you use. Make a plan to try implementing this change in your classroom. This may involve a learning curve and some deliberate practice, so be sure to include ample time to become more comfortable or adept. Be sure to include at least one checkpoint where you will reflect on what is or is not working and course-correct if necessary.

Eliciting Contributions/Responses

Consider *when* and *how* you solicit or invite contributions from students, and whether students ever contribute in an unprompted manner. Aim to put a rough percentage against the various ways students come to contribute in class:

- _____ Students contribute in a wholly unprompted manner (they simply speak up).
- _____ Students raise hands or express interest in contributing without prompting (i.e., without an explicit or implicit invitation in the form of a question or discussion-based activity; a student raises their hand to ask a question or provide a comment while the instructor or another student is speaking).
- _____ Students raise hands or express interest in contributing with prompting (i.e., in response to a question or as part of an activity).
- _____ Students are "cold-called" or invited to contribute nonvoluntarily.

For each type, note *why* this practice occurs in your classroom and your perceptions of the *strengths/weaknesses* of how this affects the classroom dynamic.

Finally, examine the overall balance of student contribution in your classroom. Carefully consider the following:

- How many different students are participating in a given class?
- How is the talk-time distributed or monopolized?
- Are few/some/all students "comfortable" contributing in your classroom? How might classroom apprehension vary among students?
- If you *do* cold-call, why is that? If you *do not* cold-call, why not? If you use a mix, what percentage of contributions are elicited by cold-calling? What role does nonvoluntary participation play in your classroom?
- Do you use adequate wait time (4–6 seconds) when inviting contributions from students?

Review the above and identify one aspect of how you approach inviting student contributions that you might change. Make a plan to try implementing this change in your classroom. This may involve a learning curve and some deliberate practice, so be sure to include ample time to become more comfortable or adept. Be sure to include at least one checkpoint where you will reflect on what is or is not working and, if necessary, course-correct.

Feedback on Class Participation

Feedback can be helpful if students are unaccustomed to participating in class. In some cases, this is best as a private conversation, particularly if

- a student tends to dominate the overall talk-time. This is even more important if they also tend to ignore the previous contributions in favor of introducing new but unrelated ideas;
- a student appears to personalize disagreement or feedback;
- a student is not effectively listening to their peers; or
- a student is unable to participate in a meaningful manner.

Other proactive framing or feedback on the questioning dynamic can target the group as a whole. It is crucial for students to understand that they are welcome to do the following:

- "Pass" on a question or request more thinking time.
- Request clarification of the instructor's question or a previous point.
- Paraphrase what they have heard before or offer a reflective restatement for the group.
- Ask questions of the instructor.
- Ask questions of each other.

Three Points to Remember about Questioning

- Instructors should consider how questioning and non-questioning techniques elicit student contributions, promote psychological safety, and foster engagement.
- Carefully framed questions promote different kinds of thinking and engagement.
- Nonvoluntary engagement, whether as a result of "cold-calling" or by "inviting contributions," is a deliberate choice. Instructors should carefully consider the potential costs or benefits and use such techniques with care.

NOTES

1. David Krathwohl was one of Benjamin Bloom's original collaborators on the 1956 taxonomy. For elaboration of the original taxonomy and proposed amendments following discussion in the mid- to late 1990s, see Anderson, L. W. (Ed.), Krathwohl, D. R. (Ed.), Airasian, P. W., Cruikshank, K. A., Mayer, R. E., Pintrich, P. R., Raths, J., & Wittrock, M. C. (2001). *A Taxonomy for Learning, Teaching, and Assessing: A Revision of Bloom's Taxonomy of Educational Objectives (Complete Edition)*. New York: Longman.

An accessible summary with discussion is found in: Krathwohl, David R. (2002). "A revision of Bloom's Taxonomy: An overview." *Theory into Practice*, 41(4): 212–218.

2. Instructor-initiation: student-response: instructor-evaluation (IRE). Initiation typically takes the form of a question.

3. Nine courses in total: four public speaking, two gender and communications, one co-cultural communication, one consultation skills, and one interpersonal communications. Six of these were treated as experimental groups where instructors explained the choice, rationale, and advantages of cold-calling without naming it as such or explaining that this aspect of pedagogy was being assessed. All courses graded participation, ranging from 10 to 22 percent of the students' total grade. One hundred ninety-two students completed both pre- and post-surveys across the courses and were included in the analysis. All data was student self-reported measures.

4. Factors highlighted as driving student comfort in the classroom include the instructor (and their flexibility and ability to foster an encouraging, respectful, and supportive dynamic; one student in particular highlighted every student being comfortable with their opinions and a lack of judgment of right and wrong opinions), the nature of the course content and course design (one student highlighted that "this class was designed for participation in discussion"), and being prepared for class and/or confident in their understanding of the material (Souza et al., 2010, pp. 237–238).

5. Data for this study was gathered in an MBA course where participation counted for 40 percent of a student's grade. The syllabus highlighted an expectation

of participation and students were verbally informed that if they did not raise their hand they would be called on. A pre-post quasi-experimental design was employed. Although fifty-four students were present in the class and completed the surveys (22% women), only twenty-seven students were able to recall the PIN that allowed direct pre-post comparison; thus, the analytical sample consisted of twenty-five men and two women (Dallimore et al., 2006).

6. Sixteen sections of an undergraduate management accounting course at a large private university were used as the cohort for this study. Each section had approximately forty students. The composition of respondees was 46 percent women and 54 percent men, with 359 completing both the pre- and post-surveys. The sixteen sections were taught by seven instructors: all were considered effective teachers (strong "teaching effectiveness" ratings on course evaluations) and capable of providing a supportive learning environment. The instructors used their natural instructional styles, including whether they employed cold-calling. One section did not use cold-calling; the rest used some combination of cold-calling and voluntary questioning—the percentage of students cold-called per section ranged from 0 to 84 percent, with an overall mean of 26 percent. Instructors were grouped as being either high (5 instructors) or low (11 instructors) cold-calling. The mean percentage of students cold-called in the "high" group was 61 percent (33–84%) compared with 10 percent (0–24%) in the low cold-call group (Dallimore et al., 2012).

7. A quasi-experimental research design was employed, gathering both observational and survey data from students. The course was a required undergraduate managerial accounting course and each section had roughly forty students. All seven instructors were experienced and noted for their ability to provide a supportive classroom environment. All had received high ratings of effectiveness and "treats students with respect" on course evaluations (Dallimore et al., 2019).

8. Minerva Schools at KGI undergraduate end-of-semester course/instructor surveys (2016–2020). Reprinted with permission.

9. While this is sometimes highlighted in student course surveys/instructor evaluations, as in the examples included, discussing these questions with students can sometimes provide insight into why they might hold such beliefs. In the case of cold-calling "keeping students on their toes" this can sometimes be driven by a strict sense of fairness (e.g., "I put in X hours preparing for class—my peers should be held accountable to the same standard"). While preparation is important for all students to undertake, students may quickly judge a lack of understanding as a lack of preparation or attention and expect the instructor to act as a source of enforcement.

10. Minerva Schools at KGI undergraduate end-of-semester course/instructor surveys (2016–2020). Reprinted with permission.

11. Here "quality" is taken to mean a discussion that represents multiple perspectives and surfaces a breadth of questions or considerations.

12. This explanation is suggested by the authors (Dallimore et al., 2012), but also identified in the broader cold-calling literature and supported by forthcoming research.

13. While not widely investigated, see distributions identified in England et al. (2017) who note that 16 percent of students reported moderately high classroom

anxiety. Bowers (1986) found 8.5 percent of all undergraduate students in their study reported classroom communication apprehension that they rated as 5 or higher on a scale from 1 (very mild) to 7 (very severe); 27 percent of their entire sampled population reported experiencing physical symptoms of anxiety in the classroom. McCroskey's study of 20,000 U.S. college students in the 1970s described 15–20 percent as experiencing debilitating communication apprehension (1977).

14. Engagement tasks that are not the focus of class activity (such as think-pair-share or peer instructors) must be used carefully to avoid interfering with students' natural ways of thinking and reflection. Examples of engagement tasks include creating a diagram or mind map, tracking arguments or "score-keeping," voting, working on an example analysis as concepts are explained, or preparing to respond to a known prompt (e.g., "At the end of the [discussion/example], be ready to . . .).

15. Minerva Schools at KGI undergraduate end-of-semester course/instructor surveys (2016–2020). Reprinted with permission.

Chapter 9

Silence Is Golden

Keeping a Handle on "Prof Talk" in the Classroom

Instructor initiation: student response: instructor evaluation (IRE) is a three-part sequence that traditionally provided the fundamental structure of the interactive classroom dynamic (Mehan, 1978). While the sequence may have some variation, particularly the nature of the instructor "evaluation," it is the most common model of instructor-student interaction (Cairns, 2006).

Previous chapters discuss both instructor-driven aspects of the interaction, namely, the form of the initiating question and the evaluative/nonevaluative response repertoire. An instructor can also reflect on the *frequency* and *duration* of this pattern of interaction in their classrooms. Two simple questions provide a basis for self-reflection:

• How frequently do you comment after student contributions?
• Why this frequency?

Identifying the underlying reasons is challenging, but several common patterns of behavior provide a clue: Is it to offer evaluation? Express appreciation? Paraphrase or extend the student's point? Offer your perspective in a "mini-lecture" or short monologue?

Bursts of "prof talk" are a common occurrence, even in a classroom that has moved beyond a dynamic focused on the instructor as the source of immediate "right answers." While most instructors aim to keep track of the balance of talk-time between students, they should also carefully consider the frequency and duration of their own contributions. This is particularly relevant when the tendency to respond to every students' contribution becomes a *habit*, which in turn begins to dominate the classroom dynamic.

The distinction between *intentional* and *habitual* behavior on the part of the instructor differentiates productive and unproductive "prof talk." Here, prof talk is defined as an instructor contribution of medium or longer duration (from around 10 seconds to more than several minutes).[1]

HABITUAL PROF TALK

Bursts of prof talk often come from good intentions: wanting to convey excitement and interest in the students' ideas, wanting to help students understand the depth underlying their contributions, wanting to add a perspective that only comes from experience. These intentions can lead to four common behaviors becoming habitual, each of which can consume a considerable amount of talk-time:

- Prolonged paraphrasing
- Offering the instructor's perspective
- Anecdote over-sharing
- "Helpful" additions

Prolonged paraphrasing takes hold when the instructor fails to differentiate between instances where extended paraphrasing is additive, such as playing back or clarifying a complex point, and situations where an abbreviated paraphrase would be sufficient. This can also lead to a tendency for *every* contribution to be paraphrased, even when no longer additive to the dynamic. Consider how this can sound in practice:

- Student contribution: "The primary conflict in this case is between respect for individual rights and collective utility. Here, the government is prioritizing utility for society as a whole over individual rights. This is signaled when the state talks about measures to 'prevent unauthorized demonstrations,' which is an individual's freedom to assemble, in order to 'maintain good order,' which is how they are defining utility in this context. I guess this idea of utilitarianism could be considered more aligned with Bentham than Mill, given that liberties are constrained."
- Prolonged paraphrase: "Utility for society, described as maintaining order, at the expense of rights of an individual, indicated by ideas such as one's freedom to assemble. With a note that this is a conception of utility that need not respect individual liberties, and thus more of a Benthamite approach. What rationale could underlie this decision?"
- Abbreviated paraphrase: "Utility for society at the expense of individual rights. What rationale could underlie this decision?"

A desire to respect every contribution to the discussion *by giving it equal attention from the instructor* makes this type of prof talk proliferate. Some instructors, at least initially, describe experiencing discomfort at spending more time paraphrasing some contributions. When this becomes a pattern such that the instructor's response is of similar length to the student's contribution, it results in the instructor unduly dominating the discussion.

The above example featured a rather in-depth initial contribution. What about when a student struggles to make a contribution to the discussion? In wanting to promote psychological safety (by treating every contribution as valued), move the discussion along, and help a student convey the depth of their thinking, many professors will offer a prolonged or sympathetic paraphrase:

- Student contribution: "There's the individual and their group of friends, which kind of shapes their motivation to behave in certain ways, I guess . . . But they contribute to the group too, because they are part of it." [Uncertain tone of voice]
- Instructor: "I can hear you articulating two levels of analysis, individual and group, and when you say "shapes" it calls out an interaction between levels: how individuals both *shape* and *are shaped by* their group norms and dynamics. Such interactions are very relevant to social science."

In some cases, it is as simple as inserting a piece of technical or difficult-to-pronounce terminology; in others, it becomes a more detailed elaboration intended to highlight points of insight. While well intentioned, and in some cases wholly appropriate when working with students who are less confident or struggling, sympathetic paraphrasing can become problematic when it becomes a pattern where the instructor is

- prioritizing the pace of discussion over student-driven clarification or critical thinking;
- taking more ownership of the idea than the original student;
- turning it into something not recognizable as grounded in the initial contribution; or
- casting oneself in the role of savior of all contributions.

The final pitfall, becoming the regular "savior" of student contributions, is a particularly challenging dynamic to break once an instructor slips into that role. In some cases, particularly when students are getting used to finding their voice in the classroom or content is technically challenging, some intentional and targeted sympathetic paraphrasing is very helpful. In doing so, however, an instructor must take care not to develop a habitual response of *over*-paraphrasing every "weak" contribution.

Consider the second type of prof talk: offering the instructor's perspective. For an instructor, offering their perspective can also be a form of expressing enthusiasm for both the topic and student's contribution. Consider again the previous example:

- Student contribution: "The primary conflict in this case is between respect for individual rights and collective utility. Here, the government is prioritizing utility for society as a whole over individual rights. This is signaled when the state talks about measures to 'prevent unauthorized demonstrations,' which is an individual's freedom to assemble, in order to 'maintain good order,' which is how they are defining utility in this context. I guess this idea of utilitarianism could be considered more aligned with Bentham than Mill, given that liberties are constrained."
- Instructor perspective: "Utility for society at the expense of individual rights. This is a common ethical conflict to encounter in examples across this course, and one we will all want to be aware of. I appreciate you highlighting it. In the context of government, it is a particularly salient tension. What rationale could underlie this decision?"

Again, best intentions drive this burst of prof talk. The instructor is genuinely delighted that the student has identified a key issue and wishes to highlight it so everyone can identify the theme in the future. The valence of such responses is impactful: When the instructor's perspective aligns with the student, it can become a form of positive reinforcement (or reward). If the instructor were to disagree while displaying a negative affect, it could be interpreted by students as a form of social punishment, and thus diminish psychological safety.

Most instructors who offer their perspective as a *habitual* pattern of behavior tend to highlight the positives in the student's contribution, or what they personally find insightful. Although experienced positively, the instructor's response typically becomes as long as, if not longer than, the student's initial contribution. This duration alone gives the instructor the dominant role in shaping the discussion.

Relationship building drives the third form of prof talk. Every instructor makes a deliberate choice regarding the depth of personal opinions and experiences they share with their classroom. These anecdotes are often positively received by students, so the tendency to overshare is strong. Consider several avenues for a personal anecdote to creep into the previous interaction, given the same student contribution as before:

- "Utility for society at the expense of individual rights. When I was an undergraduate student, about your age, there were protests on my college campus and we . . ."
- "Utility for society at the expense of individual rights. This is a common conflict, and was a theme I encountered when I was writing my thesis . . ."

- "Utility for society at the expense of individual rights. It reminds me of when . . ."

Given the positive contribution of the instructor-student relationship to the dynamic, anecdotes are not entirely inappropriate. They humanize the instructor, demonstrate interest in the topic, and provide context and framing that is both salient and memorable. Again, as anecdotes are often not a brief contribution, the instructor should consider whether they will obscure the previous (student's) point and whether every class discussion tends to turn into more of a storytelling hour on the part of the instructor.

Helpful additions, the fourth form of prof talk, occur when the instructor feels a need to add information that the students *could not know* on their own. For example,

- "You mentioned freedom to assemble as a facet of individual rights. This is related to Rawls' idea of 'equal basic political liberties.' In his seminal work, Rawls suggested . . ."

These additions are particularly common when students are just scratching the surface of a given topic, and the instructor is aware of subtleties, recent research, and further directions. Again, while some inclusion of such remarks can be additive, the temptation to share a piece of information for every contribution can become a dominating force in the instructor's response repertoire.

A significant mode of extended prof talk under the umbrella of helpful additions is the *proactive management of common confusions*, where an instructor's familiarity with a given subject means they attempt to prevent a misunderstanding or confusion *before* it can fully arise in the group discussion. This becomes particularly common when an instructor has previously taught a given course, and has, to some extent, "seen it all before."

The particularly challenging aspect of this dynamic is that a response that is wholly *authentic* to the instructor ("Aha! They are about to mistake correlation for causation in this context! I'd better warn them about that") can be perceived as *inauthentic* on the part of the students when inserted proactively into the discussion. Rather than experience the intervention as helpful, they may instead feel the instructor is making a hasty generalization ("But *we* never claimed it's causation!") or simply not find the point memorable without grounding in the *actual* class discussion.

INTENTIONAL PROF TALK

Not all prof talk detracts from the student-driven discussion, and none of the above need be dissuaded entirely. Instead, an instructor should examine when they are engaging in each type, and how frequently they are making substantial contributions to the discussion. Productive prof talk can include the above (in moderation), in addition to the following:

- Essential clarifications—given that some ideas can take a few tries to understand, offering an analogy or alternate description may be necessary
- Future directions—highlighting current trends in a given discipline, or avenues of investigation that the instructor finds particularly compelling.
- Avenues for further engagement—sharing how students can engage with this further, either in their studies or avenues outside of the classroom.
- Highly discipline-specific factors—noting what is particularly important given the nature of the discipline. This can include highlighting seminal ideas, significant debates, and proponents of particular schools of thought.

Recognizing that not all prolonged prof talk is negative, the instructor needs to be mindful of their *relative volume* and *pattern* of prof talk, and ensure they are not

- taking an overly dominant role in the discussion due to their talk-time relative to students;
- fostering a call-and-respond dynamic, where the instructor heavily mediates *every* contribution; or
- falling back on an exhaustively predictable pattern, such as too many personal anecdotes.

Productive prof talk can also relate to the overall power dynamic of the classroom, with relationship building typically relying on some measure of sharing on the part of the instructor.

Similarly, student perceptions of an instructor's charisma significantly shape how they experience prof talk, running a gamut from "painful anecdotes" or "trying too hard" to "unique experiences" or "awesome insights."

STUDENT PERCEPTIONS OF PROF TALK

How do students experience prof talk in the classroom? Deslauriers et al. explored students' self-reported *perceptions of learning* versus *evaluated outcomes* in an introductory physics course taught with either active learning or lecture-based pedagogy (2019). Interestingly, while students had a generally positive perception of the active learning environment, they rated their perceived learning lower than their peers in the passive (lecture) environment. Quantitative analysis of outcomes did not support this perception.

Instead, students demonstrated greater understanding in the active learning environment.

The authors note repeated studies have demonstrated improved student learning outcomes in active learning environments, despite the widespread use of lecturing.[2] To reconcile student perceptions with the quantitative evidence, Deslauriers et al. suggest that students may interpret the increased cognitive effort demanded by active pedagogy as a sign of inferior learning.

This previous research tends to take an all-or-nothing approach, that is, contrasting a lecture with active learning. Yet, similar student perceptions of the benefit of instructor talk-time appear to apply *within* interactive classrooms. Instructors often anecdotally report a positive response to their contributions, and students highlight them as a positive feature in course or instructor evaluations.

When asked to give an example of something their instructor does well, first-year undergraduate students in a social science course delivered via active learning responded:[3]

- "[The instructor] clearly reiterates a point made by a student and adds more to it, giving relevant examples, which makes it easy to understand. [The instructor] is also very jovial, which lightens the mood and makes learning fun."
- [The instructor] does a great job of taking each student's points and identifying the value in them. When students say their points, and it may not be particularly articulated well, [the instructor] expands on it, bringing clarity for the class and taking the student's point to another level. Really confidence boosting, and I think a great way of making each student feel valuable in class and be more willing to make contributions, even if the point is a little risky."
- "[The instructor's] discussions, questions, and clarification just make me understand each and every part of the [course concepts]."
- "[The instructor] somehow turns my half-insightful comment into a fully insightful comment when she summarises it—I REALLY want to learn this art from [the instructor]."
- "I love when [the instructor] shares [their] own experience with the subject, a personal twist in classes are always nice."
- "It is clear that [the instructor] pays attention to what people are saying, summarizing important points."

All of these responses highlight facets of prof talk, including sympathetic paraphrasing, clarifications, instructor perspectives, anecdotes, and helpful additions.

Given the power dynamics of the classroom, students who focus on the instructor as the direct source of expertise and evaluation can react negatively to active learning techniques that limit prof talk. Students expecting an IRE dynamic may feel the instructor is deliberately withholding something they deserve (immediate and direct response). This is particularly common if students are still becoming accustomed to how a given instructor uses prof talk to manage confusion in the classroom, such as through summative feedback rather than immediate intervention.

When asked how their instructors could improve, the same group of students responded:

- "Directly answer the additional questions asked in class since sometimes I didn't feel that I got the answer to what I asked."
- "I think it would be better if [the instructor] could correct us when we are wrong, because many times when an incorrect answer was not responded to it just confused me."
- "Don't redirect the questions that were directed to the professor to other students. In such situations, I really want to hear the professor's answer."
- "[Name] likes to ask the question 'What do you think?,' and it really confuses me a lot. My opinion is that the question should either be specific or not asked at all. Because when [professor] asks me 'what do I think' in the first class, I usually think that I want to sleep. However, this thought is not really related to the topic of discussion, so I need to think quickly about something else, and my response cannot adequately contribute to the discussion. I am pretty sure I am not the only one who thinks like this."
- "Provide more useful corrections in class during discussions, or perhaps clear up misunderstandings after the discussion."

Interpreting such student feedback is challenging. While some comments do suggest areas where the instructors may wish to change their behavior (clearing up misunderstandings after the discussion), others may represent an effective use of active learning (redirecting questions to other students; asking a student what they think).

For students who are more used to a traditional lecture-based dynamic, offering framing of the approach or explaining *why* an interactive environment is going to be different may be critical. This framing can take place at the outset of a course, with reference to research related to the science of learning and active versus passive environments, but also reinforced over time as a norm. This should set clear expectations about the role of prof talk in the classroom, and help students understand when and how clarification or the instructor's perspective will be offered (or not). Examples of ongoing framing in-class include the following:

- "I'll try to keep this clarification short . . ."
- "I've been talking far too much now! Let's get back to *your* understanding of this . . ."

- "I'm going to step back so you can discuss directly, but you can always 'call on me' if stuck or quite confused . . ."
- "Let's see if we can get a few perspectives on the table, do some analysis, and then summarize. I will help check we haven't missed anything from the literature as we conclude."

Statements such as the above convey intentionality behind the way the instructor is engaging in the discussion. This is essential context and reinforces norms about active learning and student participation discussed at the outset of the course.

PROF TALK AND THE SCIENCE OF LEARNING

While the benefits of active learning are widely touted, one study of introductory biology classes across seventy-seven colleges and universities had a surprising outcome: no association between student learning gains and the use of active learning instruction (Andrews et al., 2011). The authors interpreted this as a problem putting theory into practice:

> We contend that most instructors lack the rich and nuanced understanding of teaching and learning that science education researchers have developed. Therefore, active learning as designed and implemented by typical college biology instructors may superficially resemble active learning used by education researchers, but lacks the constructivist elements necessary for improving learning. (Andrews et al., 2011, p. 394)

This lack of understanding of the cognitive processes that underlie learning and memory, particularly in the context of active learning, is widespread. Indeed, a literature review found the majority of forty-eight relevant teacher-training textbooks did not mention cognitive strategies related to the science of learning (Pomerance et al., 2016).

In an extensive review of learning techniques, Dunlosky et al. (2013) found positive outcomes associated with a variety of approaches, driven by both the student (e.g., self-explanation) and the instructor (e.g., instructor-led interleaved practice). Weinstein et al. describe six common learning strategies (2018):

- Retrieval practice: repeatedly testing memory of a given concept.
- Spaced practice: distributing instances of engaging with a concept.
- Interleaving: switching between concepts and making new connections between them.
- Elaboration: explaining or extending concepts.

- Concrete examples: creating specific examples, particularly of abstract concepts.
- Dual coding: integrating multiple modalities, such as words and pictures in a diagram or mind-map.

Importantly, active learning can employ all of these techniques, yet excessive prof talk risks diminishing their effectiveness. The reason for this lies in the difference between being a passive recipient of information transmission and a cognitively engaged learner.

This cognitive engagement is summarized by two maxims that sit above sixteen principles of learning and memory (Kosslyn, 2017, p. 152 and 153).

- Maxim 1: Think it through.
- Maxim 2: Make and use associations.

Both of these maxims capture cognitive engagement on the part of a student. There is a significant difference between prof talk that aids students in pursuing these activities and prof talk that forestalls or interferes with this taking place. In general, the *more* an instructor speaks, the *less likely* they are leaving room for students to grapple with an idea. This room to think is critical: to practice retrieval, test understanding, elaborate a concept, make associations, and generate examples. Prof talk, no matter how well intentioned, can't do this *for* a student in a way that is sufficiently cognitively engaging.

DELIBERATE SILENCE: THE IMPORTANCE OF WAIT TIME AND PAUSING IN THE CLASSROOM

Building on the previous discussion of wait time (chapter 8), instructors need to understand the role of silence in their classrooms. Without training, an instructor typically allows roughly one second for a student to begin to respond to a question (Rowe, 1972, 1974).[4] If the student does not initiate a response, the instructor will repeat, rephrase, ask a different question, or call on another student. When a student does respond, the instructor will typically begin to comment on the response, ask another question, or move to a new topic within less than a second (Rowe, 1972).

In an IRE interaction, first and second wait times are present at the following points:

- Instructor initiates with a question and the first wait time begins; typically ~1 second unless trained to wait appropriately (Rowe, 1974).

- *Wait time I* ends when the instructor intervenes to restate the question, rephrase the question, or ask another student (alternatively, the student responds).
- *Wait time II* begins when a student completes their response; typically ~0.9 seconds unless trained to wait appropriately (Rowe, 1974). This wait time ends when the instructor reacts (comments or evaluates), asks a follow-up question, or moves to a new topic.

Most instructors are initially deeply uncomfortable with silence in their classrooms. Yet deliberately increasing wait time to 3 to 5 seconds has a significant impact[5] on student behavior in the classroom (Rowe, 1972, 1974, 1978, 1986):

- Student responses are longer.
- Student responses are more complex.
- More students volunteer to answer and have meaningful contributions.
- Students offer more speculative or inference-based contributions.
- Students propose more experiments or hypotheses.
- Students ask more questions.
- More students engage with each other's ideas directly.
- Student confidence increases.[6]
- Student restlessness and inattentiveness decrease.
- Students previously identified as "quiet" spontaneously speak more.
- The number of students responding "I don't know" or refusing to answer declines.
- Achievement improves on cognitively complex written measures of performance or understanding.

Instructor behaviors also change as wait time increases, positively affecting both the classroom dynamic and student learning (Rowe, 1972, 1986):

- The instructor response repertoire becomes more varied and flexible.
- Instructors ask more cognitively engaging questions.
- Instructors speak less as an overall proportion of class talk-time.
- Instructor-centered "show and tell" decreases and student-student engagement increases.
- Preconceived expectations for "low-achieving" or "quiet" students improve.

Preconceptions of students have a critical impact on classroom facilitation. Without training, instructors allow significantly more wait time for students they perceive as high-achieving (2 seconds versus 0.9 seconds for low-achieving students) (Rowe, 1974, 1978, 1996). This creates a systemic unfairness and a self-fulfilling prophecy, handicapping students who might otherwise be able to make an effective contribution.

The second wait time, ending when the instructor responds to the student contribution, is more likely to be rushed. While this wait time is critical thinking time for the instructor, it is also essential *articulation* time for the student.

A student articulating a complex thought will speak dysfluently—in short bursts that can be up to several seconds apart. A rapid reaction from the instructor is likely to occur during one of these gaps, cutting off or attenuating the student contribution rather than allowing them to finish (Rowe, 1980).

Beyond the frequency and depth of each contribution, the average duration of wait time significantly shapes the classroom dynamic. Rowe describes a game model of the classroom, where the instructor and students are players and four "moves" exist (1986, p. 46):

1. Structuring: giving directions, stating procedures, suggesting changes.
2. Soliciting: asking questions.
3. Responding: answering solicitations, expanding on a structuring move, reporting data, or continuing a line of reasoning.
4. Reacting: evaluating statements made by self or others.

In a classroom dynamic with a short average wait time, the instructor engages in structuring, soliciting, and reacting; the students are left only to respond. When the average wait time increases to 3 seconds, students engage in all four moves. Opening all the moves to all the players makes for a more positive classroom dynamic.

Wait time also interacts with habitual prof talk and evaluative responses. An instructor who frequently repeats student contributions, either in full or in part, is unlikely to include sufficient wait time. The broader impact of this "mimicry dynamic" becomes apparent when an instructor attempts to modify this behavior:

> An anecdote illustrates the unintended consequences of a mimicry pattern. In a classroom where the teacher was changing this pattern in order to increase [the second] wait time, one of the students asked, "Mrs. B. how come you are not repeating things any more?" Before she could reply, another student answered the question. "I know. She knows that we can tell from the tone of her voice which answers she likes and which she doesn't, and we can stop thinking." There are other verbal signals to consider avoiding or reducing in conjunction with wait time, e.g., "Yes . . . but . . ." and ". . . though" constructions because they signal the student that an idea is about to be rejected without the consideration due it. (Rowe, 1986, p. 46)

INCORPORATING PAUSING AND WAITING

Modifying wait time behavior is challenging and time-intensive for an instructor—typically requiring deliberate practice and external feedback to be effective (Rowe, 1986).

Ingram and Elliott elaborated Rowe's (1972) characterization of first and second wait times to highlight four distinct subtypes captured in the original theory (Ingram & Elliott, 2014, 2016):

- Wait time I(i): pause following the instructor finishing speaking and a student starting to speak.
- Wait time I(ii): pause following the instructor finishing speaking and then taking the next turn.
- Wait time II(i): pause following a student finishing speaking and the instructor taking the next turn.
- Wait time II(ii): pause following a student [initially] finishing speaking and then continuing their turn.

Such pauses are critical, yet instructors should approach extended wait time with sensitivity and framing. Wait time I conveys the importance of thinking time in general, as well as a willingness to allow a specific student to formulate a considered response. However, overly extended wait time I for simple questions may lead to impatience on the part of students accustomed to responding quickly (Kirton et al., 2007) or attentional lapses.

A study of lecture-based college science classes suggests an optimal wait time of 4 to 6 seconds (Larson & Lovelace, 2013), with instructor discretion given the type of question, specific context, or student composition of the class.

In addition to the impact on instructor and student behavior described by Rowe and colleagues, insufficient wait time II may also suggest a negative judgment. Verbal intervention in the classroom, even if intended to promote metacognition, "may be interpreted to mean that the path selected is indeed wrong—simply because of a belief that the teacher would not say anything if one were on the 'right' path' " (Lesh & Zawojewski, 2007).

While wait time describes the use of silence within interactions, pausing can structure the overall pace of information transmission or discussion.

Rowe identified four types of "mental lapses" that will affect even a dedicated student in a lecture with complex content (Rowe, 1976, 1980, 1983):

1. Overloaded working memory, where there are too many new concepts to integrate while the lecture continues.

2. Sense-making, where the student needs time to make sense of the new material, effectively relate it to existing knowledge, and scaffold it in long-term memory.
3. Unrecognized context shift, where symbols or concepts from one context are used differently in another.
4. Diverted attention, including when the lecture sparks a complementary train of thought.

To mitigate the impact of these lapses, Rowe proposes the Pausing Principle. In a college classroom, faculty should lecture for roughly 10 minutes, then pause for 2. In a high school classroom, the ratio is 8:2. Critically, this pause is not a time to field questions. Instead, Rowe instructs students to share notes and discuss their current understanding in groups of three.

While all three students will have experienced lapses, these lapses will likely have occurred at different times. While the information overlap between students can vary significantly, groups of three are usually sufficient to fill in the gaps and collectively resolve confusion. Questions reserved for *after* the pause are usually clear and pointed. This form of pausing has a positive impact on learning, test performance, and long-term retention in lecture-based science courses (Rowe, 1983).

Specific active learning activities deliberately incorporate pausing and promote wait time. For example, Rowe's Pausing Principle can also be used to create opportunities for a *ConcepTest* (Mazur, 1997) or a "One-Minute Paper" (Stead, 2005). Wait time can be created with "Multiple Hands, Multiple Voices," where the instructor poses a question and asserts, "I'm going to wait until I see hands from five [pick a number appropriate for your setting] volunteers before we hear an idea from anyone" (Allen & Tanner, 2002). These approaches can also be deliberately integrated with approaches from the science of learning, such as pausing to allow students to generate a novel example or add to a mind-map.

SELF-EVALUATION AND NEXT STEPS

Prof Talk Self-Assessment and Reflection

Reflect on a recent class (or take a tally sheet into class with you) and determine your general pattern of prof talk.

Do you tend to speak after student contributions, *beyond* what would be needed to drive the discussion forward (i.e., beyond briefly clarifying, posing a follow-up question, or inviting another contribution)?

- *If so*, why do you do this? Given the considerations described above, are you engaging in habitual prof talk?

- *If not*, roughly how frequently are you speaking? Could some further prof talk be additive to clarify complex points; include memorable examples; build relationships with students; or provide additional context related to the discipline more broadly?

When you do engage in prof talk, use a tally sheet to identify the relative frequency of different forms:

- _____ Prolonged paraphrasing
- _____ Instructor's perspective
- _____ Anecdote sharing
- _____ "Helpful" additions
- _____ Clarifications or discipline-specific explanation
- _____ Future directions or avenues for further engagement
- _____Other

Reflect on the impact of your contributions. When did your prof talk *facilitate* cognitive engagement by students (i.e., practicing retrieval, thinking it through, or making and using associations)? When did your prof talk *forestall or diminish* an opportunity for cognitive engagement by students?

Given the above, in what way might you want to try changing how you engage in prof talk?

Wait Time Self-Assessment and Reflection

Effective characterization of wait time is challenging without the ability to automate the measurement of pause durations. To create a general understanding of your teaching practice, make an audio recording of a class and use a tally sheet to *very roughly* note the number of:

Pauses between finishing a question and calling on a student, for example, "Solve for x . . . [Student]."

- Less than 3 seconds long _____
- More than 3 seconds long _____

Pauses between you finishing speaking and a student starting to speak, that is, the duration of wait time students are taking in your classroom, when allowed.

- Less than 3 seconds long _____
- More than 3 seconds long _____

Pauses between when you call on a student and then intervene before they answer, for example, to restate the question, rephrase the question, or call on another student.

- Less than 3 seconds long _____
- More than 3 seconds long _____

Pauses between when a student stops speaking and you speak next.

- Less than 3 seconds long _____
- More than 3 seconds long _____

If possible, pauses where a student appears to hesitate or finish speaking, but then continues. This is challenging to log but even a subset of responses is informative. Understanding your students' speech dysfluencies will reduce the frequency with which you cut them off before they are done.

- Less than 3 seconds long _____
- More than 3 seconds long _____

Things to Try

To Promote Extended Wait Time and Pausing

Extending wait time takes deliberate practice and persistence. An instructor attempting to change this behavior will need to monitor their use of wait time over an extended period. It is not uncommon for an instructor to revert to previously habitual patterns of short wait time (Rowe, 1986).

Review the initial assessment and attempt to characterize your use of wait time: How frequently are you likely to be offering sufficient versus insufficient wait time? How often are you likely to be interrupting students while they are thinking? How frequently might you be cutting off students who would otherwise continue to articulate an idea? Attempt to change these behaviors and periodically check-in with the self-assessment checklist or similar approach to quantifying classroom wait time.

If working from a detailed lesson plan or lecture notes, identify several complex or cognitively demanding questions that would benefit from extended wait time. When asking these questions in class, silently count to 4 to 6 seconds to promote adequate wait time (using fingers behind your back if necessary). Consider incorporating pausing or wait-time-promoting activities or prompts, such as the Pausing Principle or "Multiple Hands, Multiple Voices," in the lesson plan.

If you identified yourself as an excessive prof-talker, use the questions below to reflect on your pattern of prof talk and consider how you might wish to change your behavior.

- What is your desired amount of prof talk? Consider how prof talk can help or hinder the dynamic and learning in your particular classroom and try setting yourself a target.
- Can you identify specific circumstances that trigger your engagement in prof talk, and determine specific strategies to mitigate it? For example, "I tend to jump in when the class is hesitant to speak, particularly in response to another student's question." Reframe this as an opportunity to practice *wait time*. Write a note on the top of your lesson plan to remind yourself that pauses often *feel* longer than they actually are.
- How can you modify your response repertoire to include more deliberate redirects to students or abbreviated paraphrasing? Some instructors might even write themselves a few reminders of target behavior on the lesson plan itself ("Keep it short!" or "Pivot!" [to students]).
- How will you keep yourself on track in the future? Some instructors might keep a tally sheet next to their notes, and simply put a mark down each time they engage in prof talk (an ambitious instructor might even have columns for different types of prof talk). This can help the instructor keep track of their talk-time during class, and also provide some concrete data for reflection.
- How will you review whether your target amount of prof talk is appropriate? Some instructors might set a plan to review their pattern of prof talk after X weeks, either independently, with another instructor familiar with the challenge, or even directly with students.

If you identified yourself as a highly infrequent prof-talker and believe more could be additive, use the questions below to reflect on your pattern of prof talk and consider how you might wish to change your behavior.

- Can you identify specific circumstances that could trigger positive prof talk, and determine strategies to promote it? For example, "I'd like the students to get to know me a little more and share some anecdotes from my research and interests. This could give them some discipline-specific associations to understand the course content more deeply." After preparing for a given class, take ten minutes to reflect on where you might have personal experience that could be of interest. Jot these ideas down in the margins of the lesson plan, to be used if additive in the natural flow of discussion.
- How will you experiment effectively with prof talk? Some instructors might approach a given class session with the intent to offer one or two instances of specific kinds of prof talk. Others might keep a tally sheet and simply mark down when they catch themselves engaging in a particular

type of prof talk. This can help the instructor keep track of their talk-time during class, and provide some concrete data for reflection.

- How will you review whether your intended behavioral change has been effective? Could it be reflected in comments on instructor/course evaluations? Could you ask a colleague or teaching assistant to sit-in on a class and listen for instances of prof talk? Could you ask students to comment?

If you identified yourself as engaging in roughly the "right" amount of prof talk, use the following questions to reflect on your behavior:

- Can you examine your pattern of prof talk in more detail? What specific factors drive or trigger bursts of prof talk? What positive outcomes are enabled by your contributions? Some instructors might try keeping a tally sheet of the different kinds of prof talk they find themselves engaging in and reflect on this aspect of the dynamic in more detail.
- How does your use of prof talk compare to other instructors in your discipline? Can you sit-in on another instructor's class and track the frequency and type of their prof talk? How is their approach similar to yours? How different? What outcomes seem related to the similarities? To the differences?
- How can you be confident your prof talk is additive to the class dynamic? Do you see it referenced in course/instructor evaluations? Have students mentioned your contributions directly in conversation or when completing deliverables?

Three Points to Remember about Prof Talk

- Good intentions often drive prof talk, but it can become habitual and dominate talk-time and the overall classroom dynamic. Intentional prof talk can build relationships between the instructor and students, highlight points related to discipline-specific expertise, or promote students making and using associations in a manner supported by the science of learning.
- Students may believe they are learning more effectively in an environment with a high degree of lecturing, even though outcomes do not support that belief.
- Adequate wait time and pausing are critical for effective learning, engagement, and the classroom dynamic.

NOTES

1. While this does depend on speaking speed, at a reasonable rate, "Tell me more," takes fewer than 2 seconds to deliver. Ten seconds is typically a duration that will include a paraphrase or opinion.
2. In the domain of physics alone, Deslauriers et al. (2019) highlight:

Crouch, C. H., & Mazur, E. (2001). Peer instruction: Ten years of experience and results. *American Journal of Physics,* 69(9): 970–977.

Deslauriers, L., & Wieman, C. (2011). Learning and retention of quantum concepts with different teaching methods. *Physical Review Special Topics—Physics Education Research,* 7: 1–6.

Deslauriers, L., Schelew, E., & Wieman, C. (2011). Improved learning in a large-enrollment physics class. *Science,* 332(6031): 862–864.

Fraser, J. M., Timan, A. L., Miller, K., Dowd, J. E., Tucker, L., & Mazur, E. (2014). Teaching and physics education research: Bridging the gap. *Reports on Progress in Physics,* 77(3): 1–17.

Freeman, S., Eddy, S. L., McDonough, M., Smith, M. K., Okoroafor, N., Jordt, H., & Wenderoth, M. P. (2014). Active learning increases student performance in science, engineering, and mathematics. *Proceedings of the National Academy of Sciences,* 111(23): 8410–8415.

Hake, R. R. (1998). Interactive-engagement versus traditional methods: A 6,000-student survey of mechanics test data for introductory physics courses. *American Journal of Physics,* 66: 64–74.

Further sources of note include:

Andrews, T. M., Leonard, M. J., Colgrove, C. A., & Kalinowski, S. T. (2011). Active learning not associated with student learning in a random sample of college biology courses. *CBE—Life Sciences Education,* 10: 394–405.

Ballen, C. J., Wieman, C. E., Salehi, S., Searle, J. B., & Zamudio, K. R. (2017). Enhancing diversity in undergraduate science: Self-efficacy drives performance gains with active learning. *CBE—Life Sciences Education,* 16(4): 1–6.

Haak, D. C., HilleRisLambers, J., Pitre, E. & Freeman, S. (2011). Increased structure and active learning reduce the achievement gap in introductory biology. *Science,* 332(6034): 1213–1216.

McCarthy, J. P., & Anderson, L. (2000). Active learning techniques versus traditional teaching styles: Two experiments from history and political science. *Innovative Higher Education,* 24(4): 279–294.

Park, E. L., & Choi, B. K. (2014). Transformation of classroom spaces: Traditional versus active-learning classroom in colleges. *Higher Education,* 68: 749–771.

Prince, M. (2004). Does active learning work? A review of the research. *Journal of Engineering Education,* 93(3): 223–232.

Rocca, K. A. (2010). Student participation in the college classroom: An extended multidisciplinary literature review. *Communication Education,* 59(2): 185–213.

Wieman, C. E. (2014). Large-scale comparison of science teaching methods sends clear message. *Proceedings of the National Academy of Sciences,* 111(23): 8319–8320.

3. Minerva Schools at KGI undergraduate end-of-semester course/instructor surveys (2016–2020). Reprinted with permission.

4. Wait times can vary by context, although Rowe's findings related to wait time duration and impact generally hold across a number of studies (Ingram & Elliott, 2016; Tobin, 1987). In first-year post-secondary language courses, Shrum found average first wait time of 1.91 seconds and average second wait time of 0.73 seconds (1984). In college classes taken by education majors, Duell et al. (1992) found an average first wait time of 2.25 seconds and an average second wait time of 0.45 seconds. College students given unlimited wait time would begin to respond to the instructor's question within 3–5 seconds, but the substantive portion of their response would, on average, begin at around 8s for straightforward questions and around 30s for complex questions (Ellsworth et al., 1991). Ellsworth et al. suggest these "time-filling activities" appear to be a means of gaining additional time to think without being silent—perhaps because students equate silence with appearing unknowledgeable or a risk of the instructor moving to another student.

5. The balance of evidence is strongly supportive of wait time and the positive outcomes described here. One study by Duell (1994) reported no benefit from increasing wait time from 1 to 3 seconds, and diminished high-level attainment when wait time was increased to 6 seconds in a university context (possibly due to an excess of thinking time becoming distracting). The author notes that the study design measured wait time as the duration between the instructor finishing a question and calling on a specific student to respond (rather that the duration between a question ending and a student or instructor speaking); thus, all students in the short wait time treatment may have essentially been taking extended, if not unlimited, wait time. Other critiques of this study highlight the tightly constrained experimental context not being generalizable to actual classroom interactions (Ingram & Elliott, 2014) and investigation of the first, but not second, wait time (Ingram & Elliott, 2016).

6. Increased confidence is indicated by a decrease in inflected responses. Similar to the "uptalk" described in chapter 3, an inflected response conveys uncertainty and a sense of "Is that what you want?" This implicit question mark is also affected by reward or praise: as reward increases the incidence of inflected responses also increases (Rowe, 1972).

Chapter 10

The Bomb Squad

Identifying and Managing Challenging Dynamics

ANXIETY-DRIVEN DISENGAGEMENT

Some students do not participate as frequently as others. A psychologically safe classroom dynamic, collaborative culture, and clear participatory expectations significantly increase participation. Still, an instructor may encounter a perpetually quiet student.

Instructors must be aware of a tendency to personalize this behavior. Examples of common, but highly problematic, interpretations of quiet students include the following:

- They're lazy or generally unprepared for class.
- They don't respect their peers; why do they expect everyone else to contribute to the discussion if they aren't willing to do the same?
- They don't want to be here! This must be an elective or a class they don't want to take. If they cared, they would contribute.
- They either don't like me or don't respect me as an instructor.

These beliefs are particularly pernicious when other students seem very willing to contribute, and the instructor truly believes the classroom offers a high degree of psychological safety.

Some of these beliefs are verifiable. If an instructor believes silence is due to a lack of preparation or inattention, they can gather data to test this assumption. Is the student completing the pre-work or homework? Is the student able to make a meaningful contribution when required, or through other nonverbal or nonpublic avenues? If the instructor feels it is necessary, small changes can incentivize preparation (e.g., pre-work, homework share-outs, low-stakes quizzes, or small group activities).

If silence reflects a learning style focused on introspection and notetaking, instructors can invite summative or reflective contributions.

If silence reflects cultural differences, where the student is unaccustomed to participating in the classroom or being perceived as questioning the instructor, a private conversation may be sufficient to change behavior.

In many cases, however, *persistent* silence is a sign of classroom communication apprehension or anxiety, which is debilitating for a significant minority of students. When the instructor has done everything possible to create a warm climate and a dynamic that fosters engagement, it can be necessary to broach the topic directly and privately with the quiet student.

- Approach the student with empathy and emotional intelligence; do not personalize the behavior.
- Share your observations of their participation and invite them to comment.
- Listen carefully to how they describe the feelings that go along with participating in class, as well as any reasons they highlight for their behavior.
- Explain or reiterate why participation is essential in this context.
- Express your desire to support the student.
- Where possible, suggest specific actions each of you will take to increase participation.

For the student, actions could include a commitment to *try* or raise their hand at least a few times per class. You might also suggest specific ways they can engage with more confidence, such as by posing a question or sharing output from group discussions.

For the instructor, actions could include easing them into participation with thoughtful questioning and ensuring adequate wait time. One can also try to disarm factors that can increase anxiety, such as by discussing the brilliance belief or imposter syndrome with the class as a whole.

It is normal to experience anxiety speaking in class. Instead of simply advising the student to try and "calm down," some attempt to help students reappraise it as "excitement" and a necessary part of the learning process. Most people believe trying to calm down is the most effective way to manage performance anxiety. Yet reappraisal resulted in a more positive subjective experience and increased performance in singing, public speaking, and math (Brooks, 2014). While beneficial, this mitigation strategy does not directly diminish anxiety and may not be significantly effective for students with severe classroom communication apprehension.

While expectations to participate often need to evolve over time, a highly anxious student may initially require a very supportive and low-stakes avenue of engagement. An instructor might say to a student, "Just speak, and don't worry about what you say. This is a chance for you to practice. I won't judge or grade you. *No matter what you say, it will be okay.* If you get stuck, I can help. If you feel like you're rambling or something is unclear, I can paraphrase."

While these strategies are not going to resolve all the challenges of classroom communication apprehension, a highly supportive environment can help anxious students contribute without being paralyzed by their anxiety. Beyond enabling the student to begin to contribute voluntarily, one can expect improved learning outcomes when anxiety related to participation isn't interfering with their thinking during the class session.

Three Points to Remember about Anxiety-Driven Disengagement

- Significant individual differences exist in generalized anxiety and classroom communication apprehension, even in a safe and supportive classroom dynamic.
- Instructors should try to understand quiet students, rather than personalize their behavior or assume it necessarily reflects disinterest or disengagement.
- Rather than simply trying to help a student "calm down," an instructor can suggest reappraisal techniques or create a plan for how the student will more confidently participate in future classes.

POWER, ACADEMIC ENTITLEMENT, AND INSTRUCTIONAL DISSENT

"Teacher authority, in part defined as the right to make these decisions, is so taken for granted that most faculty members no longer recognize the extent to which they direct student learning" (Weimar, 2003, p. 50).

Whether intentionally or not, instructors wield power through a variety of sources. The particular combination employed varies significantly from person to person. Still, some facets will always play a significant role in shaping the level of psychological safety and interpersonal risk present in instructor-student interactions. Consider eight sources of power that shape the classroom dynamic:

- *Social hierarchy*: Here, the roles of the instructor and students come into play, where social expectations would have students defer to the instructor. In a college or university, the instructor's position in the formal and informal hierarchies compounds this effect (e.g., a lecturer versus tenured professor; popular figures on campus).

- *Expertise*: Here, the instructor's credibility as an expert in their field becomes a source of power. Expertise is particularly relevant in an evaluative dynamic. Here, the instructor is the judge of the "right answer" and perceived as being able to speak on behalf of their field.
- *Prestige*: In a university, an instructor's expertise ties to their professional reputation in their field. A strong reputation compounds the power of expertise and can extend perceived cachet to merely being a *student* of that professor. Prestige can also increase the interpersonal risk associated with making a contribution—who dares offer a counterargument against a construct that was *defined* by the professor? Even if the student trusts they won't be subject to punitive evaluation, it raises the perceived risk of making a "dumb point."
- *Evaluation*: The instructor's role as the source of grades adds interpersonal risk. Evaluation encompasses specific judgments or a student's belief an identity of them as an "A student" or a "B student" develops in the classroom.
- *Reward and Punishment*: Beyond formal evaluation, the instructor can also offer praise or criticism, which is particularly salient in a public forum. Even when entirely independent from grading, this plays a significant role in shaping behavior.
- *Recommendation*: Extending the power of evaluation, the instructor may have the ability to shape the career of the student through letters of recommendation or introduction to their professional network. Here, the student is concerned with the instructor's perception of them and the nature of their interpersonal dynamic. In addition to being perceived as intelligent, the student may also wish to come across as personable, diligent, or a hard worker.
- *Charisma*: Instructors perceived as charismatic can use that to shape behavior in the classroom. Instructor charisma is often strongly present in classroom dynamics described as lively, engaging, or upbeat. Students may conform to such a dynamic to avoid sanction from their peers for changing the positive climate. Charismatic instructors who foster an upbeat dynamic may wish to consider whether students feel comfortable shifting to serious issues or slowing the pace of engagement.
- *Relationships*: Similarly, an empathic relationship with students valued as individuals will further shape the dynamic of the classroom.

While it is possible to cultivate some of these sources of power, others are inherently a part of the instructor's background and the current context. Reflecting on these sources of power can offer insight into what is available for a given instructor and suggest constraints when comparing "what works" from one instructor to another. Even sources of "positive" power, such as relationships, can nonetheless introduce interpersonal risk if the student doesn't want to disappoint the professor.

As an example, consider three hypothetical instructors and the sources of power available to them:

- A senior tenured faculty member with a high-profile publication history.
- A junior tenure-track professor with a new research lab.
- A graduate student teaching a class under the direction of a supervisor.

The Senior Instructor

For the senior faculty member, social hierarchy, expertise, and prestige, reinforced by the power of recommendation, provide an immediate platform for this individual. Evaluation and reward and punishment will be highly salient and typically go unquestioned. Students perceive this instructor as experienced at assessing contributions and wholly familiar with "what good looks like" in the field. Charisma is appreciated if present (reinforcing the social hierarchy) and often forgiven if absent. The power of relationships is enhanced by student perceptions that these instructors are highly selective, for example, "They have time for me even though they are so important!"

This instructor will be considered credible *even before* setting foot in the classroom, despite students not having firsthand experience of the instructor's trustworthiness, caring, or competence. Students will tend to be more trusting that course content is well chosen for the field, and that the instructor's teaching style is appropriate to the discipline. Where particularly prized, such as in courses or subjects with a reputation for being hard, students are likely to believe they are being challenged and subjected to a particularly rigorous education. Simply being a student of this particular instructor becomes a source of pride and prestige.

The Junior Instructor

The junior tenure-track professor with a new research lab will have a somewhat different platform of power. Their expertise will likely command some respect, as students may recognize the success inherent in having reached the level of leading a research group. The evaluation provided by this instructor is likely to be taken seriously; however, it may not go unquestioned. While the senior professor could fall back on something along the lines of "You have a B+ because that's my professional judgment," more junior faculty feel compelled to provide further justification for their evaluations.

Reward and punishment are likely strongest when delivered socially (rather than simply written praise on an assignment, which would be a more significant ego-boost from a senior faculty member).

The power of recommendation is intermediate. Many students will recognize that a reference letter from this instructor will not carry the same degree of weight as one from a more senior professor. However, students may also feel that instructors at this level are more relatable and able to comment on them as a person. The fact that this individual has a research group of their own will be important through the lens of recommendation: perhaps the instructor can offer opportunities or an introduction within their professional network.

Charisma can be enhanced when the instructor is relatively young, and often leads to students considering them more interpersonally approachable than a senior professor. It's not uncommon for a social hierarchy to form around younger instructors, with students responding strongly to social sources of power. This further drives the power of relationships in this context, although extending oneself in this way may be more *expected* by students than with more senior instructors.

Consider the kinds of factors students reel off first when asked to describe younger instructors: is it that they are a great researcher? Intelligent? Insightful? Or is it more along the lines of, "They're really *nice*."

The junior instructor will be considered *semi*-credible before setting foot in the classroom. Students may question whether the course content is well chosen for the field and if the instructor's teaching style is appropriate to the discipline. Yet, students are still more likely to defer to, rather than confront the instructor, in a public forum such as class.

Instructors at this stage in their career can make deliberate choices about how they will use different sources of power. Doing so requires careful consideration of interactions that affect psychological safety—for example, relying on charisma and humor without students negatively experiencing their contributions as the butt of a joke. Five additional choices merit direct consideration by junior faculty:

First, the extent to which credibility (and power) relies on expertise. There is a potential trap in grounding one's role in the classroom in *faultless* expertise, as that makes it very challenging for the instructor to have to say, "I don't know." A classroom dynamic where the instructor's role is highly evaluative or controlling increases this challenge. While the senior professor may have an answer for every question, a junior professor should consider how to set a norm where they can comfortably say, "I'd want to look into that more before commenting too firmly—let's raise it again next time."

Second, the kind and extent of justification provided for evaluation. A more senior instructor can get away with minimal explanation when grading (perhaps unfairly). A more junior instructor can find students questioning or outright challenging their evaluations (e.g., "You gave me a B+, but I think I should have an A"). While all evaluation carries an inherently subjective quality (Wassermann, 1979, 2020), instructors can consider proactively or reactively engaging with how students respond to their evaluation.

Proactive engagement includes providing evaluation rubrics directly to students. This shifts the conversation from the fundamental basis of evaluation to a more targeted exploration of consistent application of the rubric. In many cases, the combination of a clear rubric and formative feedback linking a specific evaluation to the rubric dimensions precludes certain challenges from taking place. It can also turn the onus from the instructor to the student: rather than the instructor justifying the grade, the student explains how they fulfilled the rubric measures.

Reactive engagement, how the instructor responds to a challenging evaluation, also varies according to instructor seniority and sources of power. A more senior instructor can suggest the student come chat with them, listen, and then make a decision that is more likely to be accepted given the instructor's experience. A more junior instructor who has built an aura of expertise may be able to do this as well. In contrast, one who is transparent about having more limited expertise in a given context may find this challenging.

A more junior instructor should consider the extent to which they put themselves forward as the authority, versus redirecting to institutional policy or their peers. In some cases, a policy may be clear and, if the student continues to press, offer a course of action that is out of the instructor's hands, for example, "I can't change grades post hoc in this way; if you would like to pursue this further, the student handbook allows you to . . . ."

Alternatively, one may be able to suggest that a third party could provide a blind second evaluation—a consideration is whether this second opinion is from someone of similar seniority. This choice can subtly shape the student's perception of the dynamic: does the instructor need *help* from someone more experienced, or are they merely seeking an *alternate perspective*? Would a particular individual's second opinion satisfy the student more than another, and should that be taken into consideration?

Both of these alternatives are, to some extent, outsourcing authority. More junior instructors should consider when they would shift from directly handling a given challenge. While it is expedient to fall back on policy, such an approach can be perceived by students as uncaring or an unwillingness to provide them with a "fair" chance even if applied consistently. More generally, all instructors should consider how they respond when their evaluations are questioned: do they personalize it as calling their judgment or expertise into question? Do they relate to it as somehow disrespectful?

Some instructors engage in this as an open dialogue with students. For example, "Explain your thinking so we can re-evaluate it together." This approach is particularly effective when instructors are genuinely open to the conversation *and* have a clear answer key, rubric, or comparison examples that can be examined by the student and the instructor (rather than merely the instructor's judgment).

Even if the instructor is confident that their evaluation is appropriate, an instructor can convey many different messages. The responses below could shape a student's perception of psychological safety in interpersonal interactions with a given professor:

- "This is my evaluation [implied 'take it or leave it']."
- "This is my evaluation; let me convey why [I feel] it is sound."
- "This is my evaluation; help me understand why you do not think it is appropriate. I will try to clarify my thought process or what is considered important in this discipline."

Third, the use of charisma can interact with reward and punishment. This interaction is addressed further in chapter 7. Still, as a starting point, an instructor should be aware that how they express enthusiasm verbally ("Great idea!") or nonverbally (expressive gestures or affect) can become a significant source of reward and punishment. One should consider the degree to which specific words, tone of voice, or body language is effectively becoming a source of praise or criticism.

Fourth, the use of recommendation as an incentive to motivate students can significantly increase the relative salience of evaluation. For individual students, this can decrease psychological safety because they will become more concerned whether any contribution they offer is substantial, perfectly correct, or clever. This can also drive a competitive dynamic where students become more concerned with demonstrating the superiority of their own ideas than fostering a constructive dynamic for everyone.

While a letter of recommendation is, in essence, a form of evaluation, describing it more broadly for students can foster a more constructive dynamic. For example, stating, "To write a strong reference letter, I need to be able to comment on you holistically. If you make a point of coming to my office hours, I'm more likely to be able to support you in this way." Such framing will lead to a more robust recommendation. It also reminds students that there can be a broader relationship between the instructor and student than a purely evaluative one.

Similarly, if one is the gatekeeper of a specific opportunity, linking it overtly to evaluation makes a significant difference to the classroom dynamic. Consider the potential impact of two different ways of framing such an opportunity on the first day of classes:

- "I offer two summer research positions in my lab to top students."
- "If you're looking for a summer research position, be sure to stop by my office hours for a chat during the semester so I know you might be interested."

Finally, the nature of the instructor-student relationship shapes student perceptions of the pastoral role of the instructor. As an instructor expresses empathy for students, either in response to individual contributions or for the group as a whole, the general level of psychological safety can increase. While this is supportive of academic contributions, it can also create an environment where students are comfortable sharing more personal details.

Different instructors may have varying degrees of comfort with this type of relationship. Instructors should always be mindful of when they can appropriately engage with these kinds of issues and when they should not. As some younger professors occasionally lament, "I care about them *so much*, but I can't be their therapist or their parent." All instructors must be aware of the formal support structures available to their students and understand in advance when they may need to step back and refer students to professionals.

Gender and cultural context also play a significant role in student perceptions of junior faculty (described further below).

The Novice Instructor

For the new instructor or graduate student teaching a class, available sources of power are more constrained: expertise (limited), evaluation, reward and punishment, charisma, and relationships. Their overall platform is also far more fragile than when a junior faculty member wields the same sources of power.

Expertise becomes significantly more linked with credibility, as students may be skeptical about the instructor's depth of knowledge. An instance of misspeaking, forgiven as such on the part of the senior faculty member, can be taken as a sign of weakness. Trying to bolster perceived expertise often leads to an unsustainable amount of overpreparation. This, in turn, reinforces a fragile dynamic where the instructor feels obliged to be the source of continuous and faultless "right answers" for the class.

A graduate student needs a different response repertoire when fielding questions, supported by proactively framing the role of instructor expertise in the classroom. One approach is to set norms such that other students are ready to respond to their peers' questions or work together to clarify points of confusion. Similarly, students may ask questions that go beyond the scope of the course. Setting a norm where the instructor can freely determine whether it will be a useful digression or best saved for discussion in office hours prevents a deferral being taken as a sign of modest expertise.

Evaluation perceived as a novice instructor's *opinion* of a work product is more likely to be questioned. Here, rubrics become a form of external authority, particularly if developed for the course in consultation with a teaching team or other professors. Creating rubrics also benefits the instructor:

consulting colleagues about metrics for evaluation often results in helpful suggestions and testing. Broadly speaking, rubrics can lead to greater consistency across courses and more effective integration of curriculum and evaluation.

The novice instructor can find themselves in a double-bind when students question an evaluation. Seeking a second opinion from a colleague can be taken as a sign of uncertainty rather than merely due process, yet rigidly sticking to initial evaluation can be considered unreasonable behavior.

Given these considerations, providing as much proactive framing of evaluative metrics and setting out reactive processes and consistently following them is very important.

Charisma and relationships need to be approached more carefully in order to remain professional. Anecdotes are a double-edged sword: what is humorous and relatable from the senior professor can come across as immature from the graduate student. Similarly, extending sympathy can either be relatable or undermine expertise, depending on the level of rapport. "When I first studied this, I nearly failed the exam—it's hard!" sounds very different from the graduate student versus the tenured professor.

Students may *directly challenge* whether the course content is well chosen for the field or whether the instructor's teaching style is appropriate to the discipline. The instructor will need to be ready to rely on their emotional intelligence while building relationships that promote trust between the instructor and students.

Gender, Culture, Power Dynamics, and Teaching

Power dynamics are culturally bound and affected by institutional norms as well as the background of individual students. This becomes particularly relevant when students expect a power dynamic that is either more authoritarian or more relaxed. In such contexts, a professor deliberately nonconforming to the expected social hierarchy or behavioral norms is stressful for students.

If the instructor is too formal: perceptions of being standoffish, demanding, uncaring, or unrelatable.

If the instructor is too relaxed: perceptions of being immature, emotionally needy, or not taking their role or the course seriously.

Variability in this is tremendous. What is too relaxed in one country or institution may be perceived as reserved or unapproachable in another.

An instructor can demonstrate immediacy in formal and relaxed contexts—it does not require a first-name basis or other hallmarks of a casual dynamic. Focusing on nonverbal immediacy and demonstrating meaningful empathy rather than superficial familiarity will increase immediacy. This is particularly effective when paired with careful consideration of the degree to which one employs the power of hierarchy, expertise, charisma, and relationships.

Gender significantly shapes the availability and use of different sources of power in the classroom context. Early studies of interaction style and influence found differences that became particularly relevant in the context of persuasion, including different patterns of behavior employed with men versus women (Carli, 1989).

In a study titled "Women are teachers, men are professors," the authors found undergraduate students would overestimate educational credentials when their instructors were male graduate students and underestimate the level of formal education attained by female instructors. This relationship held even when the female instructor was a *full professor* (Miller & Chamberlin, 2000).

Female instructors encounter such misconceptions regularly. The authors of one study note, "Dr. Mitchell once received an email from a student in a course co-taught with a male professor with the greeting 'Dr. [male instructor's surname] and Miss Kristina' " (Chávez & Mitchell, 2019).

This diminished power of expertise for women has implications for both in-classroom interactions and overall perceptions of instructor competency. On RateMyProfessors.com, "brilliant" and "genius" appear more frequently in the reviews of male professors across disciplines (Rosen, 2018). Students perceive male instructors as more knowledgeable and having stronger class leadership skills despite equivalent learning outcomes (Boring, 2017).

This evaluation of leadership capability ties to gendered stereotypes beyond the classroom, including biases where male leaders need to demonstrate strength while female leaders need to show strength *and* sensitivity to be perceived as effective (Johnson et al., 2008). In large courses, opportunities to demonstrate individual consideration and sensitivity are more limited. Here, ratings of competent female instructors are impacted by the "sage on a stage" dynamic being associated with stereotypically male characteristics of assertiveness and maintaining authoritative control of the classroom (Martin, 2016).

These gender differences may extend further into students' perceptions of teaching styles. When women engage in more discussion-based teaching approaches instead of lecturing, students may inaccurately interpret that as a lack of knowledge or preparedness (Laube et al., 2007).

Such biases are supported experimentally: when individual instructors facilitating an online class adopted two different gender identities, students rated the male identity more highly, regardless of the instructor's actual gender (MacNell et al., 2015). When asked to nominate "best" and "worst" instructors, male students selected a female professor as "best" less often than expected (Basow et al., 2006).

It is difficult to provide generalizable advice for a female instructor, particularly a *younger* female instructor, facing these challenges. The first important step is awareness on the part of instructors and their supervisors, particularly given the negative impact of gender on course and teaching evaluations (Basow et al., 2006; Flegl & Rosas, 2019; Sherwell et al., 2018; Wagner et al., 2016).

Female instructors who experience devaluation of their expertise or achievements, or increased resistance behaviors from students, should consider whether this is a broader pattern rather than a personal failing. Importantly, advice for "managing" the classroom dynamic or disruptive students must incorporate the instructor's gender and available sources of power.

Female instructors should also be aware that they may face different expectations of extra favors and emotional labor. In one study of professors in the United States, women received more standard work demands (such as office hour time) and requests for special favors (e.g., redoing an assignment).

Furthermore, academically entitled students[1] had stronger expectations of female instructors *granting* their requests for special favors (El-Alayli et al., 2018). The researchers note this expectation of compliance may also lead to entitled students having stronger negative reactions when a female instructor *declines* a particular request.

The authors also note that female instructors, in general, experience more friendship behaviors from students. While these are typically pleasant and enjoyable, they nonetheless represent engagement above and beyond standard work duties and take both extra time and emotional labor.

Every instructor should consider the level of engagement that they can sustain above and beyond standard work duties, with direct implications for employing the power of relationships. Academically entitled students may behave differently with female instructors by making more requests with a greater expectation of compliance. While female instructors benefit from having clear academic standards and policies to justify their decisions, holding fast to a rule may still result in more negative student reactions than a male colleague would experience in a similar situation.

One strategy is to tackle entitlement reduction proactively by setting expectations with the class before any special favors are requested. Rather than focusing on individual requests, this also helps students see the broader communal context of needing to maintain fairness across the group as a whole (El-Alayli et al., 2018).

As leadership models shift from more transactional and authoritative to more facilitative, with growing recognition of the biases faced by women and minorities, perceptions of women in leadership roles should change as well (Kubu, 2018). Until then, female and minority instructors should be aware of the specific challenges they face, mindful of the relative strengths and weaknesses of different sources of power, and thoughtful about how they demonstrate competence, agency, and authority in the classroom.

Resistance, Challenge Behaviors, and Instructional Dissent

Instructors who misbehave, rely on antisocial sources of power, are nonimmediate, or use aversive communication techniques often experience student resistance, challenge behaviors, and instructional dissent. Here, "misbehavior" encompasses offensiveness and incompetence, including students' perceptions of bad grading or poor teaching practices, unfair application of course or institutional policies, or laziness (Goodboy, 2011a).

While perceived problems in the classroom typically trigger dissent (Goodboy, 2011a,b), distal causes unrelated to the instructor and dispositional factors, such as generalized traits of verbal aggressiveness and argumentativeness, also play a role (Goodboy & Myers, 2012).

Students' challenge behaviors and instructional dissent decrease when instructors use appropriate sources of power, display verbal and nonverbal immediacy (Goodboy & Myers, 2009), set and uphold clear expectations (Simonds, 1997), offer individual consideration and confirmation (Goodboy & Myers, 2008), and act fairly (Chory, 2007).

Younger instructors are often perceived as more willing to change course policies or reduce the difficulty of exams or assignments. Such behaviors are open to interpretation: either increasing affect for the instructor given approachability and positive impact on individual grades, or decreasing affect due to perceived unfairness and lack of being held to a high standard of learning (Semlak & Pearson, 2008).

Most negative student behavior reflects attempts to exert power over the instructor or peers in the classroom. These attempts can differ in focus or mode of expression, and include resistance strategies, challenge behavior, nagging, and instructional dissent (Goodboy, 2011a).

Resistance strategies typically describe classroom behaviors that resist instructor persuasion and demonstrate noncompliance or overtly reluctant compliance with expectations (Chory & Goodboy, 2010).

Challenge behaviors attempt to shape the classroom dynamic, expectations of students, or course policies. Kaid and Wadsworth identified four categories[2] of such behavior (1989):

- Procedural challenges: students challenge classroom rules and implicit or explicit norms.
- Evaluation challenges: students challenge evaluation procedures or assigned grades.

- Practicality challenges: students challenge the relevance of the course over-all or specific activities.
- Power play challenges: students try to influence the behavior of the instructor or fellow students.

Nagging behaviors describe instances where a student attempts to persuade an instructor by making *persistent nonaggressive* overtures to elicit sympathy, solicit student support, demonstrate frustration, suggest instructor incompetence, strike a deal, flatter, or barrage with requests (Dunleavy et al., 2008). Nagging behaviors may be verbal or nonverbal, such as sighing or rolling eyes to demonstrate frustration, and are frequently committed indirectly or off-record (Dunleavy et al., 2008). Compared to instructors, students perceive nagging behaviors to be more appropriate and effective (Dunleavy & Martin, 2010).

Instructional dissent, students expressing disagreement or complaints about course-related issues, can be expressive, rhetorical, or vengeful (Goodboy, 2011a).

Goodboy describes how some forms of dissent are directly addressed to the instructor, while others are shared with classmates, friends, and family. Each type encompasses a range of behaviors. Expressive dissent is often associated with venting emotions or frustration. Rhetorical dissent attempts to rectify a perceived injustice by the instructor, such as arguing with an instructor about a course policy or grade. Vengeful dissent takes the form of retaliation against the instructor, often by targeting their reputation (2011a).

Instructional dissent is almost exclusively triggered by student perceptions of instructor misbehavior, such as unfair evaluation, poor teaching style, offensiveness, inconsistent application of policies, laziness, or lack of feedback. A group member slacking off is a further trigger that is not a direct instructor misbehavior. However, an instructor's *response* to slacking may also trigger instructor-focused dissent. Students who engage in instructional dissent typically report decreased motivation and diminished learning (Goodboy, 2011a,b).

Challenge behaviors, nagging, and instructional dissent all have deleterious effects on instructors, including emotional exhaustion, diminished teaching satisfaction, and decreased organizational commitment (Dunleavy & Martin, 2010; Frisby et al., 2015).

Instructors have three avenues to prevent or mitigate these negative student behaviors:

- Ensuring fairness of course policies and consistency in their application.
- Using appropriate sources of power; when relevant, carefully framing the role of expertise in the classroom.

• Demonstrating credibility through competence, character, and caring.

Credibility in the classroom is multifaceted. Myers and Bryant describe how competence is conveyed through expertise, affect for students, verbal fluency, and communication skills. Character is conveyed through verbal and nonverbal immediacy, promoting understanding, flexibility, and trustworthiness. Caring is conveyed through responsiveness, individualized consideration, and accessibility (2004). These three dimensions *collectively* improve both credibility and overall student learning outcomes (Finn et al., 2009).

Resistance can also result from classroom instruction techniques that are *known* to improve learning, despite initially negative student perceptions. In his "Sermons for Grumpy Campers," Felder notes the importance of convincing students that such activities are actually in their best interest, rather than selfishness or laziness on the part of the instructor. With understanding, students will tend to lower their resistance and observe the benefits of these techniques.

Where resistance is predictable, such as group work or student-centered discussions, Felder suggests anticipating instances of dissent in order to have a reply ready. For example, consider a fairly standard response to dissent related to group activities in class:

Student: "Those group activities in class are a waste of time. I'm paying tuition for you to teach me, not to trade ideas with students who don't know any more than I do!"

Professor: I agree that my job is to teach you, but to me teaching means making learning happen and not just putting out information. I've got lots of research that says people learn through practice and feedback, not by someone telling them what they're supposed to know. What you're doing in those short class activities are the same things you'll have to do in the homework and exams, except now when you get to the homework you will have already practiced them and gotten feedback. You'll find that the homework will go a lot more smoothly and you'll probably do better on the exams. (Let me know if you'd like to see that research). (Felder, 2007, p. 184)

Three Points to Remember about Power, Entitlement, and Dissent in the Classroom

• Seniority, personality, culture, and gender constrain the sources of power available to an instructor; these factors also shape how students respond to instructors employing certain sources of power.
• Instructor misbehaviors are a primary trigger of student resistance, challenge behavior, nagging, and instructional dissent; however, these

behaviors can arise from student personality traits, academic entitlement, or other distal causes.

• Ensuring fairness, appropriately using sources of power, and demonstrating credibility help to prevent or mitigate these negative student behaviors.

THE "OBLIVIOUS" STUDENT AND CONSTRUCTIVE FEEDBACK

Some students fail to use formative feedback effectively in their future interactions and work products. For instructors, it is very frustrating to feel one is providing students with input that should lead to improvement, yet not see any changes. Worse still, while feedback is necessary for learning, a significant number of studies demonstrate certain types of instructor feedback having a *negative* effect on learning when compared to controls who did not receive feedback (Hattie & Timperley, 2007; Kluger & DeNisi, 1996; Shepard, 2019, Shute, 2008).

There is an unfortunate tendency for an instructor who puts a lot of time and effort into creating feedback to personalize this lack of progress, and in attempting to explain it fall into an explanation focused on the agency of the students. Namely, it's a student problem.

• They're failing to engage with the feedback. Are they even reading it? Do they recognize when I am providing feedback during class?
• They don't have a growth mindset. Students are stuck in a self-defeating approach to their own competency and don't engage as if they can grow and develop over time.
• They just don't care.

Students may engage with feedback to varying degrees or relate to their learning with fixed or growth-oriented mindsets. An instructor should not assume that time spent providing feedback will necessarily directly drive outcomes. Instead, a lack of improvement could result from causes related to the feedback provided. Namely, it's an instructor problem.

• Your feedback is not as constructive as you believe it is. Do you explain what is done *well* alongside what could be improved? Will strong students have a clear picture over time of what, specifically, has been working? Will weaker students understand how they need to adapt what they have been doing up to this point?
• Feedback is too context-dependent and doesn't generalize to future applications.

- Your feedback focuses on the evaluation itself rather than learning goals. You have provided feedback that justifies the grade on a work product, but the student does not understand how to adapt their previous approach for the future.
- You were providing too much feedback. It is possible that students are overwhelmed by the volume and can only take so much under consideration at any one time.
- In general, you are not treating students as if they can grow and develop over time. Your feedback may be interpreted as value judgments about them as individuals and their personal characteristics rather than input about how to improve.

Taking the first three points under consideration, one can see how instructors often provide feedback they believe is clear but may not be formative for the student (see table 10.1).

The specific nature of effective feedback varies between disciplines. However, in all cases, feedback should focus on students' performance, learning, and actions under their control rather than the individual or their characteristics (Gibbs & Simpson, 2005). In a detailed review, Gibbs and Simpson describe four characteristics of effective feedback:

- Feedback is frequent, timely, sufficient, and appropriately detailed.
- Feedback directly connects to the purpose of the task and evaluation criteria.
- Feedback is tailored to the students' level of understanding.
- Feedback focuses on learning rather than grades by relating explicitly to future tasks.

A further addition to this list is that feedback should be sufficiently motivating to the students—taking care to highlight strengths or offer encouragement and avoiding unnecessarily negative phrasing of criticism or judgments (Glover & Brown, 2006). Feedback may be more effective when it relates to previous attempts and conveys information on *correct* rather than *incorrect* responses (Hattie & Timperley, 2007).

Additionally, the *topic* of feedback encompasses a hierarchy from the task itself, to task motivation, to characteristics of the individual performing the task. Interestingly, not all feedback improves performance, and feedback generally becomes less effective when focused more on the self than the task or process (Kluger & DeNisi, 1996).

Hattie & Timperley (2007) extend this hierarchy to four distinct levels:

Table 10.1 Examples of Improving Feedback

	Less Effective Feedback	*Improved Feedback*
Verbal (Individual)	"Nope, you should get 2 cos(2x). The rest cancels out." The student made a straightforward error but may not recall the piece of information needed to correct it.	"You should get 2 cos(2x) as the rest cancels out. Check your sign changes against a table of trig derivatives."
	"The answer is −12. Check the second line in your calculation." This may be effective if the student can recognize an error in the second line.	"The answer is −12. Check how you're using the chain rule in the second line of your calculation."
	"That's more of a 'consensus history' take on it." This may be effective, provided the student has an appropriate understanding of the technical term.	"That's more of a 'consensus history' take on it, given . . ."
Verbal (Summative)	"Okay, we've covered everything we needed to talk about here." The precise *what* and *why* may not be apparent to students.	"Okay, we've covered x, y, and z, which we needed to because . . ."
	"Lots of good points. Let's agree to disagree and move on." Students may wonder whether a resolution is possible with more time, or if there is a consensus in the field.	"This is a fundamental disagreement in the field. In the future, you can craft a valid argument either way so long as you clearly state what should be prioritized and justify why."
Written	"A+ Great job!" While encouraging, this does not help the student understand what, specifically, was done well.	"A+ You brought in multiple avenues of evidence to support your position and demonstrated their coherence to the reader."
	"A Very well done! Nice use of GitHub." While encouraging, "nice use" may be unclear to the student.	"A Your code is efficient and well commented. Appropriate use of pre-existing code (not too much and well attributed)."
	"A- Effective application of the factors we discussed in class, which were appropriate to use." While the student may understand what they did well in this context, they may not know how to transfer this knowledge.	"A- Effective application of the factors discussed in class. In the future, you'll want to consider whether broader economic or political factors are suited to the context. Be sure to include a sentence or two explaining their relevance to justify your approach."

"C+ This was more your opinion than an objective analysis."
While a critical issue, the student may not know how to improve.

"C- Vague."
This notes a weakness but is not directly actionable feedback.

"C+ You identified relevant stakeholders but did not adequately evaluate their motivation for the reader. To do this, be sure to have your arguments grounded in psychological theories we discussed in class and specific pieces of evidence from their behavior. Without this, it appears to be your opinion rather than an objective analysis."

"C- The reader needs more elaboration in order to understand your argument. If you list your initial assumptions and then take the reader through each step of your case, the depth of your understanding will be evident."

Note: The initial feedback may appear "clear" to an instructor, yet is not actionable for students without improvement.

- Task level: how well tasks are understood or performed. For example, "That answer is correct" or "Your argument is not persuasive."
- Process level: the primary process needed to understand or perform tasks. For example, "If using multiple comparisons, consider a Bonferroni correction" or "When you first identify your variables, determine the type of each one."
- Self-regulation level: self-monitoring, directing, and regulating actions. For example, "It appears you got stuck here. If you feel that happening again, you can . . ." or "I appreciate your persistence—this skill requires deliberate practice in order to improve."
- Self level: personal evaluations and affect (usually positive) about the learner. For example, "Clever!" or "Great effort!" or "Lazy."

Effective feedback at the task, process, and self-regulation level is interrelated and leads to both increased confidence and effort; feedback at the self level (often in the form of praise) is rarely effective as it fails to inform the student about task goals, progress, or actions to take (Hattie & Timperley, 2007), and can lead to diminished risk-taking, minimized effort, and higher fear of failure (Black & William, 1998; Kluger & DeNisi, 1996).

Most feedback is mark-focused: serving to justify a grade rather than promote student learning. Such feedback informs students about past achievement rather than enabling future work; it doesn't matter when it is returned to students and may as well not be provided at all (Glover & Brown, 2006). Instructors who are more junior or trying to preempt conflict with academically entitled students may provide an excessive amount of this type of feedback, despite its relative ineffectiveness. In turn, even well-crafted feedback may not be read by students when buried in a flood of less-actionable remarks.

Three Points to Remember about Constructive Feedback

- Feedback focused on the *self* is significantly less effective than feedback focused on the task, process, motivation, or self-regulation. In some cases, it is counterproductive to learning.
- Feedback needs to inform future work, rather than simply justify a grade.
- Providing too much feedback may obscure important points.

CONFORMITY IN THE CLASSROOM

A Crash Course in Conformity

"Exactly what is the effect of the opinions of others on our own? In other words, how strong is the urge toward social conformity?" (Asch, 1955, p. 31)

The Asch conformity experiments of the 1950s attempted to answer this question and have become a canonical feature of how we understand conformity in social groups.

In Asch's initial study, 123 college students made judgments regarding the length of lines presented as visual stimuli (e.g., "Is this reference line the same length as example A, B or C?"). These judgments took place in a group setting where the subject believed he was one of a cohort of peers responding to the question. In fact, Asch arranged the room so that the subject always responded last, and the "peers" were confederates with instructions on how to respond for each trial. Asch wished to investigate whether the subject would conform to an incorrect answer if it were the consensus of the other individuals in the group.

Asch found that the error rate under control conditions was less than 1 percent. When presented with a group consensus, subjects conformed with an incorrect judgment in 36.8 percent of such trials. Over multiple trials and modified conditions, such as varying the number of peers, Asch concluded that 75 percent of students agree with the incorrect majority *to some degree* (1955).

Conformity appeared trait-like, with some staunch nonconformists maintaining this attitude throughout the experiment even as they exhibited signs of stress, and highly conformist individuals continuing to conform across trials. The presence of a "partner" for the subject, a confederate instructed to disagree with the consensus, decreased conformity even if the partner selected a different incorrect response (Asch, 1955).

While these experiments are often presented as evidence of the highly suggestible or conformist nature of humans, Asch himself highlighted in a subsequent publication that roughly 25 percent of subjects exhibited complete independence, and never agreed with the erroneous consensus of the majority (1956). Furthermore, Asch notes,

> While the majority effect was considerable, it was by no means complete, or even the strongest force at work. The preponderance of estimates was, in each of the experimental groups, correct or independent of the majority, evidence that the given stimulus conditions—the facts that were being judged—were, under the circumstances, the most decisive. (1956, p. 10)

A more nuanced interpretation of the Asch experiments highlights an ability to think and act independently in the face of conformity. One should consider how to mitigate the drivers of conformist behavior in the classroom if the dynamic becomes problematic. Such a dynamic is characterized by an unwillingness on the part of students to engage critically with ideas presented by their peers or present alternative perspectives of their own.

First, one should consider how and why students conform, which relates to both the drivers and goals of conformist behavior.

Drivers of Conformity

In response to early studies of conformity, such as those by Asch (1955) and Sherif (1935), Deutsch and Gerard sought to identify specific factors that underlie these patterns of conformist behavior. This approach led them to set out two distinct types of social influence, which they defined as "normative" and "informational" (1955).

Normative social influence is defined as the "influence to conform with the positive expectations of another" (1955, p. 629). In this context, "positive expectations" can mean behaving in a way that will be positively reinforced by the other individual, such as by expressing agreement or "going along to get along." Under this form of influence, an individual can conform publicly, yet dissent privately, such as agreeing with an opinion one does not personally hold.

Informational social influence captures how one is influenced to "accept information obtained from another as *evidence* about reality" (1955, p. 629). This form of conformity will often lead to internalization, where the subject *believes* the information presented. Deutsch and Gerard note that one can accept an opponent's beliefs about reality even without an underlying motivation to do so.

Employing several modified versions of Asch's experiment, the authors tested a series of hypotheses intended to dissociate the relative contribution of different sources of social influence. Across a variety of conditions, they found:

- Judgments of others are taken to be a trustworthy source of information and will shape how a subject behaves *even if* they can provide their individual judgment anonymously.
- Even a group situation where the context is trivial and artificial (such as being assigned randomly to a group of strangers for an experiment) results in normative social influence.
- Normative social influence can *promote or undermine* individual integrity. Some group norms can demand individuality and that members value their own judgments, which in turn decreases conformity.
- Perhaps most significantly for the context of a classroom dynamic: "Unless groups encourage their members to express their own, independent judgments, group consensus is likely to be an empty achievement" (Deutsch & Gerard 1955, p. 635).

While the above research is dated, more recent literature reviews in the field of compliance and conformity have upheld normative and informational social influence as two distinct, albeit often interrelated, forms of motivation (Cialdini & Goldstein, 2004).

Goals of Conformity

Can conformity be considered a form of goal-directed behavior? In their literature review, Cialdini and Goldstein set out three goals: accuracy, affiliation, and maintaining a positive self-concept. The first two align with Deutsch and Gerard's distinctions when articulated as the desire to generate an accurate interpretation of reality and behave accordingly (informational social influence) and obtaining social approval (normative social influence). These two goals are, in turn, related to a third goal of maintaining one's self-concept (2004).

Interestingly, a goal such as accuracy can both drive conformity and be a tool to diminish it. Quinn and Schlenker found that a strong goal of accuracy *coupled with accountability* resulted in individuals displaying independence, reduced conformity, and making higher-quality decisions (2002). If either component were missing, subjects would exhibit the typical pattern of conforming to the majority or to the individual to which they had to justify their position.

Affiliation is multifaceted. It is present in the chameleon effect discussed in chapter 5 as a facet of entrainment (Chartrand & Bargh, 1999). Williams et al. demonstrated that an incidence of ostracism, even with anonymity and online rather than in-person, drives increased conformity in a subsequent task (2000). Cialdini and Goldstein concluded that conformity related to a need to belong can occur without direct, personal, or public disapproval (2004). This need is reinforced by how conformity is perceived. An audience typically prefers individuals who express agreement, evaluating them as more intelligent and likable (Braver et al., 1977).

Identity and positive self-concept also play a significant role. Individuals will conform to valued groups, such as political parties, even when evidence suggests the group is misinformed (Binning et al., 2015). Individuals will also conform in ways related to their sense of uniqueness or personal identity (Brewer et al., 1993). For students, this can include in-group/out-group identity related to ethnicity or gender, but also to socially constructed facets of identity or values.

Returning to the Asch experiment, a nonconformist explanation highlights the importance of setting group norms that value individuals expressing unique perspectives, no matter how initially unpopular they may seem. It suggests that the group as a whole, by explicitly agreeing to such norms, could render everyone more resistant to both informational and normative social influence in ways that will be highly productive for the discussion. It also suggests that, given the power of informational influence, instructors may wish to consider initially allowing anonymous submission of contributions or opinions to prevent nonconscious bias.

Other Factors Shaping a Conformist Dynamic

Task Importance, Evaluation, and Conformity

Goals of accuracy and a positive self-concept also interact with the power dynamics and evaluative nature of the classroom. For many students, "bad answers" introduce personal risk and diminish their concept of themselves as a competent learner. Furthermore, even if a student can set aside the normative social influence associated with the negative experience of providing an incorrect answer, the "safest" answer when grades are at stake is surely the response held by the majority. While such an answer is unlikely to be outstanding, it would nonetheless, by definition, place the student firmly on the grading curve.

In a study that provides insight into the conformist pressures accompanying evaluation, Baron et al. (1996) found a relationship between task difficulty and the incentive for accuracy. In contexts where the difficulty of the task was low, increasing the incentive for accuracy resulted in reduced conformity. Conversely, when the task difficulty increased and accuracy was strongly incentivized, individuals conformed more to inaccurate judgments supported by the group.

This suggests that in a context where accuracy becomes more important, such as when evaluation is taking place, students are more likely to conform to their peers. As discussed in previous sections, this also has the potential to be driven by a lack of psychological safety or student perceptions of reward and punishment for correct or incorrect responses. While previous chapters describe how diminished psychological safety or reward and punishment can make students hesitate to join the conversation, one can also see how they can, given these pressures to conform, drive herd mentality.

As an instructor, one can try to test whether conformity increases when questions or contexts are more high-stakes. If this is the case, it is important to work with students to set expectations of nonconformity, reframe how they consider accuracy a goal, and reiterate the value of each individual's distinct contributions.

Culture and Conformity

The possibility of a cultural basis for conformity has fascinated psychologists for decades, with Stanley Milgram's "Which Nation's Conform Most" capturing widespread attention when first published (Milgram, 1961). In a detailed meta-analysis of 133 studies that applied Asch-like protocols, Bond and Smith drew two intriguing conclusions: first, that conformity in the United States appears to have declined since first measured in the 1950s. Second, countries classified as collectivist societies *tended to exhibit* greater levels of conformity than individualist societies, particularly when conforming to an in-group (1996).

This is consistent with the folk-psychology view of conformity and collectivism. However, significant debate surrounds the prevalence and validity of such beliefs. Specific patterns of behavior may be mediated by age and context-dependent factors (Takano & Osaka, 1999, 2018a,b; Hamamura & Takemura, 2018). When evaluating the role of culture shaping conformity in the classroom, instructors should consider the impact of norms and past experience, rather than simply ascribing behavior to fundamental personality traits.

Gender, Personality, and Conformity

While gender differences in conformity have been widely reported, with women traditionally considered to exhibit greater levels of conformity than men (Bond & Smith, 1996; Mori & Arai, 2010), more detailed analysis has revealed a variety of interacting factors.

Social framing and prosocial behavior (any voluntary behavior that benefits other people) interact, such that women can behave significantly more cooperatively in one context than another, depending on the framing (Ellingsen et al., 2013).

While mixed-gender groups typically increase the breadth of perspectives available, it is unclear whether gender diversity promotes or inhibits nonconformity (Amini et al., 2017).

The medium of communication may also affect persuasion and conformity, with online asynchronous communication (e.g., e-mail) more effective for men persuading men, and in-person communication more effective for women persuading women (Guadagno & Cialdini, 2007, 2002).

Taken holistically, differences in conformity related to gender are more complex and context-dependent than traditional stereotypes suggest (Weinschenk et al., 2018).

Trait-like aspects of personality also affect conformity. However, one cannot make a direct and straightforward prediction of conformity from a personality test. Some facets of personality may make an individual more susceptible to memory conformity (Doughty et al., 2017), and individuals who exhibit general characteristics of being kind, practical, and emotionally balanced may be more inclined to conform with a group (Kosloff et al., 2017).

Mitigating Undesirable Conformity in the Classroom

Some conformity in the classroom is positive: social norms and patterns of friendly behavior are all examples of conformity found in a pleasant social environment. When conformity constrains the diversity of perspectives that are shared or diminishes risk-taking, instructors can attempt to mitigate it by

- decreasing the emphasis on accuracy or the "cost" of a wrong answer;
- establishing class norms that promote independent thinking and risk-taking;
- reducing the normative social influence of the instructor, given the judgmental nature of their response repertoire and use of social sources of power;
- reducing the informational social influence of the instructor, given the nature of their judgmental or evaluative contributions and use of expertise-linked sources of power;
- offering avenues for anonymous contribution; or
- decreasing the availability of informational cues, such as how other students are voting on an ongoing poll.

Some of these strategies interact; for example, the perceived "cost" of a wrong answer may be related to the social influence of the instructor and how they react to student contributions. Other avenues can be a natural instructor behavior such as withholding their opinion during student discussion to reduce their informational social influence.

Subtle differences in how active learning is employed shape conformity. One study found greater response variability to controversial questions when students indicated their response via *clicker* versus hand-raise (Stowell et al., 2010). Instructors should also consider whether information is available while students are actively participating (e.g., "Everyone close your eyes and then raise a hand to vote . . ." or disabling features that show the results of electronic polls as votes are submitted).

Another study examined the common in-class activity of *polling, discussing, and re-polling* students. If students saw a bar graph of the initial poll results as part of the discussion stage, they were 30 percent more likely to switch to the majority answer when repolled (Perez et al., 2010).[3] The authors highlight that instructors could misinterpret this switch to be a result of learning from the discussion, rather than merely response bias.

Setting explicit norms around the importance of individualism and the freedom to dissent can increase tolerance for diversity in a group (Hornsey et al., 2006).

Organizational psychology often examines how institutional norms drive innovation and minimize groupthink. Some of these norms deliberately promote divergent behavior, such as Intel's "constructive confrontation" (Chatman et al., 2014).

Yet, using conformity as a tool is challenging due to interactions between norm content and personality. One study attempted to use individualism as an explicit norm, "stand out or get out," as a means of increasing creative expression. Interestingly, this norm increased creativity in groups of individuals with low levels of creativity, but diminished creativity when the group was composed of highly creative individuals (Goncalo & Duguid, 2012).

Mitigating Conformity in Asynchronous Forums

Conformity can increase as classes incorporate an online component, such as discussion boards, or move into fully asynchronous online models where the instructor never engages with the students in real time.

In five years of experience facilitating a graduate course with an online discussion component, Wang observed a tendency for some students to have "made irrelevant and shallow postings, echoed what others said, and posted long quotations without any interpretation" (2014, p. 406). She highlights that effectively intervening in this context is challenging, given the particular risk of students relating to instructors online as authoritarian (rather than simply *authority*) figures, and experience feedback as impersonal.

Specific strategies mitigate these issues but require careful engagement on the part of the instructor—weighing in too frequently can reduce the length and frequency of student posts. Instead, an instructor can create a set of questions tailored to mitigate specific patterns of student behavior, such as repetition or conformity (Wang, 2014). Similarly, an instructor can take a Socratic approach when replying to student discussion board postings (Strang, 2011). Instructors can also attempt to model desired types of engagement, such as challenging, questioning, clarifying, and hypothesizing (Choi et al., 2008).

Instructors should also be aware of the extent to which online avatars convey information about student gender, as that can significantly shape informational social influence and patterns of conformity (Lee, 2004; Wijenayake et al., 2019).

Three Points to Remember about Conformity

- Drivers of conformity can be social or informational and may interact with the evaluative nature of the classroom dynamic or the information available to students.
- Factors such as culture, gender, and the presence of in-/out-groups mediate conformity. One may need to consider the composition of a given class and

tailor approaches for mitigating a conformist dynamic to the individuals present.

- Explicit norms that value independent perspectives and risk-taking are a proactive means of mitigating some forms of negative conformity.

CONTRARIAN BEHAVIOR IN THE CLASSROOM

Most instructors have experienced a contrarian in their classroom: typically outspoken, this student can be counted on to offer disagreement with the prevailing opinion, a counterexample, or particularly pointed question. While potentially a refreshing antidote to a conformist pattern of behavior, a distinction can be made between *constructive* and *destructive* contrarians in the classroom. While the two can appear the same, at least superficially, the difference has implications for how an instructor engages with such students.

A *persistent* contrarian can introduce a pattern of behavior that is challenging, for both the instructor and students. From the instructor's perspective, "Why must they always question what I say? Oh no, here comes that hand again—we're going to run out of time!" For fellow students, "They *always* hold us up with a question! Why do they always have to disagree?"

An instructor must find a way to engage directly with the behavior, but also help it be functional within the classroom dynamic. Particular concerns are balancing the talk-time between the contrarian and other participants or ensuring class doesn't become overly shaped by a single student.

Instead of immediately personalizing a contrarian pattern of behavior as the student expressing skepticism of the instructor's knowledge or testing their authority, it is crucial to take the time to understand it. Could *needs* or *values* be driving this behavior? Understanding this is an avenue to help the student develop self-awareness of their contrarian tendencies and have fellow students perceive it as an overall positive for the classroom dynamic.

The Constructive Contrarian

A *constructive* contrarian is often entirely earnest in their disagreement, and persistent questioning may be rooted in a desire to engage as deeply as possible with the subject. When this is the case, elements of psychological safety, namely, that their contributions are valued, become tied to the contrarian pattern of behavior. Given this consideration, instructors should be thoughtful about whether they attempt to shut down the contrarian pattern or help the student channel it productively. As a starting point, consider several possible drivers of constructive contrarianism through the perspective of needs and values.

- A need to participate: the student believes that participation is essential to their success and/or the student exhibits a strong degree of extroversion in their interactions.
- A need for accuracy: the student is particularly concerned that the group's understanding is entirely accurate. They will want to raise potential edge cases, alternative hypotheses, or exceptions to ensure generalizations or conclusions are, in fact, *technically correct*.
- A need for completeness: similar to the above. The student is particularly concerned that their understanding is holistic and will push at the boundaries of a topic or insist that the class *must* consider more points before moving on.
- Valuing a perspective related to their interests or identity: the student is passionate about a particular way of approaching the subject that may not always be recognized—for example, exploring through lenses grounded in gender, ethnicity, power dynamics, or culture. They will typically raise this as a perspective that is being missed, or one that *must* be included for holistic engagement with the topic.

Constructive contrarianism, no matter how well intentioned, does not always result in a positive dynamic for the group. It can become time-consuming; derail a carefully planned activity or thought experiment; drive depth in a particular topic at the expense of intended breadth; become repetitive, if a pattern of objection becomes ubiquitous; or even lead to perceived favoritism, if a specific student's alternative perspective on a given issue is always explored.

Assuming that the constructive contrarian is engaging in good faith driven by needs or values, consider several avenues to approach shifting this dynamic. As an instructor, one can deliberately foster group norms that mitigate or prevent the negative effects of contrarianism. These can include the following:

- A shared understanding that all students are deserving of equal talk-time in the discussion. If the group as a whole explicitly values making room for everyone to participate, the contrarian may begin to self-censor the frequency of their contributions and focus on those that are most impactful. The instructor also has a clear avenue to invite another student into the conversation rather than call on every hand.
- A shared understanding that all students may have a particular perspective or lens they are interested in applying to the topics of the course. As such, no one approach will be applied to every single topic.
- A shared understanding that the class simply isn't going to be able to cover everything. There are times when the instructor must take a role in guiding

the discussion and evaluate when to pause and discuss something further. In doing this, the instructor may explicitly call out trade-offs of depth versus breadth or potential tangents to discuss further outside of class.

- Acknowledgment that a certain level of understanding of a topic is "sufficient for the purposes of the course." While further subtleties, edge cases, or exceptions may exist, they are not appropriate to draw out in full for every topic. Acceptance of such a statement will be grounded in implicit power dynamics related to both expertise and evaluation. The contrarian must trust that this is a genuine judgment on the part of the instructor, rather than a placation.

Setting group norms is a very effective way of proactively shaping the classroom dynamic to reduce the negative effects of a contrarian, but what if it is insufficient? While these norms can be reinforced by explicitly calling attention to them if a negative dynamic emerges, another method is to approach the contrarian student privately.

While the instructor should first try to identify which needs or values may be driving the contrarian's behavior and take this into account, the primary goal of the conversation is to understand the pattern of behavior from the *student's perspective*. Sometimes, the responses are surprising, for example, "I want to be a lawyer, so I like finding exceptions when I'm learning something." While the instructor may have a hunch about underlying drivers, the most important aspect of a conversation such as this is to listen to the student and ensure their sense of comfort engaging in classroom discussion is maintained.

While this can vary between instructors and particular students, some avenues to gently broach the topic and begin a conversation about the classroom dynamic could include starting with an observation:

- "I've noticed a pattern in class where you typically take the lead in offering a dissenting voice. How do you feel about that?"
- "I've noticed that you're very skilled at finding exceptions. Is that something you tend to find yourself doing in other classes as well?"
- "I appreciate your willingness to play Devil's advocate for us and help the group consider alternatives. It's quite a role to take on. Is it frustrating when we don't have time to explore the alternative perspectives fully?"
- "I noticed you often end up being the odd one out when we vote on something. Do you sometimes do that deliberately, or is that just how it has happened to turn out?"

Many constructive contrarians are self-aware regarding their tendencies and very open to understanding how their contributions are shaping the classroom dynamic.

In such cases, one can attempt to draw out how the contrarian feels about the role that they take on (perhaps they enjoy it; perhaps they wish others would also help drive the discussion). From there, the instructor can openly discuss how contrarianism can be used most productively in a given class setting. Perhaps the student should consider focusing on one major objection per discussion. Perhaps it is most appropriate in early stages of discussion rather than near the conclusion.

This idea of anchoring on a productive dynamic is particularly important when the behavior appears habitual rather than thoughtful. As an instructor, one might be able to help the student reflect on the frequency of their contrarian responses and how it affects the class. At times, the group could perceive it as being constructive, such as pressure testing or brainstorming. At other times it could be a barrier to progress, such as "shooting down" ideas for a group presentation without contributing a helpful suggestion.

In some cases, an instructor may work with the student to agree on specific avenues to shape the class dynamic productively—sometimes even identifying specific comments the instructor can use as verbal cues in class.

Consider a few different types of agreement between a constructive contrarian and an instructor:

- "Don't be shy about contributing; it's my job to manage the balance of contributions. When we simply don't have time to explore an alternative perspective fully, I will clearly call it out as a time issue by saying something like, 'I'm afraid we need to move on.'"
- "If I say something like, 'That's true; it's taking us into an edge case,' it means that you're technically correct but too specific for the class as not everyone will be able to follow. We can reconvene after class or in office hours to talk more."
- "There may be instances when I don't respond to your hand because I need to give a quiet student some talk-time and am assuming you have a 'next level' comment or want to raise an alternative perspective. If that ever happens when you need to ask a question or have a point of clarification, don't be afraid to give your hand a little wave."
- "Even if your hand is the first one up, I may need to give other students some practice offering rebuttals. If, over time, you feel like you're missing out, please do come chat with me."

Even with an agreement in place, the instructor can find themself needing to manage the contrarian dynamic publicly. When instructors have a strong rapport with the student and the group as a whole, some resort to a direct comment as a means of managing this dynamic.

- "[Student X], our master of the edge case, what could we be missing here?"

- "I can see [Student X] already has their perspective ready. How about someone else start us off this time?"

If done sensitively, this can be honoring of the student. Still, one must be very mindful of the individual and the group—particularly if other students will not be aware of one-to-one conversations between the contrarian and the instructor. Different instructors will use humor in different ways and should always do so with psychological safety in mind. The tone of voice and genuineness is critical in having it be an empathic dynamic. Some deliberately steer clear of this kind of comment entirely.

More generally, an instructor can consider adding several specific points to their response repertoire to manage a contrarian dynamic driven by needs or values. For example,

- Watch your own use of language. Could imprecise speech on the part of the instructor be driving a contrarian reaction? For example, speaking in absolutes or glossing over explanations relying on correlation rather than causation would invite student questions or pushback.
- When a contrarian pattern relates to a specific perspective, can the instructor highlight the relevance while pivoting to other students' point of view? For example, "[Student X] has shown how feminist perspectives can apply to topics throughout this course; what other approaches could we consider here?" This signals that the constructive contrarian's perspective is valued, yet creates room for other students to contribute or explore different topics.
- Can the instructor put a "sufficient" understanding in context: "For the purposes of this course, that will be a sufficient definition, although there are nuances along those lines." If possible, a few words of context can sometimes help to reinforce this, for example, "Yes, there are some alternative views from a computational approach. For the purposes of this course, that is a sufficient definition as it reflects the experimental psychology literature. When you take [subsequent course], you'll weave Bayesian models into how one can describe this."
- Can the instructor frame a "sufficient" understanding in terms of the Pareto principle, or 80/20 rule,[4] by clearly noting, "We've focused on the causes that will account for the vast majority of the effects we're interested in here, so we'll call that sufficient in this context."

The Destructive Contrarian

The *destructive* contrarian can also be called a "nagging dissenter," one who "finds fault whenever they can, picking and complaining at all but invisible stimuli. This type of [student] does not seem to be a rational dissenter, although he will oftentimes be very skilled at making up arguments when he needs them" (Raths et al., 1973, p. 176). If this is merely habitual and non-conscious, a conversation such as the one described above for a constructive contrarian may be sufficient to change behavior. In some cases, however, the dynamic is intentional and may merit another course of action.

This pattern of behavior is exhausting for the instructor and tiresome for the other students, given the constant disruption to the flow of the class. Worse still, when a destructive contrarian consistently opposes their peer's contributions, the continual threat of negative judgment can inhibit participation.

What should one do when a destructive contrarian asks a deliberately pointed question? Justifying, arguing, defending, explaining—all engage with the student at the expense of the rest of the group. To effectively triage when and how to engage, an instructor could consider, "If *any other student* asked the question, how might I respond?"

- Student: "Why are we reading this paper? It's too old!"
- Instructor: "The paper is considered seminal in the field and lays the groundwork for what comes next" or "While somewhat dated, it has the clearest explanation of the relevant theory. I'll be sure to highlight subsequent avenues of research as we go."
- Student: "Why are we covering this? It doesn't fit with the last unit!"
- Instructor: "The overall arc of the course will tie it together further, but for now, what specific links might we keep in mind?" [Other students answer]
- Student: "What's the point of this case study? We should do something else!"
- Instructor: "We're going to stick with this for now, but why don't we chat after class? I'd be interested in your suggestions for next time."

It is fair to note that other students might be very unlikely to ask such a question, and, even if they did so, would not use the same tone of voice as a nagging dissenter. When an instructor has a sense that a student is deliberately engaging in a destructive contrarian pattern of behavior, their initial response must avoid overtly personalizing the behavior. This is very challenging if the instructor feels the student is being deliberately disrespectful or is forcing the power dynamic to be driven by authority or expertise (and directly calling that into question).

As a starting point, consider whether needs or values could be driving a destructive contrarian's pattern of behavior and decide if the instructor can engage with these underlying causes to change the dynamic. In the case of the nagging dissenter, their identity becomes grounded in opposing others, particularly authority figures; "it almost seems as if [they] like to be different and thrive on contention" (Raths et al., 1973, p. 176).

This can also become compounded by a further factor (below) that provides a rationalization for their skepticism and dissent. Such factors are varied but suggest a way to mitigate the behavior.

Perhaps the student feels forced to take the instructor's course and believes it is at best tangential to their interests or what will enable them to be successful in the future. At worst, they may relate to it as a waste of time and resources. If this is the case, the instructor may wish to draw out the student's particular interests and explore how to include them in course deliverables. Maybe the student could see the opportunity to take a leading role in applying their area of interest to the topic. Maybe the student could reflect on how analytical skills in the present course may be broadly applicable, even if the specific factual knowledge is narrow.

Perhaps the student is skeptical about the fairness of evaluation practices employed at the institution and is pushing back on what is called "sufficient understanding." They could be relating to the notion of sufficient depth of knowledge as a trap, and the instructor as an agent with dubious motives. Repeated experience with the instructor's approach to evaluation may mitigate this. Still, interactions that promote psychological safety in discussion and engaging the students in conversations about outcome measures can demonstrate good faith.

Perhaps the student is skeptical about the instructor's expertise, either in their domain knowledge or how they approach structuring and facilitating the course. This relates directly to the power dynamics discussed previously, which may be mitigated by considering the interacting sources of power at play.

The borderline case between a constructive and destructive contrarian is a student who genuinely enjoys a debate. Some instructors use *gentle* direct engagement on those terms to honor the student's zeal for argument without diminishing psychological safety for the student or the group. Where this debate fixation has become a core aspect of their identity, a private conversation that directly discusses the impact on the classroom dynamic may be appropriate.

When engaging with a destructive contrarian and attempting to work with the student to change their pattern of behavior, an instructor should take action carefully:

- Do not personalize it or get "hooked" by the behavior during class. An emotional reaction may only reinforce the destructive contrarian's skepticism of the course or instructor.
- See if the group dynamic will push back. When relationships, charisma, and/or group norms that value respect are present in the classroom, students may shift the dynamic in a way that minimizes the contrarian's platform. Other students may even directly intervene to offer an alternative perspective or reinforce a more constructive group dynamic.

- If possible, talk to your colleagues: is this a pattern of behavior observed in other classes? Could other examples offer clues as to the underlying causes of the student's behavior? Have other instructors been able to work constructively with the student to address this?
- Shift the behavior outside of the classroom, for example, "I appreciate your question, but we'll have to discuss it further after class."
- Be direct when necessary, for example, "We're getting into what feels like a meta-level critique, which is not appropriate in class. Please make an appointment so you and I can talk directly."

It is, unfortunately, anecdotally more common for younger female instructors to encounter a destructive contrarian in their classroom, particularly in traditionally male-dominated fields. In these cases, no amount of listening, gently redirecting, or demonstrating competency may be sufficient to change the dynamic, and it would be unfair to the instructor and the class as a whole to let the pattern of behavior persist. Here, the instructor may have to meet privately with the student and firmly set out expectations of behavior given group norms, fairness to other students, and the desired classroom dynamic.

Three Points to Remember about Contrarianism

- Underlying needs or values can drive a pattern of persistent contrarian behavior.
- A constructive contrarian can be a refreshing antidote to conformity; however, the instructor may need to work with the student to promote their self-awareness and ensure the dynamic is positive for both the contrarian and the group.
- The destructive contrarian is not personal—until it is. An instructor may have to work hard to maintain their emotional cool, avoid being "hooked" by the behavior in class, and consider whether a stronger intervention is appropriate.

SUPPORTING SECOND-LANGUAGE SPEAKERS

A classroom with a significant range of fluency in the language of instruction poses particular challenges. In this context the basics of effective communication significantly impact comprehension. In some cases, this is as simple as reminding oneself of the *absolute* basics while teaching:

- Talk slowly!
- Pause!
- Breathe!

While straightforward, these simple actions can be challenging to maintain throughout a class. Many instructors need to record themselves teaching to understand how rapid their speech becomes when excited about a topic of discussion or pressed for time. Other fundamental techniques make speech more intelligible, such as using uptalk for questions but not statements, varying cadence and volume for emphasis, and making thoughtful use of gestures.

Approaches that support effective interactions more generally, such as wait time, are particularly important for second-language speakers. Other techniques can be used in a more targeted way to promote engagement from these students. This can include *when* you invite such students to contribute, *how* you do so, and your approach to *supporting* them as they engage.

When to Invite Contributions

While a long-term goal should be helping non-confident students become proactive contributors throughout the discussion, becoming more comfortable speaking up requires some degree of practice. Some second-language speakers do not voluntarily contribute to discussions. One approach to gently easing them into participation is inviting engagement at moments where there is a general understanding of appropriate contributions.

For example, if a lesson typically has discussion followed by a brief summative moment, and students understand the nature of this activity, the student may feel more confident contributing at this time. Some instructors even use a set of somewhat common questions. Students will understand these questions from previous experience and can focus on the content. For example,

- Initial framing of discussion: "We'll open the floor for people to share their arguments. As you listen, *identify one you find very convincing.*" Summative moment: "Student X, you've been listening to a few different perspectives on this issue. *What, in your opinion, was the strongest argument?*"
- Initial framing of discussion: "Let's work through an example together. As we do this, try to *identify general tips* that will let you use this method on your own." Summative moment: "We've been looking at one particular example. What about other cases you might encounter in the future? *What is one tip to remember when using this method next time?*"

This approach should be used with care, as students are likely to recognize if calling on certain students at this time becomes a pattern. Additionally, engaging in summative reflection is a learning moment and should be offered to different individuals throughout the class. It can be useful to set a more general norm that *any* student who has been quiet throughout the discussion is likely to be invited to offer a summative reflection.

Group work provides another avenue for engaging second-language speakers at a point where they can be more confident in their contribution. With a clear task and a group consensus, a student may be more confident sharing the agreed deliverables. The instructor can also direct complex or poorly phrased follow-up questions to other group members more able to handle them on-the-fly.

Similarly, homework or responses prepared in advance of class may be another avenue for less fluent speakers to more confidently and coherently share their ideas.

How to Invite Contributions

A dynamic that deliberately uses wait time (rather than an expectation of rapid-fire contributions) can also be a means of supporting these students. This wait time allows the student to translate the question, gather their thoughts, and communicate them in the language of instruction.

One can also reframe or repeat key questions. While too involved for every question, it can nonetheless be very effective when used strategically.

- Reframe: "Could a reductionist approach lead to insight here? If we break down the problem into subproblems, then study each in isolation, will we get to an answer?"
- Repeat: "It sounds like we're questioning whether we should solve for x or y. [Pause] What do you think—should we solve for x or y?"

If using nonvoluntary participation, cueing can help students attend to a question with the knowledge that they are going to need to respond, rather than simply focus on understanding the question. Consider the difference a straightforward change can make:

- "How is Boltzmann's constant relevant to black-body radiation, [Student's name]?"
- "[Student's name], how is Boltzmann's constant relevant to black-body radiation?"

A further extension is combining cueing with repetition when posing a question. This allows the instructor to reiterate the focus of the question. For example,

- "This leads us to consider *emergent properties* and whether they are present in this context. [Student's name], what might be an *emergent property* here?"
- "In some cases, you can calculate the *limit of a function*, and in others, you cannot. Let's examine each function from the problem set. [Student's name], were you able to calculate a *limit for the first function*, or does the *limit not exist*?"

This is very similar to an approach of restating and questioning, which gives the student a specific point with the technical language already present. For example,

- "[Other student] has described a *reinforcing feedback loop*, with a *necessary* cause. Do you agree that this cause is *necessary*; that it must be present for us to observe this effect? Or do you think it is only *sufficient*; that other causes could also lead to this effect?"

Another approach is scaffolding student responses by clearly setting out the starting point or skeleton of a response. For example,

- "There were two sides to this debate. We'll have someone share one initial position. Then, I'd like us to extend it with as many related arguments as we can. Simply say, 'And—' followed by an argument we haven't heard yet."
- "Let's look at each claim from the author. You can either say, 'I agree, because—' or 'I disagree because—.'"
- "Examine the deductive argument closely and evaluate whether it is sound and valid. When you're ready, you can say, 'It's sound/unsound, because—' or 'It's valid/invalid, because—.'"

Supporting Engagement: Norms and Paraphrasing Strategies

Second-language speakers often experience increased levels of anxiety and classroom communication apprehension. Promoting psychological safety can mitigate the negative impact on learning. A significant action is simply conveying two norms to the class as a whole:

- Everyone will have adequate time to make their contribution—even if they need to pause to find the right words or start over.
- Students won't be left "out to dry" if they stumble while contributing—the instructor is ready to help with a technical term or pronunciation, or even paraphrase.

In following up on this second norm, an instructor will want to be thoughtful in how they paraphrase a second-language speaker's contribution.

In some cases, the student's specific point may be a little unclear to the instructor. There is a tricky choice between asking the student to clarify (which they may or may not be able to do) or attempting to paraphrase or offer a reflective restatement of the contribution. In doing the latter, the instructor can consider how *they* can own the confusion and give an avenue for the student to clarify (rather than twist the point into the instructor's idea).

The instructor will want to convey that "Let me know if I'm not quite getting this right . . ." is a very genuine comment. The instructor can also consider when to engage in a "sympathetic paraphrase," that is, one that includes a significant degree of inference and extension on the part of the instructor. For example,

- Student: "I, uh, I think it's maybe emergent. Because there are all the different people. Yeah. And they have their own goals; like, they're not told what to do. So [trails off]."
- Instructor: "So [Student X] would classify it as an emergent property because they have identified a population of heterogeneous and autonomous agents interacting without a central controller. [Student Y], tell me about the characteristics you would look for in this context."

Humor in a Second Language

Humor can pose a particular challenge for second-language speakers when it becomes part of the classroom dynamic. While one shouldn't back down from being one's genuine self (puns included, if necessary), an instructor should be mindful of the struggle this can introduce for some students. As a doctoral candidate who had lived in an English-speaking country for several years once confessed, "Ugh, humor—sometimes I just don't know when people are joking."

Apparent proficiency with a given language does not necessarily equate with a nuanced understanding of interactions, even those that seem so obvious to a native speaker of the instructional language.

For an instructor, this means humor requires extra considerations. In short, they should

- be thoughtful when injecting a joke into the interaction;
- make sure everyone understands there is a joke; and
- be prepared to explain the joke.

**Three Points to Remember for Students Who Are Not
Native-Speakers of the Language of Instruction**

- The basics of effective communication require deliberate practice.
- Engagement can be facilitated by *when* and *how* the instructor poses questions.
- Supportive norms can diminish classroom communication apprehension and anxiety.

TEACHING WITHOUT DOMAIN-SPECIFIC EXPERTISE

Expertise is the primary expectation students have of their instructor and a strong source of power in the classroom. Yet, instructors often teach outside their specific discipline. How can an instructor effectively promote engagement with topics where they do not have deep domain-specific expertise? How can they do this without compromising credibility?

In such contexts, instructors should shift their role from subject matter expert to being a *facilitator*. While some measure of brushing-up on the subject is necessary, facilitation does not rely on possessing every piece of factual knowledge or current opinion in a given discipline. Instead, the instructor employs practical knowledge and experience in facilitation to guide meaningful engagement with the subject.

In this role, the instructor's skillset may resemble that of a mediator. Some elements of the response repertoire can also be borrowed from a management or strategy consultant. These individuals often work for clients who have more experience in a given industry or organization. Core skills in this context include clarifying, sense-checking, reflecting, and investigating. Instructors can describe this role at the outset of the course. Approaching every class session as a joint investigation of the topic reinforces this approach.

An instructor teaching without domain-specific expertise will eventually be asked a question they are unable to answer immediately. Two steps can manage this interaction: first, diagnose the student's question—why are they asking this? Second, determine an appropriate response.

Diagnosing the student's question requires considering their motivation and current knowledge. The motivation for asking a question varies significantly: from requesting straightforward clarification to speculation given interest or excitement. Similarly, an answer can range from necessary course content to elaboration beyond the scope of the course.

Every instructor's response repertoire in this context will depend on their relative comfort admitting their own confusion, the power dynamics in their classroom, and student propensity for instructional dissent.

Responses that pivot to other students for reflection or evaluation can provide time for an instructor to gather their thoughts. Similarly, if students develop the question further or draw out key ideas, an opportunity for a facilitative interaction is often created.

Two common scenarios are a student requesting clarification of a very discipline-specific point or a student exploring an idea not explicitly present in the readings or materials of the day. In both cases, a relevant mantra could be, *logic is your friend.* Below is an example question of each type and a sample of possible instructor responses.

Student initiation I: "I didn't understand X in the reading for this class. Can you please explain?" This is a direct request for clarification; however, if the instructor is not deeply familiar with the passage, they may not have a quick "correct" response. They may wish to buy some thinking time, source multiple perspectives, or directly consult the material during or after class. Potential responses include the following:

- "Tell me more about your interpretation of the passage, or what you found confusing?" As the student explains, the instructor may be able to determine an appropriate response. In some cases, it may be a comment on the student's thinking process rather than an absolute right/wrong answer. For example, "That interpretation is plausible, given your logic, and it is consistent with my understanding of that passage as well." More importantly, if it becomes apparent that another interpretation is more appropriate, the instructor should follow up via e-mail or in the next class.

- "Can others share how they interpreted this passage? What did it mean when you read it?" Crowdsourcing several perspectives gives the instructor a basis for a more considered response.

- "Let's open the reading and look together." When the passage in question reflects a common confusion, this can be very effective. It is, however, more time-consuming. Using this response also requires the instructor to demonstrate their thinking process "live." Some instructors may be more comfortable with this than others, given personality, power, and credibility in the classroom.

- "Let me note the passage in question, and I can email the class later." When the passage in question reflects a confusion particular to the individual or is not critical for the present discussion, this can be very effective. The instructor may frame it as being able to do justice to the question, yet need a bit of time to do their own research.

- "We can't go deeply into this now, but if you bring the reading to my office hours, we can review it together." This may put the instructor on the spot to later work through the confusion "live" with the student; however, it demonstrates individual consideration and is relationship-building. Most instructors would make sure to note this question and review the material in advance of office hours.

Student initiation II: "Would it be possible to do X?" or "Could X lead to Y?" Here, the student presents a speculative idea or hypothesis that extends a concept of the day beyond the scope of the discussion. Instructors with deep domain-specific knowledge would be able to offer an immediate response. They would know if someone has, in fact, tried that before, be able to provide comparison cases, or simply have an expert opinion.

An instructor without domain-specific knowledge might wish to acknowledge that a quick investigation might reveal an answer, for example, "I haven't encountered that specific proposal before, but it is possible someone has tried. If you look it up after class, please let me know what you find." Alternatively, the instructor may wish to prompt extension as a means of facilitating a reality check or source multiple perspectives from the group. Potential responses include the following:

- "Tell us more about your assumptions or what led you to this suggestion." In many cases, this form of student question is a hypothesis in disguise. That is, the student is framing their contribution as a question to mitigate their uncertainty or minimize the possibility of negative evaluation. As they elaborate, their assumptions and depth of knowledge become clear. The instructor may then be able to comment on either the soundness (substance) or validity (logic) of the suggestion.
- "How might one evaluate if this is plausible?" This response can address the original student or the group as a whole. Other avenues also provide focus, "How could we test this?" "What evidence would you need to gather?" "Can an analogy suggest an answer to this question?" "What is the specific information we're missing?"
- "Hmmm, [restates the idea], what do you [the class] think?" Here, the instructor pivots to the group as a whole for their evaluation rather than staying with the individual. When restating, the instructor might deliberately adjust the contribution from a question to a statement or concrete hypothesis. This approach is very similar to the previous response, but more open-ended than anchoring on a specific dimension of evaluation. This also provides an avenue for comments from students who have seen a similar question in another course or discipline.
- "I'm afraid this goes beyond what we can discuss today. If you come by my office hours, I'd be happy to explore it with you." This offer, if genuine, is often appreciated. Where the instructor knows their knowledge may be a limitation, a referral to a colleague nonetheless demonstrates

consideration, for example, "This is Prof. X's area of expertise. You could drop by their office hours to chat" [or, "I'd be happy to introduce you by email"].

Three Points to Remember about Teaching without Domain-Specific Expertise

• While teaching without domain-specific expertise can be stressful, it is also incredibly rewarding.
• Do not attempt an unsustainable amount of preparation for each class. Instead, tailor your response repertoire to facilitate student-driven exploration and evaluation; use logic and domain-general analytical tools; and make associations to your own area(s) of expertise.
• Don't be afraid to say, "I don't know," so long as followed by, "but I will find out . . ." or a suggested avenue for the student to investigate further.

NOTES

1. Academically entitled students are defined as those with "the tendency to possess an expectation of academic success without a sense of personal responsibility for achieving that success" (Chowning & Campbell, 2009). This can extend to entitled expectations of professors or course policy and externalized responsibility for their academic success.

2. Simonds (1997) includes a detailed list of example challenge behaviors. Briefly, commonly observed behaviors include the following. Procedural: disagreeing with course policy (esp. absence policy); wanting full credit for make-up work; disruptive or off-topic talking during class; providing inappropriate comments or examples under the guise of humor. Evaluation: questioning grade on an assignment; nagging or begging for a higher grade; arguing questions not valid; questioning fairness of grading practices. Power play: interrupting the instructor to reinforce their opinion; questioning instructor's expertise; refusing to participate; attempting to embarrass the instructor or fellow students. Practicality: questioning relevance of course content to everyday life or the discipline in general; questioning why a course is required.

3. This effect varied by question type: students were 28 percent more likely to switch to the majority answer on a multiple choice question and 38 percent more likely to switch on a true/false question (Perez, et al., 2010).

4. The Pareto principle is also variously known as the 80/20 rule, the law of the vital few, or the principle of factor sparsity. It captures to the idea that roughly 80 percent of a given effect is often driven by 20 percent of the causes. First identified in the realm of economics and wealth distribution, the relationship is found across a variety of disciplines, including computer programming, business revenues, and health outcomes.

Appendix 1

Example Discussion and Commentary

What follows is a brief transcript from a cognitive neuroscience class session at the Minerva Schools at KGI,[1] followed by observations of the possible effects of the instructor's responses. Durations are included for each instance; a reader may wish to reflect on the time required to articulate certain types of points.

The instructor has already introduced the topic and learning goals of the day and invited students to collaboratively develop a definition of "speech" and "language" as an initial warm-up. Pre-read for this class session included Hickok's *Computational Neuroanatomy of Speech Production* (2012), which introduced a highly specialized conceptualization of "speech," relying on the vocal tract, regions of the brain responsible for auditory and motor control, and the role of acoustic and somatosensory feedback in error correction.

This transcript occurs prior to starting specific activities from the lesson plan and relies on voluntary contribution of students' ideas, rather than recalling a particular definition from a pre-reading. In this class, the norm is that students typically raise their hands to signal an interest in contributing. The instructor invites student contributions by name, including contributions from students whose hands are not currently raised. Technology allows individual students to provide yes/no votes visible to the entire class, signal emotions or agreement with emoticons, and write in chat.

Following several contributions to the working definition, Student 1 raised their hand. Note: this is intended as an example rather than a model of best practice.

- Student 1: "This is more of a question, but do we consider sign language a form of 'speech'?"

- Instructor: "What do people think? Would we consider sign language a form of speech, by our definition? Quick vote from everyone: is sign language a form of speech?" [8 second wait as students vote] "Some yeses, some noes . . . and maybe some on the fence—and some votes are changing now that I've said that. So let's quickly chat. [Student 2], why would you say yes?" *Note: Student 2 had been visibly nodding before and during voting, although their hand was not raised.*
- Student 2: "I would say yes because speech has to do with relaying our ideas, sort of like going through the levels from something conceptual to something that we can code and express, so I think sign language does fit into that general framework." [17 seconds]
- Instructor: "That sounds like those early levels that [Student 3] was describing earlier. [Student 4], what would you say?" *Note: the student's hand was raised.*
- Student 4: "So I remember I think in one of the videos they talked about four aspects that we can look for to say that something is a language and that's what they used to justify that some animals didn't—that the crabs cracking their claws is not considered language, and I—as far as I can see, I think that sign language does account for all of those four." [24 seconds; other students are visibly signaling their agreement with this contribution]
- Instructor: "Absolutely, so we can see those characteristics [lists the four described in the class pre-read]. All of those seem relevant. I think there were a couple of noes, though, so [Student 5], where might you say something is missing or less sure?"
- Student 5: "I think sign language is definitely a language, but I wouldn't necessarily classify it as speech because I think speech has to do with producing sounds when you speak, although—I—I—I dunno . . . maybe this is a very limiting definition." [15 seconds]
- Instructor: "I think it's fair to highlight that, and have these questions of 'should we limit the definition?' and 'what does it mean to put those kinds of caveats on it?' [Student 6], I think you'd gone back and forth [when voting], and I saw a [signal of agreement during the previous point], was it a similar consideration from you?"
- Student 6: "Yeah, so, I was looking at one of the models that we were learning about for speech, like the . . . [glances at notes] what is it . . . the psycholinguistic approach to language and thought that it made sense that for any speech or language there has to be a process of thinking of a word, then forming the word, then actually withdrawing the word, so there's often this phenomenon of a word being on the tip of your tongue, but you don't exactly say it, and I thought because of that sign language may not be speech because there isn't this auditory process of you forming the word, but then I went back because when you're signing something you're sort of translating the word in your head to an actual physical manifestation

even though it's not auditory it's somatosensory so there is some sort of representation. So I think because of that it might be considered speech." [58 seconds]

- Instructor: "That is an interesting question: can we see analogous errors when the speech is being conveyed with gesture versus this (motions to mouth) articulatory system? [Student 7], what else would you like to highlight?" Note: the student's hand was raised; specific types of errors were described in the pre-class readings as being used to elucidate the nature of speech production.
- Student 7: "Yeah, just as a response to [Student 5]'s point it is definitely not speech in the sense that they cannot—for example, the findings from language-use or speech-use cannot be generalized to sign language use, I think, and I think that's because even though they are both using motor control they are using different circuits, right? Because one is muscles here and one is muscles in your hands and although you can find connections between the two I don't think it can be generalized." [41 seconds]
- Instructor: "This is another one: if it feels analogous, what are the actual underlying neural circuits, and are they similar enough or different enough that you would think about it in different ways. [Student 8] how about a final thought from you here?" *Note: the student's hand was raised.*
- Student 8: "Yeah, so from one of the graphs in the readings there was, like, articulatory control and it went to vocal tract and then speech, so I was thinking, like, speech only involves, like, the vocal tract, not, uh, full (motions with hands)." [22 seconds]
- Instructor: "So linking to [Student 7]'s point, and really looking at that diagram and again saying, if we want a stringent definition that says it has to use these processes, we can see where it's not going to directly match, but again, this question of analogies becomes quite interesting. [Student 1], thank you for the question. Do you want a final thought on what you've heard so far?"
- Student 1: "I think I agree with most of what I've heard. I was just curious because we seem to be equating language and speech, and then I was wondering if there was that caveat of 'is sign language a language but not speech' and is there kind of a distinction there." [14 seconds]

In this example the instructor may be slightly over-paraphrasing or expressing enthusiasm in a way that could be mistaken for affirmative evaluation ("Absolutely, . . ."). Further observations of the possible effects of the instructor's responses are included below.

- Student 1: The initial question
- Instructor: "What do people think? Would we consider sign language a form of speech, by our definition? Quick vote from everyone: is sign

language a form of speech?" [8 second wait] "Some yeses, some noes . . . and maybe some on the fence—and some votes are changing now that I've said that. So let's quickly chat. [Student 2], why would you say yes?" *Note: Student 2 had been visibly nodding prior to and during voting.*

- ○ Observations: The instructor avoids the obvious *why* question to the first student ("Why would you ask that?") or a direct question in return ("Do *you* think we should?") and pivots to the group as a whole rather than offering an immediate response. Eight seconds of wait time gives students the opportunity to think before responding, and all students eventually respond.
- ○ While a cold-call is employed to begin debriefing the responses, the selected student had given strong visual cues that they had an opinion ready to share. "So let's quickly chat" is applying procedural framing to the discussion, with an assumption of how long it will take to discuss the question. While that is likely driven by an understanding of time constraints in the lesson plan, it may be an element of control that is not needed at this point.

- Student 2: "I would say yes because speech has to do with relaying our ideas; sort of like going through the levels from something conceptual to something that we can code and express, so I think sign language does fit into that general framework." [17 seconds]
- Instructor: "That sounds like those early levels that [Student 3] was describing earlier. [Student 4], what would you say?" *Note: the student's hand was raised.*
  - ○ Observations: The instructor makes a declarative statement, and deliberately offers attribution to a previous student. "What would you say" may be interpreted as an invitation to extend the *instructor's* specific idea, rather than the more general invitation to contribute that was intended.
- Student 4: "So I remember I think in one of the videos they talked about four aspects that we can look for to say that something is a language and that's what they used to justify that some animals didn't—that the crabs cracking their claws is not considered language, and I—as far as I can see, I think that sign language does account for all of those four. [24 seconds; other students are visibly signaling their agreement with this contribution]
- Instructor: "Absolutely, so we can see those characteristics [lists the four described in the class pre-read]. All of those seem relevant. I think there were a couple noes though, so [Student 5], where might you say something is missing or less sure?"
  - ○ Observations: The instructor didn't interject with a question when the student faltered (in naming or describing the four aspects) or respond asking them to clarify. "All of those seem relevant" and "absolutely" may appear as unnecessarily evaluative remarks rather than a constructive

declarative statement, particularly when students who had voted "no" had yet to speak.

○ In soliciting an opposing perspective, the question "Where might you say something is missing or less sure?" is intended as a general invitation but may be experienced as narrowing the scope of desired contributions. The instructor could have simply used the student's name.

- Student 5: "I think sign language is definitely a language, but I wouldn't necessarily classify it as speech because I think speech has to do with producing sounds when you speak, although—I—I—I dunno . . . maybe this is a very limiting definition." [15 seconds]

- Instructor: "I think it's fair to highlight that, and have these questions of 'should we limit the definition?' and 'what does it mean to put those kinds of caveats on it?' [Student 6], I think you'd gone back and forth [when voting] and I saw a [signal of agreement during the previous point], was it a similar consideration from you?"

○ Observations: The response here may blend a declarative statement with a reflective restatement, although the student wasn't given wait time to re-engage (the pause before pivoting to engage the next student was 1 second). While likely helpful to note how Student 6 had signalled uncertainty, "Was it a similar consideration from you?" may anchor their contribution on the previous point in an overly controlling manner.

- Student 6: "Yeah, so, I was looking at one of the models that we were learning about for speech, like the . . . [glances at notes] what is it . . . the psycholinguistic approach to language and thought that it made sense that for any speech or language there has to be a process of thinking of a word, then forming the word, then actually withdrawing the word, so there's often this phenomenon of a word being on the tip of your tongue but you don't exactly say it and I thought because of that sign language may not be speech because there isn't this auditory process of you forming the word, but then I went back because when you're signing something you're sort of translating the word in your head to an actual physical manifestation even though it's not auditory it's somatosensory so there is some sort of representation. So I think because of that it might be considered speech." [58 seconds]

- Instructor: "That is an interesting question: can we see analogous errors when the speech is being conveyed with gesture versus this (motions to mouth) articulatory system? [Student 7], what else would you like to highlight?" Note: the student's hand was raised; specific types of errors were described in the pre-class readings as being used to elucidate the nature of speech production.

○ Observations: The instructor knew the student was *likely* grasping for the term "psycholinguistic approach" but as the student's pause was brief—and may also be related to organizing their thoughts—did not jump in.

- ○ "What else?" might signal that an "else" would be appreciated rather than a continuation or elaboration, but if a commonly generic element in the instructor's response repertoire might simply be treated as such. Again, the instructor could consider whether to simply use the student's name and wait time when inviting a contribution.
- Student 7: "Yeah, just as a response to [Student 5]'s point it is definitely not speech in the sense that they cannot—for example, the findings from language-use or speech-use cannot be generalized to sign language use, I think, and I think that's because even though they are both using motor control they are using different circuits, right? Because one is muscles here and one is muscles in your hands and although you can find connections between the two I don't think it can be generalized." [41 seconds]
- Instructor: "This is another one: if it feels analogous, what are the actual underlying neural circuits, and are they similar enough or different enough that you would think about it in different ways. [Student 8] how about a final thought from you here?" *Note: the student's hand was raised.*
  - ○ Observations: The instructor is using the question-prompt to exert procedural control and wrap-up the conversation. This may result in the student sharing their intended contribution, abandoning their contribution given further students can't engage with it directly, or switching to a summative point.
- Student 8: "Yeah, so from one of the graphs in the readings there was, like, articulatory control and it went to vocal tract and then speech, so I was thinking, like, speech only involves, like, the vocal tract, not, uh, full (motions with hands)." [22 seconds]
- Instructor: So linking to [Student 7]'s point, and really looking at that diagram and again saying, if we want a stringent definition that says it has to use these processes, we can see where it's not going to match directly, but again, this question of analogies becomes quite interesting. [Student 1], thank you for the question. Do you want a final thought on what you've heard so far?"
  - ○ Observations: As the student faltered to some degree what appears to be a reflective restatement was employed, but a slightly disingenuous one given there was no time for the student to respond to it as such. Thus, it's more of a declarative statement that summarizes the discussion from the instructor's perspective.

NOTE

1. Reprinted with permission. With thanks to the Minerva Schools at KGI.

Appendix 2

Coding Thinking Skills in Classroom Interactions

An instructor can attempt to code their questions according to the type of thinking they *intend* to solicit. Similarly, student responses can be coded according to the type of thinking they exhibit. Each row in table B.1 provides an example of a single in-class interaction (note: several unprompted student contributions are also included).

Definitions of each question/response type are found in table 8.1 in chapter 8. These examples are provided to demonstrate coding using a modified version of Bloom's taxonomy, rather than as exemplars of best practice. Key verbs or closely related words that aid coding are indicated in italics when present.

These examples highlight how an instructor's phrasing of a question may solicit a *certain* type of knowledge or thinking, how a student's response may or may not match the query, and how students' questions can also demonstrate certain types of thinking skills.

Table B.1 Examples of Classifying Questions and Student Responses Using a Revised Version of Bloom's Taxonomy

Question Type	Instructor Question	Response Type	Example Student Response
Aside	"Did you like this reading?"	Aside	"No! It was too long!" [Note: no further recall of what was in the reading itself]
N/A	Unprompted—no instructor question	Aside	"Have you seen this (related) paper? I think it's very interesting!"
N/A	Unprompted—no instructor question	Aside	"We talked about something like this in [other class]!"
Recall	"What is a necessary condition? Given your readings, how do we *define* that term?"	Recall	"A necessary condition is a condition that must be present for an event to occur." [Recall of definition]
Recall	"What were the four levels of analysis described in the reading?"	Recall	"Biological, individual, group, societal." [Recall of information without explanation or elaboration]
Recall	"Do you *remember* where the idea of 'fire together, wire together' came from?"	Recall	"That was Hebb." [Attribution of an idea]
Recall	"Here's an image from the readings. What do we call a relationship like this?"	Recall	"That's a reinforcing feedback loop." [Student is correctly supplying a label for something they have seen before]
Understanding *With a correct answer*	"*Explain* in your own words: what is a necessary condition?"	Understanding *With a correct answer*	"It's where any time you see the effect, you also see that cause. You can't bring about the effect without it, because it's *necessary*. Like how it's necessary to go to class to pass the course because of the absence policy. You can't pass the course if you skip classes." [Note: the student does not merely recall a definition from a reading]
Understanding *With a correct answer*	"Given our definition of emergent properties, what could be an example?"	Understanding *With a correct answer*	"A traffic jam is emergent because of all those cars interacting." [Note: while asked to produce an example, it is for definition or classification, rather than a more considered creation to use as the basis of further analysis]

Understanding *Without a specific correct answer*	"In your opinion, what was a key *theme* in this reading?"	"When the author was talking about cultural differences, I found that particularly compelling."
Understanding *Without a specific correct answer*	"What would you want to *highlight* about this concept?"	"I think it's important to remember that . . ."
Understanding *Without a specific correct answer*	"What key lesson would you *summarize* from this activity?"	"We need to look for interactions between levels of analysis because we couldn't fully explain any of the examples using just one level alone."
Understanding *Without a specific correct answer*	"What's an *example* of this? What system might we deconstruct to identify interactions leading to emergent properties?"	"I think a jazz combo will have that kind of complexity." [The student is demonstrating understanding of a concept by identifying a relevant exemplar]
Applying	"If '*individual*', '*group*', and '*social*' are relevant levels for human social systems, what levels of analysis could be used to analyze Conway's Game of Life?"	"Individual cells, groups of cells, the whole world." [The student is applying a concept to a specific novel context in a straightforward manner]
Applying	"How might we make a *diagram* of the causal factors we've been describing?"	[This assumes it's a straightforward application rather than more in-depth creation of something more wholly novel]
Applying	"What is the *density* of this network? Can someone *calculate* it for the group?"	[Student calculates] "It's 0.17."

(Continued)

Table B.1   Examples of Classifying Questions and Student Responses Using a Revised Version of Bloom's Taxonomy *(Continued)*

Question Type	Instructor Question	Response Type	Example Student Response
Analyzing	"How did your breakout group approach to this problem?"	Analyzing	"We broke down the problem into four sub-parts. . ." [Note: this could also be classified as recall on the part of the selected student, particularly if they were not an equal contributor and are reading from group notes]
Analyzing	"How does your group's approach compare to what we've just heard?"	Analyzing	"Well, we both used the same levels of analysis, but we identified different group agents."
Evaluating	"Your group took a different approach. What caused you to do that?"	Evaluating	"We thought this was best explained by focusing on a different level of analysis . . ."
Evaluating	"What causes you to agree or disagree with the previous point?"	Evaluating	"I disagree because . . ."
Evaluating	"In what way was this effective of ineffective?"	Evaluating	"It was effective because. . ."
Creating	"How could we design an algorithm to address this problem?"	Creating	[Student describes a novel proposal, synthesizing information or concepts]
Creating	"What is a novel analogy that embodies this?"	Creating	"If we think about an atom like a solar system, then . . ."
Creating	"What new tool can we make to help us do this?"	Creating	"I think we could combine A and B into a new framework that will satisfy all the constraints at once."

Mismatches can occur between the question/prompt and the response that is *intended* by the question/prompt and the response

Question Type	Example Questions	Response Type	Example Responses
Recall	"What is a necessary condition? How do we define that term?"	Understanding with Y/N answer	"A necessary condition is a condition that must be present for an event to occur. I think of it like . . ."

Understanding *Without a specific correct answer*	"What key learning would you take away from this activity?"	Recall	"In this activity, we did X, Y, and Z." [Note: no real synthesis and no key learning highlighted]
Evaluating	"Let's decide whether we are on board with the premise—do you agree or disagree?"	Analyzing	"Oh, I wanted to propose another similarity or difference . . ." [Note: this responds to a previous prompt]
Evaluating	"Which approach do you think is most effective, and why?"	Aside	"We talked about something like this in [other class]!"
Evaluating	"Which approach do you think is most effective, and why?"	Analyzing	"We talked about something like this in [other class] but used different levels of analysis that are specific to econometrics."
Evaluating	"Do you agree or disagree with this proposal?"	Applying	"I agree . . . it sounds right given the concept, but I'm not sure why" Note: the student has some understanding of the concept but is unable to evaluate effectively. A reply of, "I don't know" could be its own category]

A student *asking* a question may be off-topic/an aside or a demonstration of learning. It should be coded as best as can be inferred.

Unprompted		Aside	"But why does this matter?"
Unprompted		Aside	"Can you clarify X? What do you mean?" [Note: this is a straightforward request for clarification or recall, but the student does not have this knowledge]
Unprompted		Applying	"Why are we assuming there are just four levels?" [Note: this tends to indicate the desire to disagree or test out an idea related to the application under discussion]
Unprompted		Evaluating	"What about society? Couldn't we have five levels of analysis here? [Note: this could be rephrased into an evaluation, possibly with a proposal for consideration, such as, "I don't think this takes everything into account. I think we need to add a societal level of analysis." In this case, the instructor would likely paraphrase it as such.]

Appendix 3

The Response Repertoire

The response repertoire of an instructor requires an understanding of how specific prompts or reactions to student contributions can elicit a reply, affect psychological safety, and shape the overall classroom dynamic. Below is a non-exhaustive list of different types of prompts or responses for specific situations. When developing an individualized response repertoire an instructor should take care to be authentic and, where necessary, adapt the examples below into something that feels natural.

JUDGMENTAL, EVALUATIVE, AND NONEVALUATIVE RESPONSES

Many more examples exist of each type of response. As a general rule of thumb, judgmental responses include a *value judgment* and are often personalizable (such as praising effort or smarts).

As judgmental responses are typically not actionable, it is not uncommon for instructors to include both judgmental and evaluative remarks in a single comment intended as formative feedback, for example, "Great answer! An analogy effectively distills a complex context into something more comprehensible," or "Clever! Using index: match was a very efficient way to search your data. Nesting functions is increasingly useful as the data get more complex." Such combinations can minimize the effectiveness of the component intended as formative feedback. Consult chapter 7 for further discussion of such responses.

Appendix 3

Judgmental Responses

- "Perfect!" "Awesome!" "Great answer!" "Great effort—keep it up!" "I'm so pleased by your paper!"
- "Clever!" "Very smart!" "Genius!"
- "Terrible" "Poor effort" "Bad"
- "How could you think that?" "You're way off . . ." "You messed up."

Evaluative Responses

- "That's correct" [typically followed by formative feedback pertaining to the process or output].
- "That's consistent with the literature/model/framework" [typically followed by formative feedback].
- "That's incorrect [typically followed by elaboration of process/where the student may have gone wrong/explanation of why challenging].
- Reflective restatement followed by formative feedback, for example, "[You suggest that] Eigenvector centrality gives us the most insight into the network structure, compared to other approaches. In graph theory, centrality measures. . ."
- Specific observation followed by formative feedback, for example, "The way you focused on the role of dopamine is appropriate given the symptoms in question. In future, one method to link symptoms to neurotransmitter systems is to . . ."
- Synthesis followed by formative feedback, for example, "All of these examples used a linear search algorithm effectively. When deciding between linear or binary search, consider . . ." or "Most assignments focused on interest rates and the GDP. In future, one could consider other indicators by . . ."

Nonevaluative Responses

- Reflective restatement of the contribution.
- "I see."
- "Tell me more."
- "Thank you [for sharing/for your thoughts]."

COMMON PITFALLS WHEN QUESTIONING

Yes/No questions are sometimes useful as a discussion starter so long as students engage in explanation or analysis (which may require follow-up questions). Many instructors attempt to avoid questions that can be interpreted as yes/no given their tendency to inhibit explanation, even if their classroom dynamic includes an expectation of elaboration. Some questions are *effectively* yes/no questions. "Is an ANOVA appropriate here?" or "Is an ANOVA or a t-test appropriate here?" can be answered with one word. In contrast, "How can we determine which statistical test to use here?" requires elaboration.

Leading questions diminish the depth of discussion and foster a dynamic where students engage in guessing what the instructor has in mind rather than thinking for themselves.

Rhetorical or teacher-answered questions are unproductive for the purposes of discussion or promoting thinking. Instructor who find themselves frequently answering their own questions should explore whether the issue is one of wait time rather than the question itself.

Combining multiple questions is confusing and can confuse concepts that should be distinct, for example, "Let's review the reading. What is the author's thesis? What evidence does he provide? Is this cognitive or emotional persuasion?"

Disconnected questions don't follow a logical thread or build on previous contributions. They can also constitute a failure to seek elaboration or explore the implications of a previous contribution.

"Why questions," even those intended as genuine overtures for extension or critical thinking, may carry an inherently inquisitional dimension and be less productive than alternatives (Dillon, 1981b; Wassermann, 1992, 2017). Expansive why questions are also more likely to elicit "I don't know" than questions that take a more considered approach to a topic. Consider the difference between asking, "Why did you do that?" and "What suggested this approach to the algorithm?"

Instructors who deliberately avoid *why questions* believe such contexts are better served with a prompt for elaboration, such as "Tell me more," or a specific nudge such as "Perhaps you could explain the estimation to me step-by-step?" [versus "Why is that a good estimate?"] or "How might we find evidence to support that hypothesis?" [versus "Why do you think that is plausible?"].

APPROACHES TO QUESTIONING

Questions can be described by whether they are productive or unproductive, by the type of knowledge or thinking skills they solicit, and by the constrained or unconstrained nature of the intended response. An instructor's response repertoire may also classify questions according to their intended purpose in shaping the course of the class session.

Questions That Invite Framing or Focus

- "Are we focused on the right problem in this context?"
- "How would you articulate this as a specific hypothesis?"
- "Of the hypotheses suggested so far, which one should we test in detail?"

- "Of the available analytical methods—which approach should we apply?"
- "How could we broadly describe this approach? Are there others?"
- "What have we discovered here? How could you describe what is generalizable?"

Questions That Promote Reflection or Reevaluation

- "Tell me more."
- "You're saying [paraphrase]?"
- "How is this consistent with the literature/our discussion so far?"
- "How does this build on [what came before]?
- "What assumptions are necessary here?"
- "What causes could be relevant here?"
- "How might you find evidence to support your hypothesis?"
- "What evidence suggests this is (or isn't) plausible?"
- "How might we determine if our hypothesis is testable?"
- "What was the most challenging part of this [analysis/task/problem]?
- "Where were you the [most/least] confident?"
- "What is one potential pitfall or common error?"
- "What is one question you have at this time?"

Pivoting to Another Student for Extension or Evaluation

- "How is this consistent or inconsistent with your [thinking/answer/ approach]?"
- "How does this compare with the process you used?"
- "What is one strength or weakness?"
- "Given [this example/this problem/what you've heard], what is one piece of advice you'd have?"
- "What is one question you have [about this/about what you've heard]?"

Questions That Evaluate the Need for Further Discussion

- "Shall we continue with this idea, or are we ready to move on?"
- "Let's pause here. Can someone summarize what we've covered so far before we continue?"
- "How does this relate to [the learning goal]?"
- "Let's brainstorm for [x minutes], then pause to evaluate in more detail . . ."
- "Let's try this problem/question/task individually, then discuss . . ."

Questions That Bring Closure

- "Are we converging on a consensus? If so, what is it? If not, why not?"
- Given the discussion, what is [a/the] key message we should take away? [What is generalizable from this?]
- "What must be remembered to [do this/use this] effectively in the future?"
- "How could we use this in the future or in other contexts?"

Questions That Raise Questions

Rather than simply asking, "Does that make sense?" or "Any questions?" an instructor can presuppose that there are questions and instead offer the imperative, "Tell me what questions you have" (Dillon, 1988, Larson & Lovelace, 2013). This small change should be more productive as it signals that contributions are desired and expected. It also fosters psychological safety by removing the risk that needing to ask a question is a sign of being a weak student. While apprehension can make students reluctant to ask questions, at least initially, other factors related to motivation should not be overlooked (Aitkin & Neer, 1993).

Glossary

Active learning: Anything that "involves students doing things and thinking about the things that they are doing," with a particular focus on higher-order cognitive tasks involving analysis, synthesis, and evaluation (Bonwell & Eisen, 1991, p. 19). In contrast with a lecture, this requires active engagement, whether through speaking, polling, in-class activities, or engagement tasks.

Assessment and evaluation: While sometimes used interchangeably, assessment refers to gathering and interpreting data and offering formative feedback while evaluation is conclusive determination about worth or quality, often in the form of grades. This contrast can be described as formative assessment (process-oriented) versus summative evaluation (outcome-/output-oriented).

Brilliance belief: A fundamental way of relating to certain subjects, namely, those in which the general perception is that raw, innate talent enables success. Philosophy, math, physics, and music composition are all subjects with a high degree of emphasis on brilliance.

Classroom dynamic: The classroom *climate* is traditionally defined as the general quality of the atmosphere or environment, such as "hospitable" or "chilly" (Hall & Sandler, 1982). The classroom *dynamic* includes the classroom climate as well as the distribution of talk-time, frequency and style of student engagement, and degree of instructor control.

Classroom communication apprehension: Anxiety about performing inadequately in front of the instructor or peers, typically when verbally responding to a question. Sometimes called communication anxiety.

Critical thinking: Habits of mind and skills that involve or promote analysis, synthesis, evaluation, or creativity.

First question: The initial question, statement, or example that sets the overall tone and topic of the day. This starting point is grounded in the learning goals of the day and provides direction for the class. Rather than being posed and answered at the outset, it remains open as associated sub-questions, tasks, or prompts shape the course of the session and contribute to its ultimate resolution.

Framing: Context, guidelines, explanation, or "rules of engagement" (as relevant). One might provide framing for a discussion, course content, policy, or approach to instruction. For example,

- "Let's examine each claim in the reading one at a time and then discuss whether we agree or disagree with the overall position."
- "There is a trade-off between depth and breadth in this course. We're going to focus on four key topics in order to explore them in-depth, but you are welcome to explore a topic of your choice in the assignment."
- "The absence policy for this course is [policy], given [explanation of rationale]."
- "This course will be very different from lectures you have experienced in the past. Active learning . . ."

Growth mindset: Acknowledges the challenges inherent in learning and frames one's current level of skill or understanding being a work in progress. The growth mindset presumes the student is capable of growth. In contrast, in a fixed mindset intellectual ability is viewed as a trait—one either has it or one does not.

Immediacy: The perceived physical or psychological distance between individuals; often described as the sensation of "closeness" or "being close to" another individual. Immediacy can be verbal or nonverbal, such as body language, physical distance, and affect that conveys openness, approachability, and familiarity. Immediacy increases student perceptions of an instructor's credibility and charisma, increases student engagement, and positively shapes the classroom dynamic.

Imposter syndrome: Persistent feelings of inadequacy, self-doubt, or insecurity in one's ability, regardless of success. Affected individuals have an internalized belief that they are a "fraud," are less able than their peers, and have avoided detection due to luck. While present among high-achieving students in general, women, minorities, and first-generation college students appear at greater risk.

IRE: Instructor initiation: student response: instructor evaluation (IRE) is a three-part sequence that traditionally provides the fundamental structure of the interactive classroom dynamic (Mehan, 1978). While the sequence may have some variation, particularly the nature of the instructor "evaluation" or comment, it is the most common model of instructor–student interaction (Cairns, 2006).

Judgmental responses: A distinction exists between judgmental responses that capture a *value judgment* and evaluative responses that *engage with the substance* of a student's contribution. Judgmental responses rate, praise, or criticize without providing actionable information about what has occurred. For example, "Perfect!" or "Great answer!" Judgmental responses tend to be personalizable—they can be interpreted as a comment about the student as an individual, rather than focused on the contribution, process, or work product. For example, praise such as "Clever!" [i.e., you are clever] or "Great effort!" [i.e., you are good because you put in great effort].

Pivot/pivoting: An abrupt and significant change in focus, attention, or direction, more so than a gradual shift or progression over time. Pivoting typically describes a deliberate change of the subject of discussion or redirection to another individual for engagement. For example, an instructor could pivot from being the focus of answering a student's question to the class as a whole by saying,

- Student: "Prof, do you think consciousness can eventually be understood using reductionist techniques?"
- Instructor: "While I have an opinion, let's turn this question over to the class to solicit multiple perspectives."
- Similarly, an instructor might pivot the subject of a discussion or activity by saying, "That covers genetic factors, let's turn to epigenetic factors . . ." or "That's enough on Case Study 1. Case Study 2 . . ."

Prof talk: An instructor contribution of medium or longer duration *beyond* what is necessary for class facilitation. Such contributions can range from around 10 seconds to more than several minutes. Asides and anecdotes are typical examples, but prolonged paraphrasing or helpful additions to the discussion can also be considered prof talk depending on their frequency and relevance.

Psychological safety: Broadly, psychological safety refers to the perceived consequences of interpersonal risk-taking in a given context (Edmonson & Lei, 2014). In a psychologically safe environment, individuals

- feel accepted and respected for who they are;
- believe their contributions are valued; and
- feel free to express themselves, contribute, or share their beliefs without fear of negative consequences.

Reflective restatement: A statement that summarizes and synthesizes a student's contribution without instructor judgment, attempted interpretation, or further comment. While similar to paraphrasing, the reflective restatement is followed by an opportunity for the student to clarify, extend, or revise their idea (and is intended to encourage them to do so).

- "[Direct restatement of the idea]." Followed by a pause and nonverbal invitation to affirm, elaborate, or revise.
- "You are saying that [restatement]." Followed by a pause and invitation as above.
- "I understand you to say that [restatement]." Followed by a pause and invitation as above. This formulation is often employed when a student's contribution is somewhat unclear and the instructor wishes to "own" the confusion.

Salient: Something that is salient is important *as well as* attended-to or most noticeable. This term is particularly common in psychology when describing a stimulus that stands out from the rest.

Transfer: Applying knowledge or skills in a new context. *Near transfer* describes doing so in contexts that are very similar to the context in which the knowledge or skills were learned. *Far transfer* describes doing so in contexts that are very dissimilar to the context in which the knowledge or skills were learned. For example, applying principles of electromagnetism in the lab component of a physics class could be *near transfer*. Applying principles of electromagnetism learned in a physics class as analogous reasoning to explain observations in an economic model could be far transfer.

References

Agarwal, P. K. (2019). Retrieval practice & Bloom's taxonomy: Do students need fact knowledge before higher order learning? *Journal of Educational Psychology, 111*(2), 189–209.

Aitkin, J. E., & Neer, M. R. (1993). College student question-asking: The relationship of classroom communication apprehension and motivation. *The Southern Communication Journal, 59*(1), 73–81.

Alexander, R. J. (2000). *Culture and Pedagogy: International Comparisons in Primary Education*. Oxford: Blackwell.

Allen, D., & Tanner, K. (2002). Approaches in cell biology teaching. *Cell Biology Education, 1*, 3–5.

Amini, M., Ekström, M., Johannesson, M., & Strömsten, F. (2017). Does gender diversity promote nonconformity? *Management Science, 63*(4), 1085–1096.

Anderson, J. F. (1979). Teacher immediacy as a predictor of teaching effectiveness. *Annals of the International Communication Association, 3*(1), 543–359.

Andrews, T. M., Leonard, M. J., Colgrove, C. A., & Kalinowski, S. T. (2011). Active learning not associated with student learning in a random sample of college biology courses. *CBE—Life Sciences Education, 10*, 394–405.

Asch, S. E. (1955). Opinions and social pressure. *Scientific American, 193*(5), 31–35.

Asch, S. E. (1956). Studies of independence and conformity: A minority of one against a unanimous majority. *Psychological Monographs: General and Applied, 70*(9), 1–70.

Ballen, C. J., Wieman, C. E., Salehi, S., Searle, J. B., & Zamudio, K. R. (2017). Enhancing diversity in undergraduate science: Self-efficacy drives performance gains with active learning. *CBE—Life Sciences Education, 16*(4), 1–6.

Banks, G. C., McCauley, K. D., Gardner, W. L., & Guler, C. E. (2016). A meta-analytic review of authentic and transformational leadership: A test for redundancy. *The Leadership Quarterly, 27*, 634–652.

Barnes, L. B., Christensen, C. R., & Hansen, A. J. (1994). *Teaching and the Case Method: Text, Cases, and Readings*. Boston: Harvard Business School Press.

Baron, R. S., Vandello, J. A., & Brunsman, B. (1996). The forgotten variable in conformity research: Impact of task importance on social influence. *Journal of Personality and Social Psychology, 71*(5), 915–927.

Basow, S. A., Phelan, J. E., & Capotosto, L. (2006). Gender patterns in college students' choices of their best and worst professors. *Psychology of Women Quarterly, 30*, 25–35.

Binning, K. R., Brick, C., Cohen, G. L., & Sherman, D. K. (2015). Going along versus getting it right: The role of self-integrity in political conformity. *Journal of Experimental Social Psychology, 56*, 73–88.

Black, P., & William, D. (1998). Assessment and classroom learning. *Assessment in Education: Principles, Policy & Practice, 5*(1), 7–74.

Bloom, B. S. (Ed.). (1956). *Taxonomy of Educational Objectives: The Classification of Educational Goals*. New York: David McKay.

Bolkan, S., & Goodboy, A. K. (2014). Communicating charisma in instructional settings: indicators and effects of charismatic teaching. *College Teaching, 62*, 136–142.

Bond, R., & Smith, P. B. (1996). Culture and conformity: A meta-analysis of studies using Asch's (1952b, 1956) line judgment task. *Psychological Bulletin, 119*(1), 111–137.

Bonwell, C. C., & Eisen, J. A. (1991). *Active Learning: Creating Excitement in the Classroom*. Washington, DC: The George Washington University, School of Education and Human Development.

Boring, A. (2017). Gender biases in student evaluations of teaching. *Journal of Public Economics, 145*, 27–41.

Bowers, J. W. (1986). Classroom communication apprehension: A survey. *Communication Education, 35*(4), 372–378.

Boyd, M., & Rubin, D. (2006). How contingent questioning promotes extended student talk: A function of display questions. *Journal of Literacy Research, 38*(2), 141–169.

Braver, S. L., Linder, D. E., Corwin, T. T., & Cialdini, R. B. (1977). Some conditions that affect admissions of attitude change. *Journal of Experimental Social Psychology, 13*, 565–576.

Braxton, J. M., Jones, W. A., Hirschy, A. S., & Hartley III, H. V. (2008). The role of active learning in college student persistence. *New Directions in Teaching and Learning, 115*, 71–83.

Brennan, S. E. (1996). Lexical entrainment in spontaneous dialog. *Proceedings, 1996 International Symposium on Spoken Dialogue* (pp. 41–44). Philadelphia.

Brennan, S. E., & Clark, H. H. (1996). Conceptual pacts and lexical choice in conversation. *Journal of Experimental Psychology: Learning, Memory, and Cognition, 22*(6), 1482–1493.

Brescoll, V. L. (2016). Leading with their hearts? How gender stereotypes of emotion lead to biased evaluations of female leaders. *The Leadership Quarterly, 27*, 415–428.

Brescoll, V. L., & Uhlmann, E. L. (2008). Can angry women get ahead? Status conferral, gender, and expression of emotion in the workplace. *Psychological Science, 19*(3), 268–275.

Brewer, M. B., Manzi, J. M., & Shaw, J. S. (1993). In-group identification as a function of depersonalization, distinctiveness, and status. *Psychological Science, 4*(2), 88–92.

Broeckelman-Post, M., Johnson, A., & Schwebach, J. R. (2016). Calling on students using notecards: Engagement and countering communication anxiety in large lecture. *Journal of College Science Teaching, 45*(5), 27–33.

Brookhart, S. M. (2008). Feedback that fits—How to make your feedback helpful and heard by students. *Educational Leadership, 65*(4), 54–59.

Brooks, A. W. (2014). Get excited: Reappraising pre-performance anxiety as excitement. *Journal of Experimental Psychology, 143*(3), 1144–1158.

Brosi, P., Spörrle, M., Welpe, I. M., & Heilman, M. E. (2016). Expressing pride: Effects on perceived agency, communality, and stereotype-based gender disparities. *Journal of Applied Psychology, 101*(9), 1319–1328.

Brown, R. D., & Krager, L. (1985). Ethical issues in graduate education: Faculty and student responsibilities. *The Journal of Higher Education, 56*, 403–418.

Cairns, L. (2006). Reinforcement. In O. Hargie (Ed.), *The Handbook of Communication Skills* (pp. 147–164). London & New York: Routledge.

Cameron, J. (2001). Negative effects of reward on intrinsic motivation—A limited phenomenon: Comment on Deci, Koestner, and Ryan (2001). *Review of Educational Research, 71*(1), 29–42.

Cameron, J., & Pierce, W. (1994). Reinforcement, reward, and intrinsic motivation: A meta-analysis. *Review of Educational Research, 64*(3), 363–423.

Cameron, J., & Pierce, W. (1996). The debate about rewards and intrinsic motivation: Protests and accusations do not alter the results. *Review of Educational Research, 66*(1), 39–51.

Cameron, J., Pierce, W. D., Banko, K. M., & Gear, A. (2005). Achievement-based rewards and intrinsic motivation: A test of cognitive mediators. *Journal of Educational Psychology, 97*(4), 641–655.

Carli, L. L. (1989). Gender differences in interaction style and influence. *Journal of Personal and Social Psychology, 56*(4), 565–576.

Carney, D. R., Cuddy, A. J., & Yap, A. J. (2010). Power posing: Brief nonverbal displays affect neuroendocrine levels and risk tolerance. *Psychological Science, 21*(10), 1363–1368.

Chávez, K., & Mitchell, K. M. (2019). Exploring bias in student evaluations: Gender, race, and ethnicity. *Political Science & Politics, 53*(2), 270–274.

Chartrand, T. L., & Bargh, J. A. (1999). The chameleon effect: The perception–behavior link and social interaction. *Personality and Social Psychology, 76*(6), 893–910.

Chatman, J. A., Caldwell, D. F., O'Reilly, C. A., & Doerr, B. (2014). Parsing organizational culture: How the norm for adaptability influences the relationship between culture consensus and financial performance in high-technology firms. *Journal of Organizational Behavior, 35*, 785–808.

Chickering, A. W., & Gamson, Z. F. (1987). *Seven Principles for Good Practice in Undergraduate Education.* Washington, DC: American Association for Higher Education.

Choi, I., Land, S. M., & Turgeon, A. (2008). Instructor modeling and online question prompts for supporting peer-questioning during online discussion. *Journal of Educational Technology Systems, 36*(3), 255–275.

Chory, R. M. (2007). Enhancing student perceptions of fairness: The relationship between instructor credibility and classroom justice. *Communication Education, 56*(1), 89–105.

Chory, R. M., & Goodboy, A. K. (2010). Power, compliance, and resistance in the classroom. In D. L. Fassett, & J. T. Warren (Eds.), *SAGE Handbook of Communication and Instruction* (pp. 181–199). Los Angeles: Sage.

Chowning, K., & Campbell, N. J. (2009). Development and validation of a measure of academic entitlement: Individual differences in students' externalized responsibility and entitled expectations. *Journal of Educational Psychology, 101*(4), 982–997.

Christensen, C. R. (1981). *Teaching by the Case Method.* Boston: Division of Research, Harvard Business School.

Christensen, C. R. (1991). Every student teaches and every teacher learns: The reciprocal gift of discussion teaching. In C. R. Christensen, D. A. Garvin, & A. Sweet (Eds.), *Education for Judgment: The Artistry of Discussion Leadership* (pp. 99–122). Boston: Harvard Business School Press.

Cialdini, R. B., & Goldstein, N. J. (2004). Social influence: Compliance and conformity. *Annual Review of Psychology, 55*, 591–621.

Cooper, K. M., Downing, V. R., & Brownell, S. E. (2018). The influence of active learning practices on student anxiety in large-enrollment college science classrooms. *International Journal of STEM Education, 5*, ar23.

Crouch, C. H., & Mazur, E. (2001). Peer instruction: Ten years of experience and results. *American Journal of Physics, 69*(9), 970–977.

Dallimore, E. J., Hertenstein, J. H., & Platt, M. B. (2004). Classroom participation and discussion effectiveness: Student-generated strategies. *Communication Education, 53*(1), 103–115.

Dallimore, E. J., Hertenstein, J. H., & Platt, M. B. (2006). Nonvoluntary class participation in graduate discussion courses: Effects of grading and cold calling. *Journal of Management Education, 30*(2), 354–377.

Dallimore, E. J., Hertenstein, J. H., & Platt, M. B. (2012). Impact of cold-calling on student voluntary participation. *Journal of Management Education, 37*(3), 305–341.

Dallimore, E. J., Hertenstein, J. H., & Platt, M. B. (2019). Leveling the playing field: How cold-calling affects class discussion gender equity. *Journal of Education and Learning, 8*(2), 14–24.

Daly, S. R., Mosyjowski, E. A., & Seifert, C. M. (2014). Teaching creativity in engineering courses. *Journal of Engineering Education, 103*(3), 417–449.

Davidson, G. L., & Clayton, N. S. (2016). New perspectives in gaze sensitivity research. *Learning and Behavior, 44*, 9–17.

Davies, B. (1990). Agency as a form of discursive practice. A classroom scene observed. *British Journal of Sociology of Education, 11*(3), 341–361.

Deci, E. L. (1971). Effects of externally mediated rewards on intrinsic motivation. *Journal of Personality and Social Psychology, 18*(1), 105–115.

Deci, E. L., Koestner, R., & Ryan, R. M. (1999a). A meta-analytic review of experiments examining the effects of extrinsic rewards on intrinsic motivation. *Psychological Bulletin, 125*(6), 627–668.

Deci, E. L., Koestner, R., & Ryan, R. M. (1999b). The undermining effect is a reality after all—extrinsic rewards, task interest, and self-determination: Reply to Eisenberger, Pierce, and Cameron (1999) and Lepper, Henderlong, and Gingras (1999). *Psychological Bulletin, 125*(6), 692–700.

Deci, E. L., Koestner, R., & Ryan, R. M. (2001). Extrinsic rewards and intrinsic motivation in education: Reconsidered once again. *Review of Educational Research, 71*(1), 1–27.

Deci, E. L., & Ryan, R. M. (1980). The empirical exploration of intrinsic motivational processes. In L. Berkowitz (Ed.), *Advances in Experimental Social Psychology Volume 13* (pp. 39–80). New York: Academic Press.

Deci, E. L., & Ryan, R. M. (2012). Self-determination theory. In P. A. Van Lange, A. W. Kruglanski, & E. T. Higgins (Eds.), *Handbook of Theories of Social Psychology* (pp. 416–436). Los Angeles: Sage Publications Ltd.

Deslauriers, L., McCarty, L. S., Miller, K., Callaghan, K., & Kestin, G. (2019). Measuring actual learning versus feeling of learning in response to being actively engaged in the classroom. *Proceedings of the National Academy of Sciences, 116*(39), 19251–19257.

Deslauriers, L., Schelew, E., & Wieman, C. (2011). Improved learning in a large-enrollment physics class. *Science, 332*(6031), 862–864.

Deslauriers, L., & Wieman, C. (2011). Learning and retention of quantum concepts with different teaching methods. *Physical Review Special Topics—Physics Education Research, 7*, 1–6.

Deutsch, M., & Gerard, H. (1955). A study of normative and informational social influences upon individual judgement. *Journal of Abnormal Social Psychology, 51*, 629–636.

Diamond, D. M., Campbell, A. M., Park, C. R., Halonen, J., & Zoladz, P. R. (2007). The temporal dynamics model of emotional memory processing: A synthesis on the neurobiological basis of stress-induced amnesia, flashbulb and traumatic memories, and the Yerkes-Dodson law. *Neural Plasticity, 60803*, 1–33.

Dillon, J. T. (1981a). To question and not to question during discussion I: Questioning and discussion. *Journal of Teacher Education, 32*(5), 51–55.

Dillon, J. T. (1981b). To question and not to question during discussion II. Non-questioning techniques. *Journal of Teacher Education, 32*(6), 15–20.

Dillon, J. T. (1981c). Duration of response to teacher questions and statements. *Contemporary Educational Psychology, 6*, 1–11.

Dillon, J. T. (1988). Questioning in education. In M. Meyer (Ed), *Questions and Questioning* (pp. 98–117). Berlin: Walter de Gruyter.

Dollard, M. F., & Bakker, A. B. (2010). Psychosocial safety climate as a precursor to conducive work environments, psychological health problems, and employee engagement. *Journal of Occupational and Organizational Psychology, 83*(3), 579–599.

Doughty, N., Paterson, H. M., MacCann, C., & Monds, L. A. (2017). Personality and memory conformity. *Journal of Individual Differences, 38*(1), 12–20.

Duckor, B. (2014). Formative assessment in seven good moves. *Educational Leadership, 71*(6), 28–32.

Duell, O. K. (1994). Extended wait time and university student achievement. *American Educational Research Journal, 31*(2), 397–414.

Duell, O. K., Lynch, D. J., Ellsworth, R., & Moore, C. A. (1992). Wait-time in college classes taken by education majors. *Research in Higher Education, 33*(4), 483–495.

Dunleavy, K. N., & Martin, M. M. (2010). Instructors' and students' perspectives of student nagging: Frequency, appropriateness, and effectiveness. *Communication Research Reports, 27*(4), 310–319.

Dunleavy, K. N., Martin, M. M., Brann, M., Booth-Butterfield, M., Myers, S. A., & Weber, K. (2008). Student nagging behavior in the college classroom. *Communication Education, 57*(1), 1–19.

Dunlosky, J., Rawson, K. A., Marsh, E. J., Nathan, M. J., & Willingham, D. T. (2013). Improving students' learning with effective learning techniques: Promising directions from cognitive and educational psychology. *Psychological Science in the Public Interest, 14*(1), 4–58.

Dweck, C. S. (2007). The perils and promises of praise. *Educational Leadership, 65*, 34–39.

Dweck, C. S. (2010). Even geniuses work hard. *Education Leadership, 68*, 16–20.

Dweck, C. S. (2015). Growth mindset, revisited. *Education Week, 35*(5), 20–24.

Edmonson, A. C., & Lei, Z. (2014). Psychological safety: The history, renaissance, and future of an interpersonal construct. *Annual Review of Organizational Psychology and Organizational Behavior, 1*, 23–43.

Eisenberger, R., Pierce, W., & Cameron, J. (1999). Effects of reward on intrinsic motivation—negative, neutral, and positive: Comment on Deci, Koestner, and Ryan (1999). *Psychological Bulletin, 125*(6), 677–691.

El-Alayli, A., Hansen-Brown, A. A., & Ceynar, M. (2018). Dancing backwards in high heels: female professors experience more work demands and special favor requests, particularly from academically entitled students. *Sex Roles, 79*, 136–150.

Elder, L., & Paul, R. (1998). The role of Socratic questioning in thinking, teaching, and learning. *The Clearing House: A Journal of Educational Strategies, Issues, and Ideas, 71*(5), 297–301.

Ellingsen, T., Johannesson, M., Mollerstrom, J., & Munkhammar, S. (2013). Gender differences in social framing effects. *Economics Letters, 118*, 470–472.

Ellsworth, R., Duell, O. K., & Velotta, C. L. (1991). Length of wait-times used by college students given unlimited wait-time intervals. *Contemporary Educational Psychology, 16*, 265–271.

England, B. J., Brigati, J. R., & Schussler, E. E. (2017). Student anxiety in introductory biology classrooms: Perceptions about active learning and persistence in the major. *PLoS ONE, 12*(8), e0182506.

England, B. J., Brigati, J. R., Schussler, E. E., & Chen, M. M. (2019). Student anxiety and perception of difficulty impact performance and persistence in introductory biology courses. *CBE—Life Sciences Education, 18*(2), ar21.

Ernst, M. D. (2011). Active learning? Not with my syllabus! *Teaching Statistics, 34*(1), 1–24.

Felder, R. M. (1985). The generic quiz: A device to stimulate creativity and higher-level thinking skills. *Chemical Engineering Education, 19*(4), 176–181.

Felder, R. M. (2007). Sermons for grumpy campers. *Chemical Engineering Education, 28*(3), 174–175.

Felder, R. M. (2011). Random thoughts... Hang in there! Dealing with student resistance to learner-centered teaching. *Chemical Engineering Education, 45*(2), 131–132.

Felder, R. M., & Brent, R. (1999). FAQs 2: Responses to the questions: 'Can I use active learning exercises in my classes and still cover the syllabus?' and 'Do active learning methods work in large classes?'. *Chemical Engineering Education, 33*(4), 276–277.

Felder, R. M., & Brent, R. (2004). The intellectual development of science and engineering students. Part 2: Teaching to promote growth. *Journal of Engineering Education, 93*(4), 279–291.

Felder, R. M., & Brent, R. (2009). Active learning: An introduction. *ASQ Higher Education Brief, 2*, 4–9.

Felton, J., Koper, P. T., Mitchell, J., & Stinson, M. (2008). Attractiveness, easiness and other issues: Student evaluations of professors on Ratemyprofessors.com. *Assessment & Evaluation in Higher Education, 33*(1), 45–61.

Finelli, C. J., Nguyen, K., DeMonbrun, M., Borrego, M., Prine, M., Husman, J., Henderson, C., Shekhar, P., & Waters, C. K. (2018). Reducing student resistance to active learning: strategies for instructors. *Journal of College Science Teaching, 47*(5), 80–91.

Finn, A. N., Schrodt, P., Witt, P. L., Elledge, N., Jernberg, K. A., & Larson, L. M. (2009). A meta-analytical review of teacher credibility and its associations with teacher behaviors and student outcomes. *Communication Education, 58*(4), 516–537.

Fischer, A. H., Rodriguez Mosquera, P. M., van Vianen, A. E., & Manstead, A. S. (2004). Gender and culture differences in emotion. *Emotion, 4*(1), 87–94.

Flegl, M., & Rosas, L. A. (2019). Do professor's age and gender matter or do students give higher value to professors' experience? *Quality Assurance in Education, 27*(4), 511–532.

Forehand, G. A., & von Haller Gilmer, B. (1964). Environmental variation in studies of organizational behavior. *Psychological Bulletin, 62*(6), 361–382.

Fraser, J. M., Timan, A. L., Miller, K., Dowd, J. E., Tucker, L., & Mazur, E. (2014). Teaching and physics education research: Bridging the gap. *Reports on Progress in Physics, 77*(3), 1–17.

Freeman, S., Eddy, S. L., McDonough, M., Smith, M. K., Okoroafor, N., Jordt, H., & Wenderoth, M. (2014). Active learning increases student performance in science, engineering, and mathematics. *Proceedings of the National Academy of Sciences, 111*(23), 8410–8415.

Frisby, B. N., Goodboy, A. K., & Buckner, M. M. (2015). Students' instructional dissent and relationships with faculty members' burnout, commitment, satisfaction, and efficacy. *Communication Education, 64*(1), 65–82.

Gibbs, G., & Simpson, C. (2005). Conditions under which assessment supports students' learning. *Learning and Teaching in Higher Education, 1,* 3–31.

Girgin, K. Z., & Stevens, D. D. (2005). Bridging in-class participation with innovative instruction: Use and implications in a Turkish university classroom. *Innovations in Education and Teaching International, 42*(1), 93–106.

Glover, C., & Brown, E. (2006). Written feedback for students: Too much, too detailed or too incomprehensible to be effective? *Bioscience Education, 7*(1), 1–16.

Goldman, Z. W., Goodboy, A. K., & Weber, K. (2017). College students' psychological needs and intrinsic motivation to learn: An examination of self-determination theory. *Communication Quarterly, 65*(2), 167–191.

Goleman, D. (1995; 2005). *Emotional Intelligence.* New York, NY: Bantam Dell.

Goleman, D. (2004, January). What makes a leader? *Harvard Business Review, 82*(1), 82–91.

Goncalo, J. A., & Duguid, M. M. (2012). Follow the crowd in a new direction: When conformity pressure facilitates group creativity (and when it does not). *Organizational Behavior and Human Decision Processes, 118,* 14–23.

Goodboy, A. K. (2011a). Instructional dissent in the college classroom. *Communication Education, 60*(3), 296–313.

Goodboy, A. K. (2011b). The development and validation of the instructional dissent scale. *Communication Education, 60*(4), 422–440.

Goodboy, A. K., & Myers, S. A. (2008). The effect of teacher confirmation on student communication and learning outcomes. *Communication Education, 57*(2), 153–179.

Goodboy, A. K., & Myers, S. A. (2009). The relationship between perceived instructor immediacy and student challenge behavior. *Journal of Instructional Psychology, 36*(2), 108–112.

Goodboy, A. K., & Myers, S. A. (2012). Instructional dissent as an expression of students' verbal aggressiveness and argumentativeness traits. *Communication Education, 61*(4), 448–458.

Griffin, R. (1976). Worries about values clarification. *Peabody Journal of Education, 53*(3), 194–200.

Gruber, D. R. (2016). The extent of engagement, the means of invention: Measuring debate about mirror neurons in the humanities and social sciences. *Journal of Science Communication, 15*(2), A01.

Guadagno, R. E., & Cialdini, R. B. (2002). Online persuasion: An examination of gender differences in computer-mediated interpersonal influence. *Group Dynamics: Theory, Research and Practice, 6*(1), 38–51.

Guadagno, R. E., & Cialdini, R. B. (2007). Persuade him by email, but see her in person: Online persuasion revisited. *Computers in Human Behavior, 23,* 999–1015.

Gunter, T. C., & Weinbrenner, J. (2017). When to take a gesture seriously: On how we use and prioritize communicative cues. *Journal of Cognitive Neuroscience, 29*(8), 1355–1367.

Gunter, T. C., Weinbrenner, J., & Holle, H. (2015). Inconsistent use of gesture space during abstract pointing impairs language comprehension. *Frontiers in Psychology, 6*(80), 1–10.

Haak, D. C., HilleRisLambers, J., Pitre, E., & Freeman, S. (2011). Increased structure and active learning reduce the achievement gap in introductory biology. *Science, 332*(6034), 1213–1216.

Hake, R. R. (1998). Interactive-engagement versus traditional methods: A six-thousand-student survey of mechanics test data for introductory physics courses. *American Journal of Physics, 66*, 64–74.

Hall, R. M., & Sandler, B. R. (1982). *The Classroom Climate: A Chilly One for Women?* Washington, DC: Association of American Colleges.

Hamamura, T., & Takemura, K. (2018). Common view by whom? *Asian Journal of Social Psychology, 21*, 331–335.

Hattie, J. (2012). Know thy impact. *Educational Leadership, 70*(1), 18–23.

Hattie, J., & Timperley, H. (2007). The power of feedback. *Review of Educational Research, 1*, 81–112.

Heitanen, J. O., Peltola, M. J., & Heitanen, J. K. (2020). Psychophysiological responses to eye contact in a live interaction and in video call. *Psychophysiology, 57*, e13587.

Herreid, C. F. (2007). How not to teach with case studies. In Herreid, C. F. (Ed.), *Start with a Story: The Case Study Method of Teaching College Science* (pp. 331–348). Arlington: National Science Teachers' Association Press.

Hess, U., Adams Jr., R. B., & Kleck, R. E. (2005). Who should frown and who should smile? Dominance, affiliation and the display of happiness and anger. *Cognition and Emotion, 19*(4), 515–536.

Hewett, R., & Conway, N. (2016). The undermining effect revisited: The salience of everyday verbal rewards and self-determined motivation. *Journal of Organizational Behavior, 37*, 436–455.

Hickok, G. (2009). Eight problems for the mirror neuron theory of action understanding in monkeys and humans. *Journal of Cognitive Neuroscience, 21*(7), 1229–1243.

Hickok, G. (2012). Computational neuroanatomy of speech production. *Nature Reviews Neuroscience, 13*, 135–145.

Hmelo-Silver, C. E. (2004). Problem-based learning: What and how do students learn? *Educational Psychology Review, 16*(3), 235–266.

Hodges, B. H., & Geyer, A. L. (2006). A nonconformist account of the Asch experiments: Values, pragmatics, and moral dilemmas. *Personality and Social Psychology Review, 10*(1), 2–19.

Holladay, S. J., & Coombs, W. T. (1994). Speaking of visions and visions being spoken: An exploration of the effects of content and delivery on perceptions of leader charisma. *Management Communication Quarterly, 8*(2), 165–189.

Holler, J., & Stevens, R. (2007). The effect of common ground on how speakers use gesture and speech to represent size information. *Journal of Language and Social Psychology, 26*(1), 4–27.

Hopper, K. B. (2003). In defense of the solitary learner: A Response to collaborative, constructivist education. *Educational Technology, 43*(2), 24–29.

Hornsey, M. J., Jetten, J., McAuliffe, B. J., & Hogg, M. A. (2006). The impact of individualist and collectivist group norms on evaluations of dissenting group members. *Journal of Experimental Social Psychology, 42*, 57–68.

Hospel, V., & Galand, B. (2016). Are both classroom autonomy support and structure equally important for students' engagement? A multilevel analysis. *Learning and Instruction, 41*, 1–10.

Hufton, N. R., Elliott, J. G., & Illushin, L. (2003). Teachers' beliefs about student motivation: Similarities and differences across cultures. *Comparative Education, 39*(3), 367–389.

Huston, T. (2009). *Teaching What You Don't Know*. Cambridge: Harvard University Press.

Ingram, J., & Elliott, V. (2014). Turn taking and 'wait time' in classroom interactions. *Journal of Pragmatics, 62*, 1–12.

Ingram, J., & Elliott, V. (2016). A critical analysis of the role of wait time in classroom interactions and the effects on student and teacher interactional behaviors. *Cambridge Journal of Education, 46*(1), 37–53.

Jamaludin, R., & Osman, S. Z. (2014). The use of a flipped classroom to enhance engagement and promote active learning. *Journal of Education and Practice, 5*(2), 124–131.

Jarrett, C. (2016, November 28). *The Psychology of Eye Contact, Digested*. The British Psychological Society Research Digest. https://digest.bps.org.uk/2016/11/28/the-psychology-of-eye-contact-digested/.

Johnson, S. K., Murphy, S. E., Zewdie, S., & Reichard, R. J. (2008). The strong, sensitive type: Effects of gender stereotypes and leadership prototypes on the evaluation of male and female leaders. *Organizational Behavior and Human Decision Processes, 106*, 39–60.

Kaid, L. L., & Wadsworth, A. J. (1989). Content analysis. In P. Emmert, & L. L. Barker (Eds.), *Measurement of Communication Behavior* (pp. 197–217). New York: Longman.

Kajimuri, S., & Nomura, M. (2016). When we cannot speak: Eye contact disrupts resources available to cognitive control processes during verb generation. *Cognition, 157*, 352–357.

Kelly, S., Healy, M., Ozyurek, A., & Holler, J. (2012). The communicative influence of gesture and action during speech comprehension: Gestures have the upper hand. *The Journal of the Acoustical Society of America, 131*(4), 3311.

Kelsey, J. (2010). The negative impact of rewards and ineffective praise on student motivation. *ESSAI, 8*(24), 87–90.

Khanna, M. M. (2015). Ungraded pop quizzes: Test-enhanced learning without all the anxiety. *Teaching of Psychology, 42*(2), 174–178.

Kinnier, R. T. (1995). A reconceptualization of values clarification: Value conflict resolution. *Journal of Counseling and Development, 74*(1), 18–24.

Kirschenbaum, H. (1975). *In Defense of Values Clarification: A Position Paper*. Saratoga Springs: National Humanistic Education Center.

Kirschenbaum, H. (2000). From values clarification to character education: A personal journey. *Journal of Humanistic Counseling, Education & Development, 39*(1), 4–20.

Kirton, A., Hallam, S., Peffers, J., Robertson, P., & Short, G. (2007). Revolution, evolution, or a Trojan horse? Piloting assessment for learning in some Scottish primary schools. *British Educational Research Journal, 33*(4), 605–627.

Kluger, A. N., & DeNisi, A. (1996). The effects of feedback interventions on performance: A historical review, a meta-analysis, and a preliminary feedback intervention theory. *Psychological Bulletin, 119*(2), 254–284.

Kohn, A. (1999). *Punished by Rewards: The Trouble with Gold Stars, Incentive Plans, A's, Praise and Other Bribes*. New York: Houghton-Mifflin.

Kohn, A. (2001). Five reasons to stop saying "good job!" *Young Children, 56*(5), 24–28.

Kosloff, S., Irish, S., Perreault, L., Anderson, G., & Nottbohm, A. (2017). Assessing relationships between conformity and meta-traits in an Asch-like paradigm. *Social Influence, 12*(2), 90–100.

Kosslyn, S. M. (2017). Chapter 11. The science of learning: Mechanisms and principles. In S. M. Kosslyn & B. Nelson (Eds.), *Building the Intentional University* (pp. 149–164). Cambridge: MIT Press.

Kosslyn, S. M., & Nelson, B. (Eds.). (2017). *Building the Intentional University*. Cambridge: The MIT Press.

Krathwohl, D. R. (2002). A revision of Bloom's Taxonomy: An overview. *Theory Into Practice, 41*(4), 212–218.

Kubu, C. S. (2018). Who does she think she is? Women, leadership and the 'b'(ias) word. *The Clinical Neuropsychologist, 32*(2), 235–251.

Larson, L. R., & Lovelace, M. D. (2013). Evaluating the efficacy of questioning strategies in lecture-based classroom environments: Are we asking the right questions? *Journal on Excellence in College Teaching, 24*(1), 105–122.

Latif, N., Barbosa, A. V., Vatikiotis-Bateson, E., Castelhano, M. S., & Munhall, K. G. (2014). Movement coordination during conversation. *PLoS One, 9*(8), e105036.

Laube, H., Massoni, K., Sprague, J., & Ferber, A. L. (2007). The impact of gender on the evaluation of teaching: What we know and what we can do. *NWSA Journal, 19*(3), 87–104.

Lee, E.-J. (2004). Effects of gendered character representation on person perception and informational social influence in computer-mediated communication. *Computers in Human Behavior, 20*, 779–799.

LeFebvre, L., & Allen, M. (2014). Teacher immediacy and student learning: An examination of lecture/laboratory and self-contained course sections. *Journal of the Scholarship of Teaching and Learning, 14*(2), 29–45.

Lehrer, J. (2008, July 1). The mirror neuron revolution: Explaining what makes humans social [an interview with Marco Iacoboni]. *Scientific American*. https://www.scientificamerican.com/article/the-mirror-neuron-revolut/

Lesh, R., & Zawojewski, J. (2007). Problem solving and modeling. In F. K. Lester (Ed.), *Second Handbook of Research on Mathematics Teaching and Learning* (pp. 763–804). Charlotte, NC: National Council of Teachers of Mathematics.

Leslie, S.-J., Cimpian, A., Meyer, M., & Freeland, E. (2015). Expectations of brilliance underlie gender distributions across academic disciplines. *Science, 347*(6219), 262–265.

Levenson, E. (2013). Tasks that may occasion mathematical creativity: Teachers' choices. *Journal of Math Teacher Education, 16*, 269–291.

Levine, L. J., & Pizarro, D. A. (2004). Emotion and memory research: A grumpy overview. *Social Cognition, 22*(5), 530–554.

Levy, D., & Bookin, J. A. (2014). Cold calling and web postings: Do they improve students' preparation and learning? *SLATE HKS Faculty Working Paper Series on Teaching & Learning, Harvard Kennedy School.*

Lisievici, P., & Andronie, M. (2016). Teachers assessing the effectiveness of values clarification techniques in moral education. *Procedia—Social and Behavioral Sciences, 217*, 400–406.

Lockwood, A. L. (1978). The effects of values clarification and moral development curricula on school-age subjects: A critical review of recent research. *Review of Educational Research, 48*(3), 325–364.

MacNell, L., Driscoll, A., & Hunt, A. N. (2015). What's in a name: Exposing gender bias in student ratings of teaching. *Innovative Higher Education, 40*, 291–303.

Martin, L. L. (2016). Gender, teaching evaluations, and professional success in political science. *Political Science & Politics, 49*(2), 313–319.

Mason, G. S., Shuman, T. R., & Cook, K. E. (2013). Comparing the effectiveness of an inverted classroom to a traditional classroom in an upper-division engineering course. *IEEE Transactions on Education, 56*(4), 430–435.

Mayer, J. D., Caruso, D. R., & Salovey, P. (2016). The ability model of emotional intelligence: principles and updates. *Emotion Review, 8*(4), 290–300.

Mayer, J. D., & Salovey, P. (1993). The intelligence of emotional intelligence. *Intelligence, 17*(4), 433–442.

Mayer, R. E. (2002). Rote versus meaningful learning. *Theory Into Practice, 41*(4), 226–232.

Mazur, E. (1997a). *Peer Instruction: A User's Manual.* Upper Saddle River: Prentice-Hall.

Mazur, E. (1997b). Peer instruction: Getting students to think in class. *AIP Conference Proceedings, 399*, 981–988.

Mazur, E. (2009). Farewell, lecture? *Science, 323*, 50–51.

McCarthy, J., & Anderson, L. (2000). Active learning techniques versus traditional teaching styles: Two experiments from history and political science. *Innovative Higher Education, 24*(4), 279–294.

McCroskey, J. C. (1976). The problem of communication apprehension in the classroom. *The Florida Speech Communication Journal, 4*(2), 1–12.

McCroskey, J. C. (1977). Classroom consequences of communication apprehension. *Communication Education, 26*, 27–33.

McCroskey, J. C., & Richmond, V. P. (1992). Increasing teacher influence through immediacy. In J. C. McCroskey, & V. P. Richmond (Eds.), *Power in the Classroom: Communication, Control, and Concern* (pp. 101–119). Hillsdale, NJ: Erlbaum.

McCroskey, J. C., Sallinen, A., Fayer, J. M., Richmond, V. P., & Barraclough, R. A. (1996). Nonverbal immediacy and cognitive learning: A Cross-Cultural Investigation. *Communication Education, 45*, 200–211.

Medaille, A., & Usinger, J. (2019). Engaging quiet students in the college classroom. *College Teaching, 67*(2), 130–137.

Mehan, H. (1978). Structuring school structure. *Harvard Educational Review, 48,* 32–64.

Milgram, S. (1961, December). Which nations conform most? *Scientific American, 205*(6).

Miller, J., & Chamberlin, M. (2000). Women are teachers, men are professors: A study of student perceptions. *Teaching Sociology, 28*(4), 283–298.

Moguel, D. (2004). What does it mean to participate in class? Integrity and inconsistency in classroom interaction. *Journal of Classroom Interaction, 39*(1), 19–29.

Mori, K., & Arai, M. (2010). No need to fake it: Reproduction of the Asch experiment without confederates. *International Journal of Psychology, 45*(5), 390–397.

Myers, S. A., & Bryant, L. E. (2004). College students' perceptions of how instructors convey credibility. *Qualitative Research Reports in Communication, 5,* 22–27.

Myers, S. A., & Rocca, K. A. (2000). The relationship between perceived instructor communicator style, argumentativeness, and verbal aggressiveness. *Communication Research Reports, 17*(1), 1–12.

Myers, S. A., & Rocca, K. A. (2001). Perceived instructor argumentativeness and verbal aggressiveness in the college classroom: Effects on student perceptions of climate, apprehension, and state motivation. *Western Journal of Communication, 65*(2), 113–137.

Naftulin, D. H., Ware, J. E., & Donnelly, F. E. (1973). The Doctor Fox Lecture: A paradigm of educational seduction. *Journal of Medical Education, 48,* 630–635.

Neer, M. R. (1987). The development of an instrument to measure classroom apprehension. *Communication Education, 36,* 154–166.

Nystrand, M., & Gamoran, A. (1990). *Student Engagement: When Recitation Becomes Conversation.* Washington, DC: Office of Educational Research and Improvement (ED).

Oberg, M. A., Barbosa, A. V., & Vatikiotis-Bateson, E. (2011). Dyadic postural coordination and discourse structure. *The Journal of the Acoustical Society of America, 129*(4), 2683.

O'Flaherty, J., & Philips, C. (2015). The use of flipped classrooms in higher education: A scoping review. *Internet and Higher Education, 25,* 85–95.

Opie, T. R., Livingston, B., Greenberg, D. N., & Murphy, W. M. (2019). Building gender inclusivity: Disentangling the influence of classroom demography on classroom participation. *Higher Education, 77,* 37–58.

Otto, J., Sanford Jr, D. A., & Ross, D. N. (2008). Does Ratemyprofessor.com really rate my professor? *Assessment & Evaluation in Higher Education, 33*(4), 355–368.

Packer, A. B. (1970). Ashton-Warner's key Vocabulary for the Disadvantaged. *The Reading Teacher, 23*(6), 559–564.

Palmer, P. J. (1990). Good teaching: A matter of living the mystery. *Change, 22*(1), 11–16.

Park, E. L., & Choi, B. (2014). Transformation of classroom spaces: Traditional versus active learning classroom in colleges. *Higher Education, 68,* 749–771.

Peer, E., & Babad, E. (2014). The Doctor Fox research (1973) Re-revisited: "Educational seduction" ruled out. *Journal of Educational Psychology, 106*(1), 36–45.

Perez, K. E., Strauss, E. A., Downey, N., Galbraith, A., Jeanne, R., & Cooper, S. (2010). Does displaying the class results affect student discussion during peer instruction? *CBE—Life Science Education, 9*, 133–140.

Phelps, F. G., Doherty-Sneddon, G., & Warnock, H. (2006). Helping children think: Gaze aversion and teaching. *British Journal of Developmental Psychology, 24*(3), 577–588.

Pittman, T. S., Davey, M. E., Alafat, K. A., Wetherill, K. V., & Kramer, N. A. (1980). Informational versus controlling verbal rewards. *Personal and Social Psychology Bulletin, 6*, 228–233.

Polite, V. C., & Adams, A. H. (1997). Critical thinking and values clarification through Socratic seminars. *Urban Education, 32*(2), 256–278.

Pomerance, L., Greenberg, J., & Walsh, K. (2016). *Learning About Learning.* Washington, DC: National Council on Teacher Quality.

Prince, M. (2004). Does active learning work? A review of the research. *Journal of Engineering Education, 93*(3), 223–232.

Prince, M. J., & Felder, R. M. (2006). Inductive teaching and learning methods: Definitions, comparisons, and research bases. *Journal of Engineering Education, 95*(2), 123–138.

Quinn, A., & Schlenker, B. R. (2002). Can accountability produce independence? Goals as determinants of the impact of accountability on conformity. *Personality and Social Psychology Bulletin, 28*(4), 472–483.

Ramachandran, V. S. (2009). The neurons that shaped civilization. TED India.

Ranehill, E., Dreber, A., Johannesson, M., Leiberg, S., Sul, S., & Weber, R. A. (2015). Assessing the robustness of power posing: No effect on hormones and risk tolerance in a large sample of men and women. *Psychological Science, 26*(5), 653–656.

Raths, J. (2002). Improving instruction. *Theory Into Practice, 41*(4), 233–237.

Raths, L. E. (1959). Values are fundamental. *Childhood Education, 35*(6), 246–247.

Raths, L. E., Harmin, M., & Simon, S. B. (1973). *Values and Teaching: Working with Values in the Classroom.* Columbus, OH: Charles E. Merrill Publishing Company.

Reeve, J., & Jang, H. (2006). What teachers say and do to support students' autonomy during a learning activity. *Journal of Educational Psychology, 98*(1), 209–218.

Reeve, J., & Tseng, C.-M. (2011). Agency as a fourth aspect of students' engagement during learning activities. *Contemporary Educational Psychology, 36*, 257–267.

Rhodan, M. (2013, June 4). 3 speech habits that are worse than vocal fry in job interviews. *Time.*

Richardson, D. C., & Dale, R. (2005). Looking to understand: The coupling between speakers' and listeners' eye movements and its relationship to discourse comprehension. *Cognitive Science, 29*(6), 1045–1060.

Richardson, D. C., Dale, R., & Shockley, K. (2008). Synchrony and swing in conversation: Coordination, temporal dynamics and communication. In I. Wachsmuth, M. Lenzen, & G. Knoblich (Eds.), *Embodied Communication in Humans and Machines* (pp. 75–93). Oxford: Oxford University Press.

Riniolo, T. C., Johnson, K. C., & Misso, J. A. (2006). Hot or not: Do professors perceived as physically attractive receive higher student evaluations? *The Journal of General Psychology, 133*(1), 19–35.

Rizzolatti, G., & Craighero, L. (2004). The mirror-neuron system. *Annual Review of Neuroscience, 27,* 169–192.

Rizzolatti, G., Fadiga, L., Gallese, V., & Fogassi, L. (1996). Premotor cortex and the recognition of motor actions. *Cognitive Brain Research, 3,* 131–141.

Rocca, K. A. (2009). Participation in the college classroom: The impact of instructor immediacy and verbal aggression. *Journal of Classroom Interaction, 43*(2), 22–33.

Rocca, K. A. (2010). Student participation in the college classroom: An extended multidisciplinary literature review. *Communication Education, 59*(2), 185–213.

Rochester, S. (1973). The significance of pauses in spontaneous speech. *Journal of Psycholinguistic Research, 2*(1), 51–81.

Roehl, A., Reddy, S. L., & Shannon, G. J. (2013). The flipped classroom: An opportunity to engage millennial students through active learning strategies. *Journal of Family and Consumer Sciences, 105*(2), 44–49.

Rogers, C. A. (1954). Toward a theory of creativity. *ETC: A Review of General Semantics, 11*(4), 249–260.

Rogers, J., & Macbeth, A. (2015). *Throwing Shade: The Science of Resting Bitch Face.* Noldus Consulting.

Rosen, A. S. (2018). Correlations, trends and potential biases among publicly accessible web-based student evaluations of teaching: A large-scale study of RateMyProfessors.com data. *Assessment & Evaluation in Higher Education, 43*(1), 31–44.

Rowe, M. B. (1972). Wait-time and rewards as instructional variables: Their influence on language, logic, and fate control (pp. 1–32). National Association for Research in Science Teaching.

Rowe, M. B. (1973). *Teaching Science as Continuous Inquiry.* New York: McGraw-Hill.

Rowe, M. B. (1974). Pausing phenomena: Influence on the quality of instruction. *Journal of Psycholinguistic Research, 3*(3), 203–224.

Rowe, M. B. (1976). The pausing principle: Two invitations to inquiry. *Journal of College Science Teaching, 5*(4), 258–259.

Rowe, M. B. (1978). Wait, wait, wait... *School Science and Mathematics, 78,* 207–216.

Rowe, M. B. (1980). Pausing principles and their effects on reasoning in science. In F. B. Brawer (Ed.), *New Directions for Community Colleges: Teaching the Sciences* (Vol. 8, pp. 27–34). San Francisco: Jossey-Bass.

Rowe, M. B. (1983). Getting chemistry off the killer course list. *Journal of Chemical Education, 60*(11), 954–956.

Rowe, M. B. (1986). Wait time: Slowing down may be a way of speeding up! *Journal of Teacher Education, 37,* 43–50.

Rowe, M. B. (1996). Science, silence, and sanctions. *Science and Children, 34*(1), 35–37.

Rudman, L. A., & Phelan, J. E. (2008). Backlash effects for disconfirming gender stereotypes in organizations. *Research in Organizational Behavior, 28*, 61–79.

Ryan, R. M., Mims, V., & Koestner, R. (1983). Relation of reward contingency and interpersonal context to intrinsic motivation: A review and test using cognitive evaluation theory. *Journal of Personal and Social Psychology, 45*(4), 736–750.

Salter, D. W., & Persaud, A. (2003). Women's views of the factors that encourage and discourage classroom participation. *Journal of College Student Development, 44*(6), 831–844.

Sarid, O., Anson, O., Yaari, A., & Margalith, M. (2004). Academic stress, immunological reaction, and academic performance among students of nursing and physiotherapy. *Research in Nursing & Health, 27*, 370–377.

Schein, E. H., & Bennis, W. G. (1965). *Personal and Organizational Change through Group Methods: The Laboratory Approach.* New York: Wiley.

Seidel, S. B., & Tanner, K. D. (2013). "What if students revolt?"—Considering student resistance: Origins, options, and opportunities for investigation. *CBE Life Sciences Education, 12*, 586–595.

Seipp, B. (1991). Anxiety and academic performance: A meta-analysis of findings. *Anxiety Research, 4*(1), 27–41.

Semlak, J. L., & Pearson, J. C. (2008). Through the years: An examination of instructor age and misbehavior on perceived teacher credibility. *Communication Research Reports, 25*(1), 76–85.

Shepard, L. A. (2019). Classroom assessment to support teaching and learning. *Annals of the American Academy of Political and Social Science, 683*(1), 183–200.

Sherif, M. (1935). A study of some social factors in perception. *Archives of Psychology, 27*(187), 1–60.

Sherwell, G. V., Gallegos, D. P., Jiménez, F. J., & Flegl, M. (2018). Analysis of professors' evaluation in Actuarial sciences program at La Salle University. *Memorias Del Concurso Lasallista de Investigacion, Desarrollo e Innovacion, 5*(1), 48–53.

Shrum, J. L. (1984). Wait-time and student performance level in second language classrooms. *The Journal of Classroom Interaction, 20*(1), 29–35.

Shute, V. J. (2008). Focus on formative feedback. *Review of Educational Research, 78*(1), 153–189.

Silva, K. M., Silva, F. J., Quinn, M. A., Draper, J. N., Cover, K. R., & Munoff, A. A. (2008). Rate my professor: Online evaluations of psychology instructors. *Teaching of Psychology, 35*(2), 71–80.

Simon, S. B., Howe, L. W., & Kirschenbaum, H. (1972). *Values Clarification: A Handbook of Practical Strategies for Teachers and Students.* New York: Hart Publishing Company.

Simonds, C. J. (1997). Challenge behavior in the college classroom. *Communication Research Reports, 14*(4), 481–492.

Souza, T. J., Dallimore, E. J., Aoki, E., & Pilling, B. C. (2010). Communication climate, comfort, and cold calling: An analysis of discussion-based courses at multiple universities. *To Improve the Academy, 28*(1), 227–249.

Stead, D. R. (2005). A review of the one-minute paper. *Active Learning in Higher Education, 6*(2), 118–131.

Stowell, J. R., Oldham, T., & Bennett, D. (2010). Using student response systems ("clickers") to combat conformity and shyness. *Teaching of Psychology, 37*(2), 135–140.

Strang, K. D. (2011). How can discussion forum questions be effective in online MBA courses? *Campus-Wide Information Systems, 28*(2), 80–92.

Takano, Y., & Osaka, E. (1999). An unsupported common view: Comparing Japan and the U.S. on individualism/collectivism. *Asian Journal of Social Psychology, 2*, 311–341.

Takano, Y., & Osaka, E. (2018a). Comparing Japan and the United States on individualism/collectivism: A follow-up review. *Asian Journal of Social Psychology, 21*, 301–316.

Takano, Y., & Osaka, E. (2018b). "Attention, please" to situation: Replies to commentaries by Uleman, Matsumoto, Hamamura and Takemura, and Vignoles. *Asian Journal of Social Psychology, 21*, 346–355.

Tatum, H. E., Schwartz, B. M., Schimmoeller, P. A., & Perry, N. (2013). Classroom participation and student-faculty interactions: Does gender matter? *The Journal of Higher Education, 84*(6), 745–768.

Teigen, K. H. (1994). Yerkes-Dodson: A law for all seasons. *Theory & Psychology, 4*(4), 525–547.

Thomas, J. W. (1980). Agency and achievement: Self-management and self-regard. *Review of Educational Research, 50*(2), 213–240.

Tiedens, L. Z. (2001). Anger and advancement versus sadness and subjugation: The effect of negative emotion expressions on social status conferral. *Journal of Personality and Social Psychology, 80*(1), 86–94.

Tobin, K. (1987). The role of wait time in higher cognitive level learning. *Review of Educational Research, 57*(1), 69–95.

Tredway, L. (1995). Socratic seminars: engaging students in intellectual discourse. *Educational Leadership, 53*(1), 26–29.

Vogel, S., & Schwabe, L. (2016). Learning and memory under stress: Implications for the classroom. *Nature Partner Journals Science of Learning, 1*, 16011.

Wagner, N., Reiger, M., & Voorvelt, K. (2016). Gender, ethnicity and teaching evaluations: Evidence from mixed teaching teams. *Economics of Education Review, 54*, 79–94.

Wang, Y.-M. (2014). Questioning as facilitating strategies in online discussion. *Journal of Educational Technology Systems, 42*(4), 405–416.

Ware, J. E., & Williams, R. G. (1975). The Dr. Fox effect: A study of lecturer effectiveness and ratings of instruction. *Journal of Medical Education, 50*(2), 149–156.

Wassermann, S. (1979). Evaluation practices and the emperor's new clothes. *Childhood Education, 55*(5), 277–282.

Wassermann, S. (1992). *Asking the Right Questions: The Essence of Teaching.* Bloomington, IN: Phi Delta Kappa Educational Foundation.

Wassermann, S. (1994). *Introduction to Case Method Teaching. A Guide to the Galaxy.* New York: Teachers College Press, Teachers College, Columbia University.

Wassermann, S. (2017). *The Art of Interactive Teaching*. New York and London: Routledge.

Wassermann, S. (2020). *Evaluation without Tears: 101 Ways to Evaluate the Work of Students*. Latham: Rowman & Littlefield.

Wassermann, S., & Eggert, W. (1976). Profiles of teaching competency: A way of looking at classroom teaching performance. *Canadian Journal of Education / Revue canadienne de l'éducation, 1*(1), 67–73.

Weaver, R. R., & Qi, J. (2005). Classroom organization and participation: college students' perceptions. *The Journal of Higher Education, 76*(5), 570–601.

Weimar, M. (2003). Focus on learning, transform teaching. *Change: The Magazine of Higher Learning, 35*(5), 48–54.

Weimer, M. (2013). *Learner-Centered Teaching: Five Key Changes to Practice*. Somerset: John Wiley & Sons.

Weinschenk, A. C., Panagopoulos, C., Drabot, K., & van der Linden, S. (2018). Gender and social conformity: Do men and women respond differently to social pressure to vote? *Social Influence, 13*(2), 53–64.

Weinstein, Y., Madan, C. R., & Sumeracki, M. A. (2018). Teaching the science of learning. *Cognitive Research: Principles and Implications, 3*(2), 1–17.

Wieman, C. E. (2014). Large-scale comparison of science teaching methods sends clear message. *Proceedings of the National Academy of Sciences, 111*(23), 8319–8320.

Wieman, C. E. (2014). Stop lecturing me. *Scientific American, 311*(2), 70–71.

Wijenayake, S., Van Berkel, N., Kostakos, V., & Goncalves, J. (2019). Measuring the effects of gender on online social conformity. *Proceedings of the ACM on Human-Computer Interaction, 3*, 145:1–145:24.

Wiliam, D. (2014). The right questions, the right way. *Educational Leadership, 71*(6), 16–19.

Williams, K. D., Cheung, C. K., & Choi, W. (2000). Cyberostracism: Effects of being ignored over the internet. *Journal of Personality and Social Psychology, 79*(5), 748–762.

Wiseman, R., Watt, C., ten Brinke, L., Porter, S., Couper, S.-L., & Rankin, C. (2012). The eyes don't have it: Lie detection and neuro-linguistic programming. *PLoS ONE, 7*(7), e40259.

Wisniewski, B., Zierer, K., & Hattie, J. (2020). The power of feedback revisited: A meta-analysis of educational feedback research. *Frontiers in Psychology, 10*(3087), 1–14.

Zurer, P. S. (2002). An educational experience: Duke's chemistry department regroups after experimenting with an innovative first-year course. *Chemical & Engineering News, 80*(34), 31–32.

Index

Page references for figures are italicized

About the Author

Dr. Katie A. L. McAllister completed her PhD in neuroscience at the University of Cambridge, following an interdisciplinary BSc in cognitive systems at The University of British Columbia. As a student, she was an elected member of the UBC Senate appointed to the Teaching and Learning Committee, a member of the Cognitive Systems Program Committee, and a graduate student representative to the Graduate Education Committee of Cambridge's Graduate School of Life Sciences.

A four-year hiatus from academia allowed her to develop a broad skillset as a management consultant with the London office of the Boston Consulting Group. Consulting across varied industries and strategic challenges required engagement and constructive interactions with individuals ranging from those "on the ground" to the leadership of global flagship organizations and government.

She is passionate about interdisciplinary approaches to undergraduate education, particularly focused on developing critical thinking, creative problem solving, and effective interaction skills.

Dr. McAllister is currently the head of the College of Social Sciences and associate professor of cognitive neuroscience and complex systems at the Minerva Schools at KGI.

Made in the USA
Monee, IL
14 May 2021

68566634R00142